How to Win Over
DEPRESSION

Revised Edition

How to Win Over
DEPRESSION

Revised Edition

TIM LaHAYE

ZondervanPublishingHouse
Grand Rapids, Michigan

A Division of HarperCollinsPublishers

Contents

Acknowledgments 7

Introduction 9

1. The Problem of Depression 13

2. Struggles Against Depression 21

3. The Symptoms of Depression 27

4. The Cycles of Depression 33

5. The Causes of Depression 49

6. Testing Yourself for Depression 61

7. Is There a Cure for Depression? 65

8. The Place of Anger in Depression 93

9. Self-Pity and Depression 103

10. How to Overcome Self-Pity 117

11. Depression and Your Mind 129

12. Depression and Your Self-Image 141

13. Depression and Your Temperament 163

14. Grief Is Not the Same as Depression 185

15. Depression and the Occult 193

16. Depression and Music 199

17. Ten Steps to Victory Over Depression 205

18. How to Help Your Children Avoid Depression 225

19. How to Help a Depressed Friend 237

20. The Miserable Majority 245

21. An Eighty-Five-Year-Old Optimist 253

Notes 259

Bibliography 263

Acknowledgments

The author is indebted to many people for assistance in the writing of this book. Many depressed counselees have provided insights into the problem of depression and given me ample opportunity to test the validity of the formulas for victory over depression found here.

Dr. James DeSaegher, a member of the English department at Point Loma University, San Diego, has helped immeasurably in the grammatical preparation of the manuscript. Mrs. Barrie Lyons, Linda Dukes, and Mrs. Bonnie Perry have typed and transcribed my hastily scrawled notes or dictation done primarily while flying en route to speaking engagements. Doctors William Halcomb of San Clemente, Nelson Bell and William McCandless of San Diego, along with Ruth Erne, R.N., have advised me on the medical aspects of the subject, carefully reviewing the first six chapters. Flight attendants, businessmen, and passengers who engaged me in conversation after noting the subject matter on which I was writing have voiced positive comments and convinced me this book was sorely needed.

Finally, my wonderful wife and children, who have so graciously indulged my mental preoccupation during the months of its creation, have earned my heartfelt gratitude.

Introduction

When *Newsweek* magazine devoted its cover page and lead article to "Coping with Depression," that was the last straw! For some time I had contemplated writing a book on how to win over depression, but that article finally motivated me. When I read, "For there is no doubt that depression, long the leading mental illness in the U.S., is now virtually epidemic—and suicide is its all too frequent outcome,"[1] it confirmed my own observations. If my counseling room was any indication, depression was on the rise. That article and the recent surge of books on the subject indicate that our country has no corner on a problem that is sweeping Western civilization.

For several years I have made a special study of this life-destroying emotional malady. In my training and research I was confronted with a mass of confusion, contradiction, and psychologically disguised suggestions that were hard to pin down. As the flow of depressed persons began to increase, I was forced to help them as best I could. Gradually, a therapeutic formula was developed, which many found beneficial. Occasionally I had thought about writing this book in the hope that readers could likewise benefit from the formula, but my intention was not serious until I experienced the second most traumatic experience of my life.

Not usually prone to depression, I could not readily identify from personal experience with the emotional disturbances of my counselees. But in the midst of the most dynamic opportunity I had ever experienced, all my dreams were shattered in the most devastating event of my life since my father died when I was ten years old. (This event is described later in this book.) In the aftermath I was struck with my first serious wave of depression. For the first time, I could truly identify with the cold, apathetic, hopeless feeling of the depressed.

That first depression passed within a few days, but during the next two and a half years I experienced four more depressions, all stemming from the same source. Looking back, I find that each time I used the formula I had given to others, the depression passed. It returned whenever I failed to heed that formula.

Once I realized that depression had reached "virtually epidemic" proportions nationally and that many counselees were helped by the therapeutic formula I had developed, and since I had learned something about it by personal experience, both through success and failure, I decided it was time to publish this book. It was my prayer that it would help many others realize the true cause of a major emotional crippler and offer a workable remedy. It has been twenty-two years since the book was first published and I must say, with praise to God, that it became a best-seller with over one million copies printed in English. And only God knows how many have read it in the thirty some languages into which it has been translated.

The response to the first edition has been unbelievable. For example, a French woman in Paris came to a Family Life Seminar my wife and I were conducting. She embarrassed me at first with an emotional outburst and ended up throwing her arms around me in an effusive embrace, all the while jabbering in French. I looked to the missionary in charge of the conference for help and he interpreted for me, "Your book, *How to Win Over Depression*!. . ." Then she related how she had been depressed so long, seen so many doctors, and felt so hopeless that she decided to commit suicide by throwing herself in the Paris River. En route she passed a Christian bookstore and saw this book prominently displayed in the window. She stepped into the bookstore, bought the book, read it, and accepted Christ as her Lord and Savior. Then she used the techniques I describe in the book to overcome the problem and was literally transformed. Just seeing the smile on her face made the hours of writing all worthwhile.

Of one thing I am confident: You do not have to be depressed. If you or someone you love has this problem, you will welcome the good news of a means to gain victory over it. I am convinced that by using the formula in this book, you can avoid ever being depressed again.

Twenty-two years ago when I wrote the first edition of this book I was certain that most depression was caused primarily by sin, a faulty thinking pattern, or some failure on the part of the individual to claim the promises of God. Medical science has made enormous strides in helping the depressed during the past twenty-two years, more than in any other field of medicine that deals with the everyday lives of people. Excellent medicines (many with few or no side effects) have been discovered to help the severely depressed. In addition, many studies of the function of the human brain have unveiled intricacies about that complex organ's mysterious functions that have been most helpful in treating depression. Some research has indicated that depression can be genetic, that it can be passed on from parent to child, which accounts for the fact that it is known to have followed families for four generations or more.

When I was writing the original book, like other counselors at that time, I assumed that only one to five percent of cases of depression were caused physically. Today experts assume that somewhere between ten and fifty percent are induced genetically or physically. However, even then, the formula that I offer to help avoid depression still works for the other fifty to ninety percent and can even help to reduce the effects of that debilitating emotional illness in those who can trace its cause to physical or genetic sources.

Many doctors are quite sanguine in their attitude toward the new medications available. Some suggest that all depression is treatable. If that is true, and we shall show that it seems to be, then I am even more convinced than I was twenty-two years ago that depression does not need to dominate your life but can be avoided and remedied. That it is increasing in our society, and that it is invading our young even to the point of suicide cannot be denied. But the good news is, regardless of its cause, depression is treatable. Having counseled hundreds of depressed individuals since writing this book and having received hundreds of letters from readers, I am even more convinced than I was back then that you do not have to be depressed. There is hope for even the most severe cases. I am confident that by using the formula in this book to avoid or overcome depression, or in the few physically or genetically induced cases, by following your doctors prescription and using this formula, you can avoid ever being depressed again.

A nurse stopped me after a speaking engagement to ask that I sign her copy of this book. It was a mess! Not only was it dog-eared and well marked, it fell apart in my hands, for there was a complete cut down the binding that split it into pieces. When I asked, "How did this happen?" she sheepishly admitted, "A friend gave me this book when I was in a deep depression. I browsed through it and angrily decided it was too simplistic, so I threw it against the wall so hard it split in two. Somehow it was put on the shelf in my library where I ignored it for several years as I sought every other source but God for a remedy. Then about ten years ago I found it when I was really desperate for help, read it from cover to cover, and I am happy to say that it changed my life!"

It is my prayer that this new updated edition will reach out to help even more than the first, enabling millions of people to win over the mind and emotionally numbing disease called depression.

Chapter 1

The Problem of Depression

A woman sat in my counseling room and heaved that long and somewhat discouraging sigh I had come to associate with the depressed. Her name could have been "Mrs. Everything"—you name it, she had it.

Leaving her expensive ranch-style home and a wardrobe filled with stylish clothes, she drove her troubles to my office in a brand new car. She had three lovely school-age daughters and a dynamic executive-type husband who had "never been unfaithful." Even though she possessed almost everything she wanted, she was not happy. Three times a week for two months she had been seeing a psychiatrist, yet only two nights before coming to me Mrs. Everything had almost taken her life. In a state of depression she had lowered the shades in her bedroom, crawled back into bed as soon as the girls had left for school, and pulled the sheets up over her head. Her well-groomed appearance to the contrary, she claimed that she had climbed out of such a bed to visit my office.

Although that young mother's case of depression was severe, it was not the worst I had ever seen. In fact, her emotional condition was not at all uncommon, for the majority of people I counsel are depressed. In talking to other counselors, I find this to be the general rule. On almost any day the average counselor is confronted with several cases of depression. A prominent psychologist recently observed, "Every one of us is depressed at times. It is perfectly normal." A medical doctor, lecturing to other doctors on how to diagnose depression, commented, "In a sense, depression should be expected in every individual."

For many years depression has been the nation's number one emotional illness and it is on the increase. At more than forty Family Life Seminars I have conducted in various parts of the country, my cassette lecture on "The Cause and Cure of Depression" has without exception sold more than any other lecture—even more than "Sexual Harmony in Marriage," "Overcoming Worry," "Why Opposites Attract Each Other," and ten other selections.

In late June of 1995, CNN News carried the report of the one-thousandth person who leaped to his death off the San Francisco Bay Bridge. The reporter went on to assert that "over half a million people attempt suicide each year in the United States of whom close to 30,000 are successful." Then he said, "Even though we have a skyrocketing murder rate in this country, more people die by suicide than in all the nation's homicides." I had never thought that suicide was more frequent today than murder, but statistically, between five and six thousand more people die by their own hand every year than by someone else's.

What would cause a reasonably normal person to climb up onto that beautiful San Francisco Bay Bridge and leap to his or her death? Momentary depression! At the point when a person's depression becomes so intense that it overpowers the natural self-preservation instinct, potentially anyone can take his or her own life. That is one reason I always take people seriously if they threaten to commit suicide—unless they have a history of using that ploy to gain attention. But even then I would be reluctant to ignore that threat.

Some counselors say that a large number of these self-inflicted deaths could have been avoided, and that is probably true. For that kind of depression is usually short-lived, and if the person is given physical or spiritual help when they have lost all hope, there is a very strong possibility that he or she can be helped out of that slough of despond and go on to live a long and productive life. I believe there is hope for the depressed. That is why I wrote this book—and it is probably why you are reading it. You either want hope for your depression or suggestions on how to help a loved one who is depressed.

Although increasing at an alarming rate, depression is not new. History and literature clearly indicate that it is as ancient as man. The oldest book known, the book of Job, introduces a great man in a serious state of depression, exclaiming,

> So I have been allotted months of futility,
>> and nights of misery have been assigned to me.
> When I lie down, I think, "How long before I get up?"
>> The night drags on, and I toss till dawn.
> My body is clothed with worms and scabs,
>> my skin is broken and festering.
> My days are swifter than a weaver's shuttle,
>> and they come to an end without hope.
> Remember, O God, that my life is but a breath;
>> my eyes will never see happiness again.
> The eye that now sees me will see me no longer;
>> you will look for me, but I will be no more.
> As a cloud vanishes and is gone,
>> so he who goes down to the grave does not return.
> He will never come to his house again:
>> his place will know him no more.
> Therefore I will not keep silent;
>> I will speak out in the anguish of my spirit;
>> I will complain in the bitterness of my soul.

Job 7:3–11

After reading what happened to Job (loss of family and fortune, boils covering his body), who could say that he or she would not have reacted similarly under like circumstances?

The first writer on record to categorically describe depression was Hippocrates, the Greek physician and philosopher. In his ingenious classification of the four temperaments, he labeled one "melancholia," proposing the erroneous explanation that it was caused by black, heavy blood passing through the patient's veins.

A physician named Aretaeus in the second century described the depressed as "sad" and "dismayed." He suggested that they became thin, agitated, and sleepless. If the condition were allowed to persist, they complained of "a thousand futilities" and desired to die.[1]

Another second-century man, Plutarch, created a distinctly religious context for a person with "melancholia": "He looks on himself as a man whom the gods hate and pursue with their anger. A far worse lot is before him; he dares not employ any means of averting or of remedying the evil, lest he be found fighting against the gods. The physician, the consoling friend, are driven away. 'Leave me,' says the wretched man, 'me, the impious, the accursed, hated of the gods, to suffer my punishment.' He sits out of doors, wrapped in sackcloth or in filthy rags. Ever and anon he rolls himself, naked, in the dirt confessing about this and that sin. He has eaten or drunk something wrong. He has gone some way or other which the divine being did not approve of. The festivals in honor of the gods give no pleasure to him but fill him rather with fear or a fright."[2]

A careful study of these ancients reveals a constant similarity to modern descriptions of depression. Dr. Beck, for instance, explains,

> The cardinal signs and symptoms used today in diagnosing depression are found in the ancient descriptions: disturbed mood (sad, dismayed, futile); self-castigations ('the accursed, hated of the gods'); self-debasing behavior ('wrapped in sackcloth or in filthy rags ... he rolls himself, naked, in the dirt'); wish to die; physical and vegetative symptoms (agitation, loss of appetite and weight, sleeplessness); and delusions of having committed unpardonable sins. The foregoing descriptions of depression include the typical characteristics of this condition. There are few psychiatric syndromes whose clinical descriptions are so constant through successive eras of history.[3]

DEPRESSION IS UNIVERSAL

It is safe to say that everyone becomes depressed at some point in life. Oh, he may not be so despairing as to attempt suicide, but he has experienced depression at some time or other. During the past few years I have taken polls in audiences totaling at least 100,000 people, inquiring, "Is there anyone here who has never experienced depression in his or her entire life?" So far not one person has indicated that he has escaped this problem.

Naturally, all of the people were not conceding that they were mired in the Slough of Despond. Many of them were thinking of light stages of depression which they called the "blues," or, as one woman said, "I have the weeps." But they were all conscious that at times in their lives they had been unhappy. Obviously, there is a great difference between unhappiness and mental illness. However, even the mildest form of depression dulls the keen edge of life.

Depression not only is universal, but it also is no respecter of persons. Recent studies show that the poor suffer with it just as much as the rich. As we shall show in this book, depression is not caused by circumstances, possessions, or position in life; therefore, all people are susceptible to it. Perhaps the greatest single change in the field since the first edition of this book was published, in addition to the many excellent medical treatments that have been discovered, is the way depression has invaded the young. While I was writing the book I was impressed that the authorities were amazed to see it sweep like an epidemic through the college campuses. Today it has invaded the once happy haven of the junior high and middle schools. In fact, apparently 15,000 middle school children commit suicide each year, and it is estimated that at least five attempt suicide for every one that succeeds. Generally speaking, more people are unhappy today than ever (particularly children from divorced or contentious families), and consequently depression and even suicide has increased graphically.

Depression is no respecter of persons or professions. I have met depressed cab drivers, homemakers, businessmen, school teachers, construction workers, and contractors. Many fear that confessing they are depressed is tantamount to acknowledging they have some mental deficiency. Although it is indeed related to thinking patterns, it has nothing to do with IQ. If anything, people with higher IQs are more vulnerable to this malady. For instance, almost every authority I have consulted in this field refers to the fact that Sir Winston Churchill, a bastion of strength to England at a time of great national crisis, was given to serious bouts of depression. Abraham Lincoln was bothered by it, as was Theodore Roosevelt, Napoleon Bonaparte, and far more than we know. Some of the world's greatest geniuses were plagued with the problem. After a notable work of art or feat of creativity, they fell into an apathetic period of depression.

Most high school students remember the short story by Edgar Allen Poe entitled "The Pit and the Pendulum." It is said that after completing this product of his genius, the great author fell into a four-day depression. Some, like Stephen Foster, buried their creativity in alcohol; various poets shortened their lives through wanton sex; and other artists wasted their genius in equally bizarre conduct—Van Gogh even cut off his ear in a fit of despair.

When we say that everyone has experienced depression, we are speaking generally of the many forms it takes, which will be dealt with later. These range from the "blues" or minor mood swings, common to all individuals, to the most severe psychosis. Life itself is unpredictable, and every human being will necessarily experience unhappiness. One psychiatrist has admitted, "We seem to be starved for happiness most of the time." For most people, happiness is a rare commodity which, as we shall see, depends more on mental attitude than on circumstances, but whenever a person is unhappy he has a tendency to feel depressed to some degree. It is unrealistic for any human being to think he or she can escape life's natural causes of unhappiness. If, therefore, to live is to experience varying degrees of unhappiness, and since depression is the opposite of happiness, then all of us are bound on some occasions to feel depressed.

Students of human behavior have long wrestled with two questions: (1) Why are some people more frequently depressed than others? and (2) What is the true cause of depression? Both of these questions will be addressed in subsequent chapters. Many like to think it is a physically induced illness, thus relieving themselves of any responsibility for it. In so doing, they seriously jeopardize their chances of recovery.

I have observed happy and contented people whose joy radiated amid life's most unhappy circumstances, whereas others turned the circumstances of joy into beds of depression. Unless individuals are willing to face the fact that their mental attitude toward the circumstances, not the circumstances, causes their unhappiness and depression, they are, in my opinion, incurable.

Chapter 2

Struggles Against Depression

One of the first things a sophomore psychology student learns is that self-preservation is the first law of life. When a person injures an arm, he shields that injury with other parts of his body. If he injures a leg, he will consciously and subconsciously place an additional amount of weight on his good leg. The natural struggle for existence will automatically cause emotional shifting that produces changes in behavior and, in some cases, changes in appearance.

This is particularly true in the area of depression. Subconscious maneuvers are designed, in some cases, to avoid depression or to extricate one from its grasp. People use different techniques, gradually developing habit patterns that become characteristic of their personality. These defense mechanisms may manifest themselves as a change in mood, altering their relationships with other people. Their attitude toward circumstances may become regressive or narcissistic and, if protracted, will ultimately result in escape from reality. We speak of this as "losing contact with reality." Such a person may be able to hear but seems incapable of movement or speech. Obviously, the severity of the depression will determine the severity of the struggle against it, which in turn produces what we are prone to call abnormal behavior. It is not uncommon for suicide to be the final attempt to rid oneself of the awful tyranny of depression.

The form this struggle takes in a person's life can be seen as early as infancy, as will be shown later. One of the primary causes of depression is separation from a love object, which is what makes a well-fed, dry, and comfortable baby begin to cry when his parents leave the room. The contact with the love object, in this case the mother, produces the happiness. Separation begets loneliness, which ultimately results in depression. Consequently, the child's natural struggle against depression causes him to cry. If the mother is immature and becomes irritated at what then seems to be unreasonable behavior on the part of the baby, she may scream at the child, which seriously compounds the problem. In this case we find two immature persons whose struggle against depression is in conflict. The child's insecurity is magnified by the sound of the mother's angry voice, and the mother's intemperate behavior produces guilt and loss of self-image, which will also contribute toward the child's depression.

The other possibility is that the child's initial cry cannot be accepted by the young mother, prompting her to rush to the child's aid, lovingly pick him up, and thus eliminate his cause for depression. This action, however, ill prepares the child for life, which of necessity forces all people to periodic separations from their love objects. It not only creates a habit pattern of dependency in the child but also makes the mother an unnecessary slave of her infant's expectations. This ultimately becomes a source of irritation to the mother, which may not only produce depression in her life but ultimately, if indulged, will generate feelings of hostility that she cannot indefinitely keep from expressing. The infant may in turn sense this feeling and, as a result, become depressed.

To digress momentarily concerning a cure for this most common problem, I suggest that you compare emotional and mental development to the physical act of learning to walk. Because it is tangible, we seem better able to cope with the physical side of life than the mental or emotional, which is probably why learning to walk affords such a good illustration. When children begin to walk, of necessity they repeatedly fall down. It doesn't matter how often they fail, and within certain limits it doesn't matter how hard they fall. But it is important that they be given loving approval and encouragement to try again. Ultimately, all normal children learn to walk. Similarly, normal children learn to separate from their parents. We admit that it can be a painful process, but it is a necessary part of life. Therefore, a wise parent lovingly and tenderly starts early to train his child to stand on his own emotionally for short periods of time, taking short psychological steps that equip him for the longer steps of separation that eventually become necessary.

Infantile manifestations of the struggle against depression take on behavior patterns which, although associated with children, are neither universal nor necessary.

Naturally, as a person matures physically, their mental and emotional maturity does not maintain consistent growth. In fact, their behavior may fall further and further below the standard of normalcy.

EXHIBITIONISM

In childhood this problem manifests itself in temper tantrums, showing off, and other forms of attention getting, including withdrawal. Later in life, it commonly reveals itself in an obsession toward gambling, not only with money but also with one's life. For a teenage boy it may involve recklessly driving a car or motorcycle; for a teenage girl it may include hitchhiking a ride or being sexually promiscuous; for their parents it may encompass a spending spree or a wasteful visit to the gambling tables of Las Vegas. Quite possibly this obsessive compulsion to gamble one's life, reputation, or material assets is a subconscious tempting of fate caused by the feelings of guilt over one's evil thinking patterns, which have been induced by separation from or loss of a love object.

Exhibitionism is almost universally an expression of the struggle against depression. The child who feels she is losing the love or acceptance of her parents will often lash out in vile or profane words. If the parents wisely and lovingly discipline the child, the parents not only help establish the foundation for self-discipline and self-control, but they aid the child in relieving her sense of guilt, which she will certainly feel, having mentally and verbally abused her parents. (Never underestimate a child's intuitive sense of right and wrong.) Unless checked, this spirit of rebellion will turn against society, manifesting itself in obscene words written in public places and in loudly expressed profane and vile utterances usually considered socially unacceptable. As she grows up, this attitude may express itself in devious plots against society, withdrawal from humanity, and eventually suicide.

Sexual promiscuity may likewise reflect the battle against depression. The secure, loved, and accepted woman does not dress in a provocative manner, but subconsciously prefers modest attire. Among those who dress to seek attention, it seems that a woman's security level can often be measured by the length of her skirt. This may also be true of the woman who is insistent on wearing men's apparel. For some reason she dislikes being a woman (probably because in her childhood her father rejected her for being a girl, at least that's the reason she believes); therefore, she does everything possible to disguise her femininity. She not only dresses like a man, but she walks like a man, swears like a man, and indulges in many other unfeminine practices. Such a woman is particularly vulnerable to lesbianism. If, on the other hand, she finds it easy to accept herself as a woman but not as a person, she will express her struggle against depression by being flirtatious, suggestive, and, in some cases, promiscuous. Studies have indicated that nymphomaniacs are really not oversexed women, but overly insecure women. The sex drive in a woman is not sufficiently strong enough to explain such behavior. Even the most sexually indiscriminate women I have counseled have indicated that it wasn't their sex drive that motivated them, but their tremendous need for love. Sex was the price they paid to gain the love they craved.

Sexual exhibitionism in men does not take the form of indecent exposure as frequently as it does in women, partly because the fashion industry does not cultivate this problem as much and partly because of the man's stronger sex drive. The male ego usually leads a man to find gratification in sexual conquest. The emotionally immature male tends to equate manhood with profane and obscene speech and the number of women he has taken to bed. The emotionally mature male reveals the absence of his struggle against depression by treating women with dignity and respect, confining his expressions of sex to the special object of his love, his wife.

CLINGING

Another common manifestation of the struggle against depression is called "clinging." Most parents have had the emotionally traumatic experience of forcibly extricating themselves from the clinging arms of their child. I shall never forget my five-year-old son's first day in a San Diego kindergarten. He had spent three weeks getting used to a kindergarten environment in Minnesota before we moved to California, and he was very reluctant to enter a new school situation. It was hard enough to forcibly remove his loving, clinging arms from around my neck, but one of my most difficult tasks was to force myself to walk away from him amid his loud and piteous cry, "Daddy, don't leave me!"

The "clinging" process that in some homes occurs every night just before the light is turned out carries over into adulthood. Naturally, it takes on a more sophisticated behavior. In some cases it adopts the form of excessive generosity well above a person's means. This is nothing more than a subconscious attempt to buy the love of his love object. It may also take the form of making oneself indispensable. Rejection by a boss, or father figure, is so abhorrent to some insecure men that they work long hours and neglect their family. Occasionally one will encounter a compulsive hostess who at first seems to be the "hostess with the mostest," but in reality is clinging avidly to her friends. By wining and dining them she seeks to place them in her debt so that, hopefully, they will not leave her.

This clinging mechanism is sometimes the motivation of women who serve as foster parents. Their maternal instinct is increased by their insecurity, and they are obsessed with the yearning to be needed. Consequently, they cannot tolerate not having babies or children dependent upon them. Quite possibly this is one area in which the struggle against depression may be helpful to the recipient, for unless the affection is excessive, the experience of being raised in such a home is preferable to that of being raised in an orphanage.

Another stratagem of clinging includes insistent conversation, whether person to person or on the telephone. A doctor friend noted, "Some people have compulsive telephonitis." One final adult form of clinging is helplessness or sickness for effect. Naturally, these are silent cries for help.

ATTACK

An intimidating symbol of one's struggle against depression involves attack—either aggression against someone who rejected them or, more frequently, an attack on themselves. The thought pattern usually proceeds as follows: "Since it is my fault that I am rejected, I must not be any good; consequently, I deserve to be punished." And since no one else will do it, the person often punishes himself—a pathetic practice, to say the least.

Although these defense maneuvers ride the waves of an individual's moods, they are bound to affect a person's behavior in direct proportion to the severity of the mood. Therefore, the best way to remedy the situation is not to change the expression but discover what causes the mood, as we shall show in a later chapter. Thought patterns produce feelings, feelings produce actions. Therefore, any permanent reduction in depression must of necessity deal with the problems of thought patterns. Unless the person's thinking pattern changes, this struggle against depression is bound to produce increasing degrees of erratic behavior.

Chapter 3

The Symptoms of Depression

The tremendous increase in the number of depressed persons today justifies a brief study of the symptoms of the problem. Almost everyone who reads this book has friends or loved ones who manifest these symptoms. If you don't need to recognize them for yourself, then for their sake you should learn to discern these critical signs quickly and offer your love and support in their time of need.

Three stages of depression are acknowledged almost universally by counselors. Most designate them as "mild, severe, and serious." We shall label them discouragement, despondency, and despair. In a later chapter we will show how they affect us mentally, emotionally, and physically, but here it is sufficient to say that most depression commences with discouragement, grows into despondency and, unless the thought pattern is changed, results in despair. Once the line of despair has been crossed, it is possible for the depression to become so acute that the individual loses contact with reality and must be given medical treatment even to stay alive.

As we shall see, a negative or harmful thinking pattern, if indulged over a period of time, can actually trigger the production of harmful hormones from the pituitary gland and can cause damaging physical illness that can make the depression worse.

The effects of depression are experienced physically, mentally, and emotionally. The layperson recognizes the physical symptoms first, but the specialist can often detect the mental symptoms before they become physical. Unfortunately, the depressed are not usually brought to his attention until they manifest physical symptoms. Too many physical symptoms of depression exist for us to consider in this brief book, so we shall review only the most common.

PHYSICAL AND MENTAL SYMPTOMS

(1) *Erratic sleep behavior.* The most common physical symptom of depression is a marked change in sleep patterns. Although some depressed people oversleep and awake tired, it is usually more common that they can't sleep at all. If they do, they will awaken in the early hours of the morning and cannot go back to sleep. In a taped panel discussion on depression, several medical doctors agreed that the first red flag to look for in insomnia patients is depression.

(2) *Apathy, lethargy, the blahs.* Another common symptom of depression is reflected in the statements "I feel tired all the time" or "I don't even feel like enjoying my favorite hobby." Depressed people tend to awaken tired and remain unmotivated. Although they are capable of fulfilling their responsibilities, their work performance leaves much to be desired. In addition, they tire easily. One man complained, "My feet feel like they're set in concrete."

(3) *Loss of appetite.* Food loses its charm for the depressed. They listlessly play with their food, which seems tasteless to them. The more severe the depression, the less the appetite grows. Consequently, if the problem is not checked, the depressed may experience a serious weight loss, which will compound their difficulty. Sometimes the first stages of depression result in constant raiding of the refrigerator for snacks, but usually those in despair can persist for days without food.

(4) *Loss of sex drive.* All drive functions or basic activities come to a standstill when one is depressed. This includes even the sex drive, particularly in women. Some women have been

known to get so depressed that even their menstrual function stops. Except in mild depression, when a man may become sexually aggressive because of the threat to his ego, most men lose interest in sex when they are depressed.

(5) *Unkempt appearance.* Whenever a fashionable friend loses interest in his or her appearance, look for depression. The loss of motor drive, due to the negative self-image of the depressed person, makes a man less concerned with shaving and neatness and causes a woman to skip her hairdresser's appointment. The unkempt attire is a reflection of the way the individual sees himself or herself. Clothes are revealing! They often broadcast a person's self-concept. They probably are covering up an inferiority complex if the person is overdressed. If one is well dressed, as appropriate, clothes often communicate a satisfied self-image. However, if depressed persons dress sloppily when neatness is called for, it usually is because they have given up on themselves.

(6) *Many physical ailments.* It is quite common for the depressed to suffer from many physical maladies, both real and imagined. Some of the common problems are tiredness, weakness, aching, dizziness, heart palpitation, tightening of the chest, trouble with breathing, headache, constipation, heartburn, and sweating.

EMOTIONAL SYMPTOMS

Although depression begins in the mind, it will deeply affect a person's emotions. The following are among the most common:

(1) *Loss of affection.* The almost universal tendency of depressed people to withdraw from others is a result of their loss of affection. It begins with a lessening of their love for their spouse or children and grows until they really do not care about themselves, about others, or about anything. This is a most harmful emotional state, induced by either a glandular malfunction or a faulty thinking pattern of self-occupation. In

either case, such a person needs help. Unless their thinking pattern is changed, the depression will increase. Someone has cautioned, "Love or perish." Unless you love others and yourself, you will destroy yourself.

(2) *Sadness.* Joylessness and gloom become a way of life to the depressed. It is so deeply etched on the table of their heart that it shows on their face. You will look in vain for a smile on the face of the depressed. When they are discouraged, joy and merriment fail to bring them pleasure. As the depression increases, they lose all ability to respond to humor and may become resentful at the joy of those around them.

(3) *The "weeps."* A frequent symptom of the depressed is an involuntary tendency to cry. Even those who haven't cried in years may burst into tears or wish to cry but cannot. One woman admitted, "I can always tell when I'm going to be depressed—I get the weeps." Then she demonstrated her depression.

(4) *Hostility.* As we shall see in a later chapter, every case of depression includes a component of anger, at least in the initial stages. At first it is directed at the person who has rejected or insulted them. Later it is turned inward because the depressed person feels that he or she caused the rejection. It is not uncommon to hear a depressed person mutter, "I hate myself" or "I get so disgusted with myself."

(5) *Irritability.* Passive people are easily irritated, particularly by those with energy and vitality. They resent individuals who feel good, resist those who try to activate them, and may lash out furiously at routine household noises. Music that normally soothes them may produce discomfort. They can even become agitated at the solicitations of their friends, for they don't feel worthy of someone else's time and concern.

(6) *Anxiety, fear, and worry.* The feelings of loneliness and despair that grow during depression lower the fear threshold. Everything becomes an excuse to worry. The individ-

ual will fear being left alone, although he may disguise it. He will flee the past and shrink from the future. Not uncommon is a strong apprehension of death. The wise man of Proverbs said, "An anxious heart weighs a man down, but a kind word cheers him up" (12:25).

(7) *Hopelessness.* Most depressed people are overcome by a sense of hopelessness. They feel trapped by the circumstances that brought on the depression and can envision no way out. Their past is filled with rejection and grief, their present becomes anguish personified, and their gloomy outlook on the future contemplates no solution. Unless someone can inject hope into their thinking apparatus, the depression will gradually deepen. Typical in the counseling room is the lament, "I am totally discouraged, and no hope is in sight!" That is not true! There is hope.

Chapter 4

The Cycles of Depression

MOODS

Many things can affect our moods: the weather, the time of year, politics, social events, and a host of other things. Certainly color and music are important factors. One lady I know picked out the color scheme for her home when she was in a bad mood. Shortly after painting the inside of her home, she came in for counseling regarding "the increasing severity of depression." When I found that her color scheme combined various shades of blues and grays, I suggested that she redecorate the house, using bright colors of yellow, white, or pink, colors that communicate warmth, light, and life.

The *Newsweek* article previously mentioned touched on the seasonal problem of depression.

> This is the time of year when the affliction cuts deepest in those who are prone to it: the holidays are over, gone, and the bright promise of Christmas, often painfully unfulfilled, has given way to the bleak reality of the winter that lies ahead. Psychiatrists' telephones jangle with calls for help. An executive oppressed by the incessant gabble of his children has begun drinking heavily. A young housewife, physically exhausted by weeks of anticipatory tension, by gift buying and meal planning, suddenly finds herself in the grip of insomnia. A widow, alone in a

small apartment, is racked by protracted fits of sobbing. Now the days are gray, the nights long and spring is far away.

Psychiatrists are so familiar with the phenomenon of post-Christmas depression that they have given it a name: the Holiday Paradox. There are a number of obvious reasons why the depression occurs. The holiday season inexorably stirs up deep-seated childhood and family associations and traumas. The exchange of gifts revives the stabbing pain of sibling resentments over who got the most or the best. The holidays are also often a time of reassessment, when the expectations of a youthful past are compared with the realities of adulthood, often with painful results. "The holidays," says Dr. Arthur Prange, Jr., of the University of North Carolina, "are organized to guarantee disappointment."

Even the most well-adjusted personalities suffer the pangs of the Holiday Paradox at one time or another—and then go on to an uneventful recovery. But for those predisposed to depression, the holidays can be tragic, even fatal. Although December and January do not rank high as suicide months, suicides do peak sharply just after Christmas Day and New Year's. "The really bad depressions and suicides hit on the second, third and fourth of January," says Dr. Robert Litman, co-director of the Los Angeles Suicide Prevention Center. "It's the worst week of the year."[1]

Not only are depressive moods seasonal, but they can be induced in a whole population as a result of world events. This was graphically illustrated in America as we saw the terrible devastation in Oklahoma City after the bombing there. We were stunned by the scenes of stark destruction. We were deeply saddened as we viewed hurt children, frantic parents, and weeping rescue workers. Then, as the story unfolded, all America pulled together financially, emotionally, and physically to help those most closely associated with the disaster. Stories of sacrificial giving and love for fellow human beings filled us with hope and raised the spirits of the entire nation.

Such mood fluctuations vary in intensity and length depending upon the conditions involved. Most people are more susceptible to low moods after suffering emotional or physical stress and particularly when they are tired. When people do not eat properly (either too much in the evening or the wrong kind of foods), work too hard, or stay up too late, they are more vulnerable to low moods. In marriage counseling I always advise couples against talking about anything negative, particularly in the area of family finances, after 9:30 P.M. It is amazing how much larger our problems seem when we are tired.

Low moods seem to warrant no exceptions. Even the most sanguine person, valued for his good humor and cheerful spirit, will occasionally feel down. In women this is frequently attributed to their menstrual cycle, which takes a toll on them physically and often drains them of needed vitality. However, we should recognize that men also pass through a mood cycle on a regular basis. With women it seems to be every twenty-six to twenty-nine days, but some feel that in men it is more likely to occur every thirty-four to thirty-eight days. Since the male cycle does not include the physical causes for loss of vitality in women, it is not usually as pronounced though nevertheless disturbing.

Analytically gifted people have reported an annual low-mood cycle. One national youth worker has charted his so that he anticipates it every year and prepares himself mentally, emotionally, physically, and spiritually to either offset it or shorten it.

Sydney J. Harris, syndicated columnist, reports that nothing seems to account for his moods; they just come. Since he has learned this, he anticipates them and does not let them upset him. He sits them out quietly and thus "cancels the harm they can do." He confesses that sometimes in the depth of a low mood he thinks his writing is so poor that he hopes the editor will throw it in the waste basket. "Actually," he adds, "the columns I knock out when I am feeling bad are often better than the ones I write in a good mood." He concludes that a depressed person cannot judge his own work accurately.[2]

Learning to live with and win over one's vacillating moods and periods of depression is the primary concern of this book. I am convinced that if we understand the problem, we can take specific steps to avoid becoming its incessant victim. Although low moods do not always produce depression, we are more vulnerable to depression during those periods.

During a low mood, things that ordinarily are absorbed and cause no emotional distress suddenly become a source of irritation that brings on depression. The more we know about the function of human nature, the better able we are to cope with both its positive and negative tendencies. This is particularly true when we apply its general principles to ourselves so that instead of resorting to some of the reactive defense mechanisms that produce the abnormal behavior covered in the preceding chapter, we can take positive preventive measures as we detect the symptoms. For example, when we are blue, we accentuate the mood by giving in to it. As William James, the psychologist, stated, "The physical expression of an emotion deepens the emotion; while the refusal of expression diminishes the emotion."[3]

This would suggest that whistling or singing when one first recognizes the blues could conceivably chase them away, whereas the downcast, pessimistic outlook would perpetuate them. The psalmist must have had this in mind when he experienced the sense of exaltation I can have when "I lift up my eyes to the hills" (Psalm 121:1), even when I do not feel like it. The downward look is merely self-defeating.

CYCLES

Not only is everyone subject to mood swings within the framework of his temperament, personality, life circumstances, and mental attitudes, but he also is liable to cycles of depression. That is, during certain cycles in life people are more susceptible to depression than during others. Human individuality will cause one person to bypass such a period, whereas another may be engulfed by it. Allowing for these individual characteristics, the cycles can be separated into the decades of life. Naturally, everyone does not experience all of the cycles, but because of the changes in lifestyles and stresses these decades produce, they may occur.

The First Decade of Life

The initial decade in a child's life is usually very happy, unless, of course, he comes from a broken home where, instead of enjoying the security of his parents' presence, he is subjected to separation and insecurity. These are without doubt the most important years of a child's emotional and character building development that later produce maturity. One educator submitted that fifty percent of a child's character and personality development are established by the time he is three years old, seventy-five percent by the time he is five years old. The child that is treated to love, discipline, integrity, responsibility, and good examples by his parents during this decade is rich indeed!

The Second Decade of Life

The first two or three years of the second decade are pleasant for most children, although they soon erupt into what for many is the most traumatic period of their entire life—adolescence. It is marked by emotional instability because an early teenager feels and acts like a child one minute, like an adult the next. His behavior seems almost spontaneous and in some cases out of control. He not only embarrasses and rejects himself, but he also tends to alienate himself from others. One famous children's worker said of junior high young people, "They get to a place where only their mother and father can love them, and sometimes the father wonders how the mother can put up with them." Their excessive behavior induced by their emotional volatility not only makes them insecure about themselves, but causes them to react seriously to the rejection of those they love. They often develop an argumentative spirit, rebellious attitude, sullenness, or obnoxious behavior, which makes them more unlikable and heightens the rejection, producing more hostile behavior which may lead to their first real experience with depression.

Our present culture is no friend to teenagers. With its music and movies filled with anger and rebellion it intensifies the rebellion that often seems universal among them during those precarious years.

The last thing they need is a school system or teacher that encourages that rebellion by stressing their "rights," which often brings them into conflict with the rights of their family and parents.

Teenagers also experience difficulty in their blossoming sexual development, which creates new drives they often find difficult to control. Since society and moral principles require that they regulate these drives and their accompanying behavior, teenagers often develop a problem of guilt that produces depression. Guilt is occasioned because they either kick over the traces and violate moral principles or indulge in sexual illusions that lead to masturbation, for which they are later ashamed. Guilt is a cruel taskmaster that often reveals itself in depression.

Explicit sex education classes that put more emphasis on using condoms rather than on abstinence leave that door wide open to sexual experimentation beyond belief. Girls as early as twelve are having babies and some are reported to be grandmothers at age twenty-four. What these young people need to know is responsibility that when ignored can introduce adult problems into their adolescent lives. Many go into their adult years depressed.

Another cause of adolescent depression is the increasing consciousness of ultimate separation from parents and loved ones. As we have seen, this seems to be the first emotional pressure spot in an infant's life, one that every mature person must ultimately learn to cope with. Some in their late teens escape the seriousness of the problem by becoming emotionally attached to another love object of the opposite sex (usually near their own age), which becomes a stronger desire than that of staying with their parents. This emotional involvement is often called "love," which frequently is interpreted to mean that the couple is ready for marriage. All too often the experience is based on little more than emotional need, fanned by association and passion.

Having been involved in the field of education for several decades, I have watched a number of high school young people year after year go through a rather short-term depression that is almost predictable. On the night of graduation they are subject to a euphoric, blissful ecstasy that causes uninhibited weeping and laughing, an emotional reaction often bordering on hysteria, as they say good-bye to teachers and friends. Frequently such an experience is followed by a state of depression within one to ten days. This, like other depression syndromes, often can be attributed to the removal of a goal—in this instance, graduation. Unless the young person has sufficient goals that go beyond graduation day, they are prone to experience a severe letdown that produces apathy. The young person who begins a job he relishes the day after graduation tends to escape the problem, as does the young lady who immediately plunges into plans for her impending wedding.

The Third Decade of Life

Depression in the third decade usually is associated with marriage, particularly in the case of married women whose primary mental attention is fixed on the home during this period. Married men in their twenties are more prone to give their attention to education or vocational endeavors, thus remaining mentally stimulated. In addition, their youthful energies usually keep them athletically active. Therefore, they do not normally experience as much depression as women in this third decade of life.

Brides frequently give in to depression either shortly after the wedding or upon returning from the honeymoon. There are many reasons for this. One is the psychological letdown that routine living often produces when contrasted with the exciting preparation prior to the wedding. Another cause for this depression is that her dreams and expectations were so idealistic that real experience becomes disillusioning. This is particularly true if she encounters severe discomfort in intercourse. Some girls find that the consummation of the act of marriage is somewhat painful and unfulfilling. Instead of recognizing that this is a common experience that will soon be overcome by repetition, she may build up a fear or dream of the experience which will destroy the couple's relationship. This often leads to depression. Couples have come to my office within four days after their marriage. Usually such problems are resolved within a short time if both parties are loving and considerate of each other's needs.

If the young bride escapes post-wedding depression, she may experience it after the birth of her first baby. Psychologists call this "postpartum depression." Most women sustain a letdown after child-birth, but not necessarily after each child. Although a depression-prone woman is more likely to have this experience, it is not uncommon for a sanguine mother to be weepy for several days after childbirth. This can be explained by the separation of the child from the mother or by the severe emotional strain the mother undergoes at childbirth. Even natural childbirth can throw a woman's hormonal system out of whack for a time. In some cases this depression becomes protracted and serious if the mother looks upon the child as an intruder. More than one young woman who later went on to be a loving mother indicated that her depression became so severe that she was afraid she might do something harmful to her child. This is usually a temporary malady.

An induced abortion is often much worse and many testify to serious problems of depression after an abortion.

Occasionally a young father experiences a mild depression induced by having to share the love and attention of his wife with the "little stranger" and by becoming sharply aware of his increased financial responsibilities. More intense periods of depression will usually occur on the first or fifteenth of the month!

If the couple has two or three small children close together, it is not uncommon for the mother in the late part of the third decade to experience depression and frigidity. This is simply her reaction to confinement with small children and an aversion to feeling like a prisoner. Her frigidity is not caused by a lessening of her desire for the love of her husband, but by the fact that her subconscious fear of pregnancy overpowers it. In addition, heavy demands are made on her emotionally, and she may be physically exhausted from the two or three births and the tremendous workload her children entail. If she begins to feel sorry for herself in such circumstances, she will soon experience serious problems with depression, which may cause her to lose interest in her appearance, creating a loss of self-image and thus increasing depression. She also risks the chance that her husband may lessen his concern for her because of her unkempt appearance. Incidentally, since men are stimulated by sight, a young mother should make sure that the best-looking woman her husband sees all day is his wife when he opens the door at night. This spruce-up just before 5:00 is not only good for him, but also very beneficial to her own sense of self-worth.

Still another occasion for depression may occur in the third decade of life when the last child goes off to school. The mother who felt so needed by her preschool child no longer sustains that need from 8:30 A.M. to 3:00 P.M. Consequently, she is vulnerable to depression unless she finds some creative use for her energies.

The Fourth Decade of Life

Most people function as parents of teenagers during the fourth decade of life. Presently, less than fifty percent of the mothers in this country are homemakers; the others are working outside the home. Consequently, a major portion of the mothers of teenagers are very busy women. The father during this time is an active businessman, perhaps an employee on the way up. It is a lively, busy time in the life of a family whose major attention often revolves around the emotionally volatile behavior of teenage children. If the parents have anticipated this period by conferring proper amounts of love and discipline together with moral principles on the child, this can be a happy time. But if they have indulged and pampered their children, they may be confronted with rebellious young people, anxious to develop their lives and impatient with parental restrictions. If so, even the active thirties can produce periods of depression. In spite of the hectic family pace during this stage of life, however, it has a surprisingly low incidence of depression.

The Fifth Decade of Life

Most psychiatrists agree that an increase in depression is common during the fifth decade of life. Dr. Mortimer Ostow, a neurologist and psychiatrist serving on the staff of Mount Sinai Hospital in New York City, states,

> There is an increase in the frequency of depression and of suicide in the fifth and sixth decades of life. At that time, there may be an initial attack of depression, or a return of depression which first occurred earlier in adult life, or there may simply be an increase in the frequency or depth of a series of depressions which have been recurring for some time.
>
> I believe that depression at this period in life may be ascribed to the gradual decrease in vital energies which starts relatively early in adult life but which becomes more abrupt in the fifth and sixth decades. It is this decline in energies which produces the temperamental changes that we ordinarily expect in the fifth and sixth decades, namely, mellows, a decline in ambition, relaxation of aggressiveness, and a lessening of interests in the new together with a heightened attachment to the old.
>
> I imagine that this change is part of the normal biology of human life. It may be the effect of the reduction of the secretion of gondola hormones, of pituitary hormones, of secretions of the pineal gland, or simply of aging of the brain, and especially the central and basal sections of the brain called the basal ganglia.[4]

Men probably face the greatest tendency toward depression in this fifth decade. In fact, it is not uncommon for men who have never known depression to experience it for the first time during this period, either vocationally, sexually, or both. Vocationally, most men feel like one depressed man who confided to me, "I always said if a man doesn't hit it vocationally by the time he is forty, he never will. I'm forty-five, I haven't hit it yet, and it doesn't look like I ever will." Although his case was more severe than most, the man whose job has lost its challenge or whose early dreams will not be realized may slip into a period of depression. These periods will increase in frequency until he restructures his thinking patterns and finds realistic challenges and goals within the framework of his education, talents, and opportunity.

During this period the gradual decrease in his vital energies may cause a drop in his sex drive and performance. It is not uncommon for him to experience his first trace of impotence or difficulty in performance. Because nothing is a greater threat to his male ego, he may begin to fear total impotence and be cast into a state of depression. Such men often begin to chase women in an attempt to reclaim their lost sex drive. Quite possibly that is why the period has earned the title "the foolish forties." The mature man in this state learns to content himself with slightly less frequent relations with his wife than during his twenties. He also discovers that sex is more meaningful and enjoyable as an expression of love rather than an attempt to satisfy his male ego.

Women in their forties also have their particular problems, not the least of which is the graduation of children from the home. In addition, even more frequently than brides experience depression after the ceremony, their mothers are prone to give in to this problem. Adjusting to the loss of a daughter in the home, coupled with a severe drain on her nervous energy caused by the frantic wedding preparations, often leaves her exhausted. The severity and length of depression is determined by her plans from that point on.

When the last young person at home goes off to college, enters the armed services, or marries, mother is faced with a tremendous adjustment period. Unless she gets involved in helping other people and recognizes that she is still a productive human being needed by others, she will experience frequent periods of depression. Her insecurity may cause her to be more sexually aggressive than usual, and if not afforded the love and acceptance of her husband, which she needs at this time, she may give in to temptations of infidelity unless, of course, she possesses strong moral principles to the contrary. Once yielding to infidelity, she is often buffeted by the guilt neurosis that produces depression.

The Sixth Decade of Life

It has been my observation that two distinct categories of people live through their sixth and seventh decades of life. The first includes those who have accepted the fact that they are more than halfway through life and have learned to cope with their gradual decrease in vital energies. These individuals enjoy their work, often at an increased tempo, because they know that their accomplishments in life must be achieved quickly. They usually engage in hobbies, particularly golfing, bowling, and the less strenuous activities which tend to give them genuine pleasure. They make friends with others their own age, with whom they have much in common; this creates an enriching way of life. They also have grandchildren by this time, and if they have maintained good rapport with their children, this can develop into an exciting relationship that injects a rewarding dimension into their lives. Consequently, even though they may have experienced waves of depression in the fifth decade of life, they may completely bypass it in the sixth and seventh.

The other group of individuals living during this sixth decade tend to reject the inevitable. Refusing to face the fact that they have reached their fifties, they become depressed. One man who had not learned the beauty of maturity lamented, "I am no longer the man I once was." This form of self-rejection will rapidly cause depression. As a consequence, the depression will tend to make him undesirable, and he will withdraw into a complaining and often neurotic state. It is not uncommon for marriages of over thirty years to go through a period of turbulence initiated either by the narcissistic wife who is afraid of her loss of beauty or the formerly energetic husband who rejects the natural maturing process of life. Fortunately, this is a temporary period of depression for most people; once self-acceptance is achieved and new and realistic goals are projected for the future, the individual's fluctuating moods begin to stabilize.

This is the decade when most women begin their change of life, if they have not already begun in their late forties. Many experts, including a number of women authorities, suggest that the problems of this stage are unrealistically exaggerated. If a woman expects to go to pieces during this period, you can be sure she will. However, if she anticipates taking it in stride with a minimum of discomfort and complaining, it is often much less severe. Unquestionably, her hormonal functions are altered, and she will sense some changes in her emotional responses, the degree of which varies with the individual. But the sooner she learns to cope with hers, the better off she will be. She should certainly consult her physician and read such wholesome material as he recommends. Much of the problem can be resolved not only by medication, but also by exchanging old wives' fables and misconceptions for scientific information.

Women must learn one basic essential: the change of life does not make them sexually inhibited or undesirable. There is strong indication to the contrary that after going through the change, many women find the greatest sexual pleasure of their married life. Again, more important than biology is the individual's mental attitude.

The Seventh Decade of Life

There are two major events that may occur in the seventh decade of life: retirement and the separation of spouses through death. Both of these may contribute to depression.

Retirement

Because of the affluence of our society, many people are retiring after their sixtieth or sixty-second birthday. If the individual's goal has been to take his ease, sit in a rocking chair, and do nothing when he reaches this stage, he is likely to become not only a depression-prone person but also a mortality statistic.

Everyone is familiar with the industrious businessman who lived a very productive life but died within eighteen months after his retirement without any real physical cause. In most cases the problem stemmed from the lack of goals and interests he should have projected for his years of retirement. Business firms have found that sixty-five-year-old men should not necessarily retire, for they may yet be able to offer several years of productive contribution to their company. Recently I spoke with a man who sold a multimillion-dollar company which he had built over a fifty-year period. At five o'clock in the afternoon I found him still in his office, busily managing the affairs of his life at seventy-five years of age. He is still used as a consultant in his former firm, computers and modern technology notwithstanding.

My uncle, at seventy-five years of age, refused to retire as a Baptist minister after fifty-three years of service. In fact, the church he was pastoring at that time experienced its greatest growth level in its one-hundred-year history. He had learned to cope with his maturity and continued to make a much needed contribution to life. Consequently, he was not plagued with depression.

It seems that depression-free living during the seventh decade of life is determined by one's contribution to the well-being of other people and society. No person should retire without including that dimension in his thinking. Everyone needs to be needed. I know a happy, well-adjusted, seventy-year-old former sea captain who teaches Sunday school and is an active leader with senior citizens.

Beware of the retirement obsession! The human mind can adapt to almost anything, with the exception of idleness. That is doubtless the reason for the ancient Chinese curse, "I hope you are confined to eternal idleness!"

Plan your retirement to be an active and productive time; you will enjoy it longer. Very few people "wear out"—most people "rust out."

Separation Through Death

The second major problem in this seventh decade of life concerns the difficulty of coping with the loss of one's life companion. Statistically it is said that fifty percent of those over sixty-five are either single, divorced, or widowed. Of all the traumatic experiences a person faces in life, the most critical seems to be the loss of a life partner through death.

Many people, particularly those without spiritual reserves, are incapable of making the necessary adjustment to this tragedy. If they refuse to accept it and indulge in self-pity for having been left behind, they will experience increasing periods of depression that can shorten their life. Friends of mine were in their midseventies when they celebrated their fifty-sixth wedding anniversary. The husband, who had been ill for about nine months, passed away a few weeks later. His wife, who had faithfully nursed her husband, died two days later for no apparent reason. But she had a reason! She lost her desire to live when she lost her husband. The understand-able grief and depression was more than her tired old body could take, and thus their funeral services were held simultaneously.

The Eighth Decade of Life

The eighth decade is not significantly different from any other except that senility may become a problem, which may result in depression in the life of a marriage partner. Declining health and an increase in physical maladies are apt to make individuals more con-scious of themselves and their feelings than anything else. If they are depression-prone, this will intensify feelings of hypochondria and make their infirmities worse. In addition, their circle of friends is apt to grow smaller through death, and they may not be able to keep pace with the energetic society around them.

Preoccupation with self during this period is a natural and dan-gerous threat to well-being. It is not uncommon for such people to be thrown back on their own responsibility. At a time when they are declining physically and financially, this is a tailor-made environ-ment for self-pity. Their children have families of their own, and the retired senior citizen tends to withdraw into the shell of his or her own apartment and live in the past.

The Ninth Decade of Life

Surprisingly enough, the ninth decade of life does not seem to be generally infused with the depressions of the other decades. Some suggest that this is because people return to a childlike atti-tude toward life at this age. Personally, I am inclined to think that it is because the depression-prone, introspective types have already brought on a premature death and that most people living at this age maintain an optimistic outlook on life.

A lengthy survey was made some years ago among octogenarians. Answering over 300 questions to see what they shared in common, they reflected unusual agreement on only one point: a positive antic-ipation of the future. Somehow they had learned the secret of enjoy-ing today and looking forward to an equally interesting tomorrow. My wife's mother was a good example. She married for the third time at age 84, having outlived her previous partners, then died herself at 94. She always possessed an optimistic outlook and never said anything negative about anyone. This seems to be the secret of longevity.

CONCLUSION

In retrospect, we find that each stage of life offers its own potential cause of depression. Yet many people live through them all unscathed. Their lack of depression is not due to lack of problems, however, but to a healthy mental attitude amid whatever stage of life they occupy.

Chapter 5

The Causes of
Depression

In chapter 4 we reviewed some of the general causes of depression according to the decades of life. Obviously these do not include all the reasons even the average person could give for his depression. A number of specific causes arise within every decade. Besides, everyone does not mature at the same rate; consequently the general pattern suggested in that chapter may take place before or after the decade mentioned, or an individual may elude the stage altogether.

COMMON CAUSES OF DEPRESSION

Most depression is triggered by some external experience. For that reason it is very helpful to become aware of the most common causes of the problem so that if they occur in one's life, one need not be engulfed in the potential depression. As nearly as possible we shall attempt to list them in the order of their importance and frequency.

Disappointment

Of the hundreds of depression cases I have examined, without exception they began with a disappointment or experience in which the individual was displeased. Hardly anyone becomes depressed when everything is going his way. But to live is to experience the disappointment that something or someone has not performed up to expectations.

The cause of the disappointment can be almost anything. One woman's depression began when her favorite rosebush died. Another individual's depression was triggered by her husband's expression of irritation while Christmas shopping. More than one parent has become depressed over the poor grades of his child, and some children get depressed over the negative reaction of their parents to their grades.

One of the most common sources of disappointment in life is people. Because of pressure, physical exhaustion, or a dozen other reasons, they may become irritable, thoughtless, or unkind on a particular occasion. If love for ourselves is greater than love for the individual who insults us, we will take offense, become displeased, and progress quickly along the road to discouragement—the first stage of depression. If the hurt or insult is contemplated and nursed long enough, it will produce vexation and, ultimately, despair.

The more important the object of the insult, the more grievous the discouragement. Since the need for love is so great in all of us, it follows that the greatest source of discouragement is the rejection of someone we love. The root problem with those caught in despair is almost always rejection by the person they love most.

Several years ago, a newspaper article recalled the experience of a schoolteacher father whose wife suddenly divorced him and remarried. He had been so occupied with his work that he had overlooked his wife's discontent with their relationship. He testified, "It took me almost a year to get over it! I had never been depressed in my life until my wife left me. Suddenly the carpet was jerked out from under my whole life. For weeks I just wanted to die." I have seen the most self-sufficient of men lapse into depression after such an experience.

A singular love object—namely, the parent—often triggers depression in children. Whether the child's perspective is real or imagined, once she suspects that the parents do not approve of her or, worse yet, wish they had never given birth to her, the child becomes a likely subject for depression. Loving encouragement with an ample administration of discipline when needed is a parent's most profitable investment in the life of his or her child.

Loneliness is not a cause of depression, but a result. The individual whose love object has rejected him, or has been snatched from him by death, will be plunged into depression-producing loneliness. This psychic pain occasioned by the emptiness of loneliness can be healed only by the love of another person. Unfortunately, the depressed person is apt to withdraw from people who in turn are so interested in themselves that they tend to be insensitive to the love needs of others.

Lack of Self-Esteem

Another almost universal characteristic of the depressed person is his lack of self-esteem. Unfortunately, this deficiency tends to be exaggerated to an extreme, often because his unrealistic expectations make him incapable of self-approval. This is particularly true of the perfectionist individual, who is never fully pleased with his accomplishments.

One of my sons is an excellent pianist. In the ninth grade he played his first piano solo in our evening church service; I was elated with his performance and, needless to say, quite proud of him. After the service I gave him a bear hug and exclaimed, "Lee, you played superbly tonight!" He didn't crack a smile. "No, I didn't," he replied. "I missed a note!" Failure to him was one bad note out of five hundred. It all depends upon your frame of reference.

"I get so disgusted with myself" or "I'll never amount to anything" are typical cries of the depressed. This temperament-induced tendency is so important that we will devote an entire chapter to it later.

Unfair Comparisons

Every time you compare yourself with someone who scores more favorably than you do, depression may ensue. Discontent with what you have and are will direct your thoughts inward and generate depression. Most of the time, of course, you pursue an unfair comparison, matching an area of your deficiency against that of someone else's strength. What makes the comparison particularly ill-advised is that you are not cognizant of the other person's weaknesses, and thus your envy fastens your interest almost exclusively on your discontent.

Comparisons involving material possessions are especially dangerous. King David of Israel wisely admitted, "I envied the arrogant when I saw the prosperity of the wicked" (Psalm 73:3). We may understandably crave a friend's personal warmth or sense of humor, but we must not envy his possessions, popularity, talents, or looks. The wise man heeds the admonition, "Be content with what you have" (Hebrews 13:5).

Ambivalence

Some psychiatrists, like Dr. Ostow, consider ambivalence "the most common precipitate cause of depression." He defines ambivalence as "the sense of being trapped, that is, being unable to remedy an intolerable situation."[1] The individual may shift into ambivalence in his mental attempt to escape his present situation, adopting a position between love and hate—an attitude of indifference.

Feeling trapped is not only one of the causes of depression, it is also a major reason for divorce. For instance, if a couple feels forced by an unwanted pregnancy to get married, the young husband or wife may feel ensnared, and a period of ambivalence may eventually erupt into anger. This is particularly true if the unplanned marriage destroys their long-range educational or vocational goals. Many couples who experience no such trauma at their wedding still feel "trapped." Having several children early in the marriage, lacking proper vocational skills, or enduring heavy weights of responsibility may create an ambivalent depression that develops into an increasing animosity toward anyone who, according to their perspective, devised the trap. In marriage, of course, this is the partner. In adolescence the parent bears the brunt of the young person's wrath when he is "trapped" by school, authority, or responsibility.

The capable career woman who is confined to the home with preschool children commonly feels trapped. Her situation becomes particularly difficult if she is experienced in the business world and thoroughly enjoys that challenge. Because housework, diapers, and baby talk do not stimulate her, she may feel trapped by the very people she loves most.

The modern emphasis on women's rights and careerism for all women will seriously compound this problem. When I asked one woman, "What do you do?" she replied rather sadly, "Oh, I'm just a homemaker and mother!" Women who feel unimportant and worthless because they do not have a career or job outside their homes are likely candidates for depression. Actually, when considered in the light of one's lifetime, what could be better than being a "homemaker and mother," or a husband and father? Faulty mental values often lead to depression.

Sickness

Everyone has a breaking point. We have already seen that some people can endure more pressure or depression-producing circumstances than others. But whatever your tolerance level for depression, it will be lowered through illness. Protracted periods of illness make you even more vulnerable, and the side effects of some drugs may amplify the problem. Dr. Ostow explains this dilemma at great length.

Some of the factors which can trigger depression are entirely organic. For example, individuals who have had infectious hepatitis are apt to discover that despite good physical recovery, they are left with a profound enervation which leaves them not only inert, but often depressed. Infectious mononucleosis has a similar though perhaps less pronounced tendency to favor depression. . . . the brain disorder called parkinsonism usually includes depression as one of its component elements. Drugs may have a depressing effect too. For example, the drug called reserpine is often prescribed for high blood pressure. It is effective in lowering blood pressure but, in susceptible individuals, it may precipitate clinical depression. Because of this depressing tendency, it functions as a true tranquilizer and can be used in the treatment of schizophrenia, for example. Other true tranquilizers, when administered for one purpose or another, may also precipitate depression. Cortisone and similar steroid drugs often make an individual seem more energetic and livelier. However, given in large enough doses and over long enough periods of time, these drugs may precipitate depression. It has been reported by a number of physicians that regular use of oral contraceptive drugs tends to facilitate depression. This claim has not been substantiated but, on the other hand, it cannot be dismissed.[2]

In addition, when a person is weakened or debilitated by illness, things that would not ordinarily be bothersome tend to be unduly magnified. It is probably easier to drift into self-pity during an illness than at any other time.

Biological Malfunction

Many authorities attribute a sizable number of depressions to biological or glandular malfunctions. Abnormal thyroid is often one of the first things considered; others dispute this claim, asserting that depression is brought on by an improper reaction to some traumatic experience.

A college classmate of mine had become a leading pastor in his denomination in his midforties. He was a devoted family man, a good father, and an example of Spirit-filled living. Suddenly he found himself in Ward 7 of a local psychiatric hospital, one he as a pastor had visited many times before—in an attempt to comfort others. Now he was the patient. He was depressed, dangerously so. During that time, he lost not only the joy of living, he lost the desire. Eventually he resigned from the patient church that prayed for his healing, but nothing worked. In his book, *Depression, Finding Hope and Meaning in Life's Darkest Shadow,* he tells the heartrending experience that changed his life. Naturally he suspected the Christian community assumed it was a "sin problem" or a "spiritual problem." Sometimes even he thought so.

He also tells how a doctor friend who loved him helped to discover that his depressions followed certain eating habits. This led to the realization that he was hypoglycemic. If he skipped meals or went too long between meals his blood sugar dropped so low it took his emotions with it, and he ended up too depressed to eat, the very thing he needed most. Actually, it was more complex than that, but he was relieved to discover his problem was physical not spiritual. All the spiritual disciplines in the world will not keep a hypoglycemic person from depression if they don't follow a strict eating program as prescribed by their doctor. Today he is living a normal life. He is still hypoglycemic, which he has learned to live with, but he is not depressed. His book is good reading for anyone who is depressed or anyone who wants to help those who are.

Hypoglycemia is only one of several physical malfunctions that can set off a wave of depression, which is why anyone who experiences depression for ten days or two weeks without a known cause should see a medical doctor. For as we shall see, ten to as high as fifteen percent of those who become depressed do so because of some physical or biological malfunction. If they have a negative or self-pitying thinking pattern it can exacerbate the depression by lengthening it and making it more intense. For in some cases, the self-destroying thinking pattern can bring on the biological problems, compound them, or even induce harmful changes in the operation of the body and thus adversely affect the body's delicate chemistry and hormonal balance. Again I say, seriously depressed people should see their doctor. By following his medical suggestions and by using the thinking patterns offered by this book, even those whose depression may be attributed to physical problems can be helped.

Postpartum Depression

Practically every book on depression available today includes the problem of postpartum depression. Even a sanguine young mother may experience depression shortly after the birth of her child, quite often because of the emotional exhaustion that follows childbirth. In varying degrees the mother is conscious for nine months that a new life is growing within her. Suddenly she is empty, and in addition, she is pressed quickly into a new way of life. It should be of comfort to new mothers to know that the letdown feeling or exhaustion is quite normal and soon passes. (One added word of warning in this regard: A mother may escape this experience after her first child but encounter it with her second or third.)

Fantasies and illusions never seem to be as good as the real thing. Within a couple of days the new mother discovers that babies are not "cuddly little things" and soft bundles of love, but noisy, fussy, smelly, demanding creatures. She may even resent nursing the child if the process becomes painful. Her depression may cause her to feel guilty and inadequate, which in turn will protract her dilemma.

The best medicine I know for postpartum depression is tender loving care from the baby's father. If he is a mature young man and loves his wife more than himself, he will shower his emotionally spent wife with patience, kindness, and affection. She may be irritable, unreasonable, and difficult to live with at this time, perhaps even hard to love, but the husband must remember he contributed to her condition and should now seek to boost her morale and self-confidence. For this reason I usually urge the young father to take a week of vacation when the baby is born and give himself to caring for his wife. Such a love investment reaps wonderful dividends in the future. Many women who tend to resent their husband's solicitation the first week or two later come to appreciate it after the depression passes. As one woman admitted, "I treated him like a dog right after the baby was born, but later I came to realize what a wonderful man he was."

Occasionally this period of depression lingers on too long. Until better medical evidence to the contrary becomes available, I suspect that the mother's thinking pattern is the problem. If ample time for her vitality and energy to return has passed, but her depression has not departed, she is probably indulging in self-pitying thoughts. Many women who turned out to be wonderful mothers have confessed that for a long period after the birth of their child, they resented the child. They chafed at the constant drain on their energy, nerves, and time. They were even irritated at having to share the affections of their husband or the limelight with their friends.

Believe it or not, some women enjoy being pregnant! I shared that with a mother of six who retorted, "You must be kidding!" There are various reasons for this delight, but some women relish the *attention* they receive when "great with child." However, after delivery the baby gets all the attention. Some depression-prone women, driven by a feeling of emptiness, delight in the "full" feeling they experience during pregnancy but are engulfed with an empty feeling after childbirth. Such women create severe difficulties for themselves because of their faulty thinking patterns.

Hyper Mental Activity

The active, productive person occasionally encounters a rather strange form of depression during the fifth or sixth decade of life. Not prone to depression by nature, he experiences great difficulty in coping with it. Not much has been written on the subject, but in recent years it has been increasingly under study. By the time the active, choleric individual reaches the fifth or sixth decade of life, his lifestyle is so cluttered with detail, promotion, and energy that it is difficult for him to rest mentally. Thoughts seem to short-circuit one another, and for the first time his powers of concentration begin to fail. This is an unnerving experience for a usually secure person. Reacting with annoyance and frustration because he cannot sustain his focus on an important matter, he fails to realize that the more he fusses at himself and anticipates the problem, the longer it will persist. If he does not learn efficient methods of managing his time and personal affairs, he is apt to continue this short-circuiting with increasing severity.

An apparent symptom of this form of depression is sudden irritability for no obvious reason. One father, arriving home from work to a house he enjoyed and to children he loved, suddenly became aware of the teenage hubbub and jangling. Responding with hostility and rage, he spoke sharply to the children and then hurried to his bedroom to reflect upon his unusual behavior. "What's wrong with me?" he wondered. "The children have acted this way for years. Why should I respond so harshly now?"

Some doctors feel that the problem is caused by a hormonal or chemical change in the system, which is quite possible. Yet unresolved is whether the intense mental activity of the person gives inadequate rest to the brain, causing it to react this way and in turn establishing a chain reaction in the glands, all of which could create the hormonal or chemical imbalance. In any case, such depression usually responds well to medication. One doctor has put more than 500 such patients on a mild form of Dilantin, which he feels is the best means of treatment. In fact, he acknowledged that he himself was taking the medication and approved its results. Some doctors prescribe a form of tranquilizer to reverse the activity syndrome immediately and then suggest a reduction in work schedule and an emphasis on leisure activity as a further means of remedy. Most active people, however, tend to prefer the medication so as to maintain their increased workload.

Rejection

At the risk of becoming unduly repetitive, I would like to reassert the tremendous love need in every human being. When that need goes unfulfilled, depression is the escape hatch people use to cope with it. Such depression begins early for the unwanted child who fears rejection by his parents. It occurs in the adolescent who feels rejected by his peer group, the wife who senses the rejection of her husband or a woman she admires. Men share the experience when they forfeit the affection of their wife, lose their job, or suffer the betrayal of a trusted friend. Many times the depression is out of proportion to the rejection, especially when the individual concentrates on the injustice of the rejection and his subsequent loneliness.

Inadequate Goals

In my chapter on depression in *Spirit-Controlled Temperament,* I wrote, "There is a natural psychological letdown whenever a great project has been completed." In the years that have passed since I wrote that, I have become inclined to feel that the problem is really one of inadequate goals.

Human beings are clearly goal-driven creatures; without goals we cease to struggle. That is the way our minds were created. But whenever we let a project become our primary goal, we inevitably experience a letdown after its attainment. For that reason we need to maintain long-range, as well as short-range, goals, frequently reassessing and modifying them. Extremely goal-conscious people are rarely depressed. Prior to finishing one project, they originate three others! We could all learn a lesson from them: Never indulge a mental vacuum. Instead, cultivate the art of setting goals.

One self-pitying woman used to wail, "I have nothing to look forward to." Obviously she was spending too much time thinking about herself. A world so filled with moody, problem-laden people documents the fact that too many individuals lack worthwhile goals.

WORTHWHILE GOALS

Never settle for second-rate or selfish goals. Earl Nightingale, who probably has helped to motivate more people than any other living person, advises that people desiring success should never try to get rich. Above all, set goals for yourself that involve helping other people, the riches will follow. He has certainly captured the biblical principle, "Give, and it will be given to you" (Luke 6:38). The richest people I know are those who have given themselves unselfishly to other people. Such motivation will affect the way you sell, cook, teach, or ply your particular trade. True riches, of course, are totally unrelated to money or material reward. In fact, if a person has earned money without helping people, his money will not contribute to his happiness.

A perceptive realtor friend, who sold rather expensive homes, observed that a big house never brought happiness. But if the people bought a big home with money they earned helping other people, they tended to enjoy that home. He expressed his homespun philosophy in these words, "Instead of being a status symbol, a home should be an expression of how much help a person has been to his fellowman." Of one thing I am sure: Happy people have strong goals, and somehow these include helping other people. They can also be assured that they will never run out of people to help.

SUMMARY

Depression does not just happen. It always has a cause. Even in the case of postpartum depression, when there seems to be no explainable cause, the birth of the child triggers it. As basic and common as these causes are, except for the biological functions mentioned in this chapter, they do not really comprise the true causes of depression. For many people have faced all these problems without becoming depressed. Why is it that some people escape the problem while others are engulfed by it? Actually, several of these causes of depression are not causes at all. They are excuses for depression. These causes are to depression what meringue is to a pie. It looks good and tastes good, but meringue is no substitute for pie. These reasons, then, are often merely the covering for the real problem, which will be analyzed in the next three chapters.

Chapter 6

Testing Yourself for Depression

Assuming that the experts are right (and I have no reason for believing otherwise) when they say that "everyone at some time is depressed," you may wish to take a simple test that I have developed (based on many other such tests) to see if you are experiencing depression right now.

It is not foolproof, but it can give you an indication if you need help—from your pastor, doctor, counselor, or a friend.

By reading the first five chapters of this book you may already have recognized that you have several of the symptoms we have covered. Please do not feel guilty! Feelings of guilt are common to nearly all depressed individuals. Somehow a person can accept a heart attack or other debilitating physical problem without guilt, for "after all, we are all human." Yet the same person is prone to feel guilty if he is depressed.

The truth is, depression can be cured—either with the spiritual therapy that I present in chapter 17 or by one of the other therapies we shall examine. Keep in mind, there is help for you!

Before taking this self-scoring test, realize that emotional depression may be the body's means of coping with traumatic experiences. For example, you would not expect a person to grieve the loss of a loved one, a job, a marriage, or financial security without feeling depressed for a period of time. However, when the healing process does not occur or is delayed the danger of serious depression grows. Therefore, weigh such calamities realistically before taking this test.

Please answer the following questions carefully. Circle the number that best describes your present state.

0 You rarely or never have the feeling described
1 You occasionally feel this way (once a month)
2 You feel this way twice a month or more
3 You feel this way most or all of the time

1. 0 1 2 3 I seem to be tired much of the time.
2. 0 1 2 3 I can't find any activities that really interest me.
3. 0 1 2 3 I have difficulty making decisions.
4. 0 1 2 3 Sex doesn't interest me at all anymore.
5. 0 1 2 3 I don't like the way I look.
6. 0 1 2 3 When something goes wrong, I know it is my fault.
7. 0 1 2 3 I doubt the future will improve my circumstances.
8. 0 1 2 3 Sometimes I think about actually killing myself.
9. 0 1 2 3 I have difficulty sleeping.
10. 0 1 2 3 I cry for no apparent reason.
11. 0 1 2 3 I have difficulty going to sleep at night.
12. 0 1 2 3 My present work bores me; I work because I have to.
13. 0 1 2 3 I worry about circumstances beyond my control.
14. 0 1 2 3 I worry that my physical appearance is declining.
15. 0 1 2 3 Everyday activities give little satisfaction.
16. 0 1 2 3 I don't enjoy going out after work or on weekends.
17. 0 1 2 3 I often become irritable with family and friends.
18. 0 1 2 3 I am sensitive to criticism.
19. 0 1 2 3 I am really unhappy.
20. 0 1 2 3 I really do not enjoy being around other people.

Total _____

How to Score Your Test Results

0–19 Suggests you are basically a happy person and seldom disposed to depression.

20–29 Indicates you may have some mild depression. You will find the recommendations of this book very helpful.

30–39 Indicates you may have moderate depressions on occasion and should consider going to your pastor, your family doctor, or a Christian counselor. The next few chapters will be of particular value to you.

40 + May indicate you have severe depression and need help.

After finishing this book, if your depression persists longer than ten days to two weeks, make an appointment with your family doctor to see if it is physical or biochemical. Follow his directions carefully, and use the mental and spiritual suggestions offered in the book on an ongoing basis.

Special Note: If your present depression is not characteristic of your life, yet you have not experienced any known traumatic experience like death of a loved one, divorce, rejection of a love object, loss of a job or investment, or even a move to another city, you may have a physically induced depression. You need a complete physical exam; your condition may be easily treatable, and you may return to normal quite quickly. Please do not put off making an appointment with your doctor! I have known of people who went for years before discovering their depression was not caused by sin or some other spiritual weakness but instead was the malfunction of their thyroid, a hypoglycemic condition, or a hormonal change in their body. Don't waste your life on needless depression when, as we shall see in the next chapter, there is help available.

Chapter 7

Is There a Cure for Depression?

For at least 2,500 years man has made serious attempts to cure depression. In recent times medical science and motivational studies of the mechanism of the human mind have produced rather significant attempts to remedy the problem. Whether these cures are really valid is a matter of controversy among equally competent experts.

The three most popular attempts to cure depression today are drug therapy, electrotherapy, and psychotherapy. Each method has its loyal devotees, and some analysts use combinations of them. We shall look at each of them in turn and, in addition, consider the one I believe is even more successful most of the time—spiritual therapy. Keep in mind that the treatment for depression depends upon the cause of the depression, the resources of the one to whom the depressed person has gone for help, and the depth of the depression.

DRUG THERAPY

Drugs have been utilized in an attempt to help depressed people since the beginning of recorded history. "More than 2000 years ago Hippocrates prescribed hellebore for the emotionally ill."[1] Before that the Chinese used ephedrine for nervous disorders. Medical literature also reports that in many of the older civilizations opiates, herbs, and other plant and berry extracts were selected for their sedative effects. Interestingly enough, the medicine men of primitive cultures used extracts of cocoa leaves, peyote root, and poppy seed for their hallucinogenic effects in counteracting the pain or lethargy of anxiety or depressive states. Far more sophisticated, chemically manufactured drugs are produced today by pharmaceutical houses as the result of painstaking research and experimentation. Most of the drugs currently prescribed by doctors have been introduced into the market since 1955. Dr. Mortimer Ostow, New York neurologist and psychiatrist, has this to say about drug therapy.

We can list the following among the advantages of drug treatment. . . . It can be used even in patients too miserable to cooperate in psychotherapy. . . . The patient usually obtains relief after about four to six weeks of daily medication. (It has been observed that by administering the drugs by injection for the first few days, one may obtain a therapeutic result within days rather than weeks.) Drug treatment can be continued, so far as we know, indefinitely. Compared to psychotherapy it is quite inexpensive. It can be used for the treatment of large numbers of patients for whom psychotherapy is not available. *After some experience, general practitioners and internists learn to use these drugs and are therefore able to care for their depressed patients without referring them to psychiatrists.*

Among the disadvantages of drug therapy we can list the following. It does nothing to remedy the patient's difficulty in object relations. It does nothing to repair family relations. It gives the patient a false sense that his problems have been solved and sometimes that he is even "supernormal." Therefore it frequently discourages patients from undertaking psychotherapy which most of them urgently require. Drugs have some side effects which may be distressing and which may make treatment impossible, and a few drugs have some serious toxicity. Perhaps fifteen or twenty percent of patients do not respond to drug therapy. If object relations continue to deteriorate and to generate a greater and greater degree of ambivalence, the ambivalence may overcome the effect of the drug and the patient may relapse. Since depletion of psychic energy protects against psychotic detachment, the administration of energizing drugs may precipitate schizophrenic psychosis.

The antidepressant drugs, evidently, do not offer the ideal solution to depression. Since they require four weeks or more before they become effective when given orally, they leave the patient exposed to suicide risk for at least that period of time. The effective dose cannot be ascertained in advance. Therefore the doctor must choose between starting with a small dose and gradually increasing it in order to prevent side effects, and starting with a good dose to speed the effect and thereby risking distressing side effects. Sometimes the side effects can be so distressing that the patient will resist taking the drug (emphasis added).[2]

Several years ago, a woman informed me that she had found her husband's diet pills to be the perfect solution to her depression. She did not realize, however, that those diet pills were probably a form of amphetamine which was never intended for permanent use, but for short periods to help in food intake reduction. In addition to cutting down on one's appetite, they also stimulated the "pleasure center" of the brain just above the hypothalamus gland, producing a feeling of euphoria in direct proportion to the amount of amphetamine taken and the user's natural immunity level.

The trouble with amphetamines is that they become addictive—even dangerously so. The body's natural immunity level responds to this drug, making it necessary to increase the dosage to continue the same effects. In addition, the exhilarating "high" that amphetamines produce is followed by a corresponding "low" which, not surprisingly, sends the individual into a worse depression than before he began to take the drug. The woman mentioned above, like scores of others, compounded her problems by taking her husband's pills. Not only did she feel worse after taking his "diet pills," but her husband was upset that his pills had disappeared. I have repeatedly observed that people on diet pills are usually irritable and the pills tend to aggravate a bad situation. Her first visit concerned an emotional problem. After taking the amphetamines she added a marital problem.

Dr. Leonard Cammer, another psychiatrist, favors electrotherapy and is somewhat critical of drug therapy. In his classic book, *Up From Depression,* he states,

No drug will always do exactly and only what is asked of it for everyone. An aspirin may relieve a headache in one case. In another, it can irritate the stomach and induce heartburn; or it can also cause ringing in the ears. The latter two symptoms are side effects.

Antidepressants, tranquilizers, and stimulant drugs, all powerful and complex chemicals, can give rise to quite a few side effects in different people or in the same person at different times. Most of them are not serious. For example, an antidepressant may cause the person to perspire and develop dryness of the mouth, mild constipation, and some blurring of vision. While these side effects can be distinctly annoying, they are not critical.

But what if the person's special sensitivity to the drug produces side effects that signal more than this? Perhaps danger? While the incidence of such sensitivities remains small they can occur. For example, some drugs may raise or lower the blood pressure when combined with alcohol, certain foods, or other medication. Still others can destroy blood corpuscles and leave the person open to infection, liver trouble, or other complications. To be sure, none of this need go to serious proportions if [the patient], when placed on a drug program for depression, remains under medical care and observation.[3]

Dr. Cammer further reports that only thirty-five percent of those with acute depressions were cured by drugs.[4] More recently, Dr. John Rush wrote in his book on depression: "Tricyclic antidepressant medications are reported to be effective in some 60 to 75 percent of the patients treated."[5] Doctors Depaulo Jr. and Ablow, already mentioned, suggest "70 percent."[6] In the 1990s, exciting new medications have been discovered that, if they do not assure a much higher percentage of cure, give promise of one in the near future. This is why every severely depressed person should be under the care of a doctor.

THE WONDERFUL WORLD OF PROZAC

Prozac burst into the world market in 1988 and has seemingly revolutionized the drug treatment for depression. Within three weeks, most patients experience a remarkable mood change that make some act like they have had a temperament change. One man testified: "Not only did the depression lift, so did my uncontrollable anger." The author of an article in *Christianity Today* claimed, ". . . sixty to eighty percent of clinically depressed patients benefit from prozac. . . . Sales reached $1.7 billion world wide in 1994. . . . Five million people are on prozac in the United States and 10 million people worldwide."[7] It should not be considered a wonder drug, but few harmful side effects have surfaced so far, and those that have are more than offset by the claims of millions who are experiencing the first relief of their lives.

PHYSICAL FITNESS AND DEPRESSION

During the past twenty-five or thirty years we have seen a growing interest in physical fitness. Men and women are walking, jogging, swimming, participating in aerobic dance and other fitness programs in record numbers. Subsequently, there has been a marked increase in good health and longer life (some suggest as much as three years greater longevity for those who jog or exercise regularly). Exercise also seems to produce more stable emotions and a feeling of well-being or optimism among those who are consistent.

I can personally testify to the truth of this. Thirty years ago, I read an article by Billy Graham in *Reader's Digest*. He told how he tended to get colds and flu frequently until he took the advice of a doctor friend, who encouraged him to jog regularly. I started jogging the next day. Gradually I built up my distance to three and a half miles a day, which I have maintained ever since. It has not only kept me in excellent physical condition, I am also much more optimistic, creative, and mentally alert for the first three hours after jogging. But I am not unique. Anyone who enjoys basic good health would improve their quality of life by participating regularly in some form of aerobic exercise, whether it be jogging, walking, swimming, aerobic dance, or any other type.

Unfortunately, depressed people are often so apathetic they refuse to engage in physical exercise. I have encouraged many to force themselves to walk and jog alternately for one mile a day for two weeks and then gradually increase their time and distance. Those few who had the mental toughness and self-discipline did so by faith in my recommendation for the first month then began to do so regularly because of the feeling of well-being it produced. Exercise is not a "cure-all" for everything, but it is certainly a supplement to any other therapy a person tries and can enable many people, along with spiritual therapy and proper nutrition, to avoid ailments that cause others their age long-term and expensive treatment. The apostle Paul told Timothy that "bodily exercise profits little" (1 Timothy 4:8 NKJV). He did not say profits nothing! God told Adam he must earn his bread "by the sweat of [his] brow." If God commanded us to sweat, somehow sweating must be beneficial to the proper functioning of our bodies. Jogging and other forms of moderate exercise are excellent ways for people in good health to reduce or even eliminate depression. (Note: If you are *not* in good health or have not been exercising consistently, please consult your doctor before starting any exercise program.)

ELECTROTHERAPY

During the forties and fifties the most prominent method of treating depression involved electric-shock treatments. Dr. Mortimer Ostow, who seems to favor drug therapy, notes,

> Until the advent of antidepressant drugs, the only organic treatment for melancholic depression was the procedure we call electric-shock therapy. In this treatment a brief electric shock is administered to the brain, and it produces an instantaneous convulsion and leaves a temporary amnesia. As it is ordinarily administered, these treatments are repeated about three times a week until a total of five, ten, or twenty treatments is administered. As the treatments continue, the amnesia becomes more and more intense. The energizing drugs have replaced electric-shock treatment to a large extent, though the replacement is more complete in some institutions than in others.[8]

It is obvious from the above quotation that Dr. Ostow does not regard electric-shock treatment as the best method in use today for treating depression. Others, apparently just as well qualified, are much more favorable toward the practice. Consider Dr. Cammer's enthusiastic appraisal.

> An abundance of recorded evidence and validated experience has shown that EST [electric shock therapy], in accordance with recognized medical standards, is considered to be a safe procedure. This is especially true when it is given by a trained and competent psychiatrist who can evaluate his patient's condition and is prepared to deal with any expected contingency that may arise during the treatment. I, along with many other psychiatrists, prefer to be assisted by an anesthesiologist. In my opinion, this further insures an uneventful recovery from the treatment.[9]

To a layperson, electric-shock treatments seem quite frightening. However, the patient is asleep for the procedure, feels no pain, and does not remember anything about the treatment. Within twenty minutes, the anesthetic has worn off, and about forty minutes later, the patient's grogginess has left, and he or she is free to go home.

The two major complaints of electric-shock patients is that they experience a loss of memory and they fear that the process might be harmful to the brain. Dr. Cammer attempts to cancel these fears by assuring us,

> I have found no convincing clinical or research evidence to confirm that EST impairs the brain. . . . It is plain that in a large majority of cases EST *benefits* the person. By means of it he or she becomes rational and well. But if you put it this way—does EST *alter* brain function?—yes. When the brain is stimulated by electricity or chemicals in the dosages required and the duration called for, the treatment clearly modifies brain activity toward improvement. Indeed, *it is given in order to create responses that are part of this modification.*
>
> If there are any permanent side effects on brain tissue as a result of EST, these cannot be demonstrated by any reliable tests. To me it is apparent that electric and chemical application to the brain produces stimulatory effects that help the depressed person return to normal function.[10]

Dr. Cammer's view of EST became more popular during the eighties and nineties, because the decreased voltage made possible by modern technology lessens the harmful side effects and the degree of memory loss experienced. Additionally, in many instances the lost memory does seem to return in time. Besides, any negative effects from either drug therapy or EST must be considered in light of the high suicide rate among the depressed (estimated to be between 27,000 and 30,000 annually). Obviously it would be tragic if a depressed person refused drug or EST treatment because of the possible side effects and then committed suicide.

As a nonmedical counselor, it has been my observation that electric-shock therapy, like drug therapy, will provide only minimal success unless one of two things occurs. Either there is a change in the circumstances that caused the depression or the patient experiences a change in the thinking pattern that induced it. Otherwise, in spite of the therapy used, the depression will recur in time.

One of my counselees had shock treatments on two occasions separated by a five-year interval. Apparently feeling a retrogression, she came in for help. After analyzing the problem, we found that the shock treatments had only cured the symptoms, not the problem that caused them. Consequently there was a recurring need for more treatments. Her difficulty was one of intense guilt. When her guilt consciousness was removed, then indeed she was capable of a normal happy life. It never became necessary for her to undergo the third set of treatments.

PSYCHOTHERAPY

Even before the days of Sigmund Freud, psychotherapy was the most common method of treating the depressed. In fact, it was used almost exclusively until EST came into view during the 1940s. Simply defined, psychotherapy is "talk treatment." It consists of a depressed patient speaking freely to a counselor. Because the counselee is depressed due to a faulty thinking pattern, the counselor must examine the patient's values and judgments toward other people so as to help him understand himself better and learn how to relate properly to others.

Since a high percentage of depression is kindled by the rejection or loss of a love object, a warm and empathic counselor can frequently provide the counselee with an adequate substitute. Probably the most therapeutic part of psychotherapy is that the despairing individual who feels rejected, hopeless, and alone has access to the patience, understanding, and concern of a counselor in confidentiality and privacy. If the counselor can sufficiently meet his patient's needs by suggesting corrective measures the counselee can take to change his thinking patterns, counseling can often provide a very meaningful crutch upon which the depressed person may lean.

Significant drawbacks to psychotherapy include its painstakingly long and exceptionally expensive process. Most people cannot afford a lengthy series of counseling sessions from $75 to $150 an hour. The nondirective counselor believes that he should never impose his perspective or concepts on the individual, but merely serve as a sounding board to the counselee, who should organize his own principles for living. Psychotherapy often becomes an exercise in futility because it assumes that the solution to the counselee's problem lies deep within the patient and the counselor's task is simply to help draw it out. Usually the individual does not have the answer within himself. Frequently, protracted sessions of nondirective counseling may result in frustration for both the counselor and the counselee.

Psychotherapy may become dangerous when, in the case of a humanistic psychologist, the counselor seeks to impose his humanistic principles and values upon the counselee, who is soliciting help because of his desperate condition. If the counselor is an amoral individual and finds that the counselee has serious guilt problems that cause his depression, he or she may try to explain away the patient's guilt and accordingly deny the person's moral principles. When such advice comes from a professionally trained psychiatrist, it may sound quite convincing. Unfortunately, I have observed that the new style of immoral behavior usually brings a short period of exhilaration, but in many cases is followed eventually by an overwhelming consciousness of guilt that far exceeds the original problem.

Several years ago I read an article by a psychiatrist who was critical of his own profession. He stated that he had observed fifty to seventy percent of the depressed people who consulted a psychiatrist being helped during a two-year period. In addition he noted that fifty to seventy percent of those who consulted a minister, medical doctor, or good friend gained relief. But he was particularly disturbed in that fifty to seventy percent of those who received no aid whatsoever improved over a two-year period.

This does not suggest that depressed people do not need help. But many of us who have been counseling people for many years are not convinced that psychotherapy has the answer. In fact, some of the results of group therapy, sensitivity therapy, and other humanistic fads now being propagated can be downright dangerous.

One thirty-year-old single woman's depression drove her to psychotherapy. Her "Victorian ideas" were so blasted during group therapy that she later submitted to intercourse with four different men within two weeks. When she came into my office, she was not only depressed but staggering under an overwhelming load of guilt. In addition, she was pregnant. For this kind of treatment she should pay $75? There must be a better way!

CHRISTIAN PSYCHOLOGY

Usually a Christian prefers a Christian psychologist when they need psychotherapy. We seem to understand that God's ways are not man's ways and man's ways not God's (see Isaiah 55:8–9). Therefore, we should not be surprised when the theories of Freud, Adler, Skinner, Spock, and others are diametrically opposed to God's ways as stated in the Bible. While we may not hesitate to go to a heart or brain surgeon who is not a Christian, a doctor of the mind is something else. In several of my books I show the vast difference between the "wisdom of this age" and the "wisdom of God." Paul detailed that thoroughly in 1 Corinthians 1:18–31. Therefore, humanistic psychologists have little to offer Christians, for they are committed to helping people with only the humanistic tools or concepts available to them.

Christian psychologists or counselors are different—or so most Christians think. What the individual must consider however is that both humanist and Christian psychologists are required to take most of the same courses and submit to the same training in order to get their degrees and certification. Some Christians are strong enough to sort out the humanistic man-centered principles, discard them, and go on to use the biblical principles that he has come to accept. However, many Christians are not sufficiently grounded in the Word of God to do mental battle with the very persuasive professors they encounter in graduate school. Consequently, they embrace some humanistic concepts. When they put up their counseling shingle, they often provide humanistic counseling in a Christian environment.

One counseling center near Christian Heritage College, which I had a hand in founding in San Diego, California, is a case in point. I invited Dr. Henry Brandt, a biblically based Christian counselor, to set up a biblical counseling department to train Christian counselors. As we produced counselors, it became obvious that there was another center in town that used different principles. So the head of our department went to the head of that counseling center, which was sponsored by a good, Bible-believing church that appealed to the Christian community for clients. The department head asked the following question, "What place does the Bible have in your counseling technique?" The answer was revealing: "Nothing!" Although it is hard for me to believe that a Christian would never use the Bible in his or her counseling profession, it is, of course, possible. And that is the problem. It is not enough for a Christian to go to a "Christian counselor." We must seek out those counselors who test the theories of psychology by the Word of God and then accept or reject them accordingly. Humanism tries to solve the problems of man independent of God. That is simply impossible! Jesus said, "Without me you can do nothing." If a Christian counselor is going to help people in areas of mind and emotions, particularly those that spill over into their life values, he or she will have to know the principles of God.

The Bible challenges us to "test the spirits" (1 John 4:1). True Christian counseling is a matter of gently helping those who are thinking and acting contrary to the Word of God to put on the mind of Christ, as it is revealed in the Bible. Please go to a counselor with your "spiritual eyes" open. If you feel that the person is misrepresenting or ignoring the Bible, *do not go back to that counselor* before you get a second opinion. Consult your pastor for a Christian counselor in your area.

THE TOTAL PERSON

The form of therapy most commonly neglected by secular doctors, psychiatrists, and counselors today is spiritual therapy. Because our educational system is overwhelmingly secularized and based on atheistic humanism, little or no consideration is given to the highly significant spiritual side of our nature. The secular view of people as body, mind, and emotions is *completely inadequate,* and we will never solve the problems of humanity on a permanent basis until we recognize that void. We are intensely spiritual beings, which distinguishes us from the animal kingdom. Unless therapy includes a remedy for our spiritual nature, it will offer only minimal or temporary results.

All forms of therapy agree on one principle: A depressed person must be aided externally. Whether involving drugs, electric shock, or a counselor, all current therapy involves something or someone outside of the individual to support and sustain him or her. Those of us who utilize spiritual therapy in our counseling technique similarly acknowledge the need for this external power, for we have found it to be a forceful tool in reaching the total person.

The following diagram illustrates the four distinct parts of the total person. No one is complete without all of them. No one can function to the maximum without all of them. We are all aware of the mental, emotional, and physical, but few realize the tremendous importance of the spiritual dimension.

One of the great tragedies of our times is that atheistic humanists have so brainwashed our culture into thinking human beings are really just animals without a spiritual dimension to life. Because of this popular but erroneous way of thinking, most people possess few spiritual reserves upon which to draw in times of mental, emotional, or physical distress. Instead, the giant God-shaped void within them seriously compounds their problems and hampers their recovery.

To illustrate the power of spiritual therapy to change a person's life, we shall consider briefly the other three sides of man's nature.

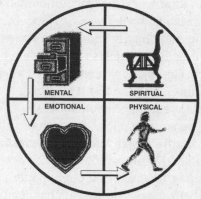

THE FOUR PARTS OF A PERSON

Physical

Everyone is conscious of the physical aspect of life—the part of our being on which we spend hundreds of thousands of dollars during a lifetime. In truth, it is the least important part, for unless the other three parts of our nature function properly, our body will malfunction. As we shall see, our physical body is controlled by our emotions.

Emotional

Of the three parts of our nature that are widely accepted today, the least understood is the emotional. Everyone is sensitive to love and hate, and we have all heard of "the heart" as the seat of the emotions. This heart is not located in the chest, of course, but between one's temples slightly behind the forehead. Scientists call this "the emotional center." This emotional switchboard seems to work electronically in conjunction with every organ of the body. If a person is emotionally at peace, his body will function normally. If his heart or emotional center is upset, he will feel the effects throughout his body.

We are all familiar with the term "emotionally induced illness." Doctors have indicated that seventy to eighty-five percent of all physical ailments are provoked by emotional disturbance. Such debilitating diseases as heart trouble, high blood pressure, ulcers, asthma, and some forms of arthritis derive from emotional tension. Dr. S. I. McMillan in his excellent book *None of These Diseases* states that there are fifty-one emotionally induced diseases. That is why a depressed person usually feels sickly if he indulges his depression for a protracted period. His emotional center sends a depressed signal to the other areas of this body. The result is lethargy.

Emotions are not generated spontaneously. Our emotions flow from our thinking patterns. Suppose, for example, that you are asked to come to the platform and spontaneously address a large audience. If you are not trained for that kind of experience, your mind will immediately set up self-conscious thought patterns producing fear, which in turn will effect a physiological change in your body. Your uneasiness may occasion knocking knees and restricted saliva glands. Your normal voice may be completely restricted, creating a high or screechy sound. Thus emotional tension, fashioning a rapid chain reaction, affects the entire body. Another common illustration relates to worry. Whenever our minds are confronted with such problems as unpaid bills or indefinite circumstances, we begin to worry. Emotional tension protracted over a long period can bring about a physical breakdown or sickness.

Since people's emotions control their body, we must examine what controls our emotions—the mind.

Mental

The mind is a phenomenal tabulating mechanism. Some have designated it "the most complicated computer in the world." The memory capability of the human mind is almost beyond belief. There are strong indications that the subconscious mind retains every thought, every sight, and every sound. When hypnotists have regressed their subjects back to the early days of infancy, amazingly accurate details of their life are revealed. The best estimates today suggest that only a very few people use more than ten percent of their mental potential.

The mind is composed of the conscious and the subconscious. Although the subconscious mind cannot be controlled, as we shall show in a later chapter, it is highly responsive to visual suggestion. "You are what you think!" accurately conveys the situation, for thinking incites our feelings. Whatever we put in our mind causes responses in our emotional center, which in turn activates a physical response. Note the symbols shown in the following chart.

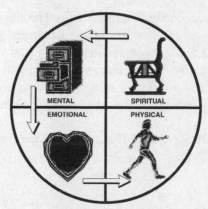

MENTAL SPIRITUAL

EMOTIONAL PHYSICAL

THE FOUR PARTS OF A PERSON

Follow the arrows to comprehend how powerfully the mind influences the emotions and body. The five senses are the windows to the mind, particularly the eyes and ears. Be sure of this: Whatever you put into your mind through your eyes or ears initiates a response in your heart and in turn motivates your body.

We may clearly illustrate this principle with the effects of pornographic literature. The reading of such literature will fan the passions that motivate and prepare your body for sexual action. By contrast, if you read clean, wholesome literature, you will enrich your emotions, producing wholesome desires and motivations in the body.

Every young man I have counseled concerning sex problems has acknowledged that he had been aroused repeatedly by reading sexually inflammatory material or viewing suggestive or X-rated movies. His drives were not spontaneous but clearly traceable to his reading or viewing matter.

The same can be said for violent action. Long before a person erupts into an angry response, he has seen, heard, or thought about those things that produced the emotions of hate that finally were put into motion. That is why the Bible says, "Anyone who hates his brother is a murderer" (1 John 3:15). No physical murder can exist without emotional murder, and the mind is responsible for the entire sequence.

As we shall see, depression (an emotion) produces physical apathy. Since feelings are caused by the mind, depression is usually initiated by a mental thought pattern. Instead of just treating the results or symptoms (apathy, sleeplessness, and so forth) with drugs or working on the emotions using substitute love objects, counselors, or EST, we may confer lifelong relief only by changing a person's thinking pattern.

The mind is the problem! But how does one control the uncontrollable mind?

Spiritual

Although a few people possess sufficient strength of mind to reverse negative or harmful thinking patterns in order to produce good emotional feelings, which in turn occasion normal body function, they are very scarce. Most people require external help in this area. Those who void their spiritual nature make themselves slaves to their own mental weakness. Most of the people who come to me for counseling have tried drugs, electrotherapy, or psychotherapy with negative or minimal results. In my opinion, such persons can be helped only by availing themselves of spiritual therapy.

A professional boxer would never enter the ring with a black patch over one eye and one arm tied behind his back. Such a sight, nevertheless, graphically illustrates the dilemma in which many people find themselves. By neglecting the spiritual side of their nature, they have blinded themselves to the tremendous power available to them in overcoming depression, fear, anger, and other detrimental emotional maladies.

Their problems are further compounded by the God-void in their lives that remains empty due to their own spiritual neglect. Pascal, the great French philosopher, once said, "There is a God-shaped vacuum in the heart of every man that can be satisfied by none other save God himself." That God-shaped vacuum keeps man on a treadmill of restless activity and propels him on a constant quest for identity and peace. It is impossible to achieve contentment on a lasting basis through the mind, the heart, or the body!

Evidence that we are intensely spiritual creatures is not difficult to obtain. Of all living creatures, only human beings undertake a universal quest for God. We alone reflect a natural, built-in religious instinct and a universal guilt consciousness.

In my travels around the world, I have made a special effort to examine the archaeological ruins of ancient civilizations. Before long I began to recognize that the oldest buildings were temples, shrines, or houses of religious worship, indicating a universal religious hunger. What produces that hunger? It is the natural, God-given spiritual instinct or nature.

Even communist leaders, who brand religion as the "opiate of the people," have had to wrestle with the fact that man is "incurably religious." That was graphically demonstrated soon after the disbanding of the Soviet Union, when millions flocked to churches and to faith in Christ even after living under communism for seventy years. This universal religious quest of humankind must have a discernible cause. Just as we experience the physical needs of hunger and thirst, emotional needs such as love, and mental needs as evidenced by curiosity, so we have deep spiritual needs, manifested by our quest for God.

Some of the most hardened atheists have demonstrated their spiritual instinct at the moment of death. We have all heard of prayerless individuals who lived totally unconscious of God during their lives, in some cases even antagonistically to him, but when confronted with death, they called for God. When I was a boy, a notorious community atheist, a bricklayer by profession, fell down a chimney he was erecting. After many unsuccessful attempts were made to extricate him, other bricklayers were summoned to take the chimney apart, brick by brick. Our local newspaper reported the next day that when they reached him, they found him praying for deliverance. Jean-Paul Sartre, the humanist French philosopher, embarrassed his fellow humanists by calling out to God on his deathbed. Rather than attribute these prayers to personal weakness, we must accept them as verification of man's natural spiritual instinct.

Anyone who neglects his spiritual nature does so at his own peril. God has given us this part of our being to stabilize and motivate our mind, heart, and body. Those who ignore this mighty power station within themselves are like a four-cylinder car functioning on only three cylinders. They do not need to improve their emotions, mind, or body. They need to empower or restore their inoperative spiritual nature.

THE GOD-VOID

The spiritual side of our nature contains our will, one of the unique characteristics that distinguishes us from the animal kingdom. God has given a free will to each of us. With it we can ignore or reject God, or we can accept and cooperate with him. We alone

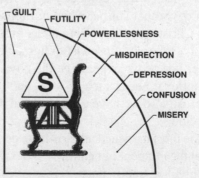

GUILT
FUTILITY
POWERLESSNESS
MISDIRECTION
DEPRESSION
CONFUSION
MISERY

A PERSON'S SPIRITUAL NATURE

make that decision, but be sure of this: Our lasting happiness depends on our choice.

The throne in the spiritual quarter of our nature symbolizes this free will. The "S" on the throne represents our ego-nature, generating the self-conscious or "self-oriented" person. God gives to each of us the opportunity to be master of our own fate, captain of our own soul. The "S" on the throne exhibits our "self" making its own decisions independent of God.

The various dots in the diagram represent the many decisions we make in our lifetime. Every individual must decide such things as where to live, where to go to school, where to work, what vocation to pursue, and whom to marry. Life is made up of a myriad of decisions, but happiness will ultimately be decided by the propriety of one's choices. If one lives an egocentric self-life independent of God, with self supreme on the throne of the will (meaning he makes his own decisions independent of God), he is going to experience varying degrees of frustration, confusion, guilt, and fear.

I have shared this diagram with hundreds of people through the years and have yet to find anyone over forty to argue with me, and even the young will often admit such a need. Some time ago, I shared it with an airline ticket agent as I was returning from a two-week vacation in Hawaii. She indicated that at twenty-two years of age she had everything to live for, but when I asked if she felt this frustration and futility in her life, she put her face in her hands and burst into tears. She wept so profusely that the tears flooded from between her fingers. Although more dramatic than most, her experience is not uncommon.

Most miserable or depressed people are not conscious of the fact that their misery emanates from the God-vacuum within them. This spiritual deficiency or God-void makes them vulnerable to a variety of mental, emotional, and physical maladies or disorders. Whether they are antagonistic to God or just neglect his presence in their lives seems to make no difference. They experience an empty hunger within them for God, and they lack the spiritual resources to help them cope with the problems caused by their self-centered decisions.

This God-void is universally as old as humanity itself. The Bible calls it "death." In the Garden of Eden when Adam and Eve rebelled and disobeyed God, they died spiritually. That spiritual death has been transmitted from generation to generation, conferring a serious void within the life of every human being. Although we can gain momentary happiness on the mental, emotional, or physical planes of life, we will never attain lasting happiness as long as the God-void in our spiritual nature is unfulfilled. We will never know abiding joy or have power to control those weaker parts of our nature.

JESUS CHRIST FILLS THE GOD-VOID

Jesus Christ is God's special remedy to fill the God-void in every human being. That he lived over 1,900 years ago is a matter of historical fact. Why he lived, however, is too often a source of confusion, even though the only authentic record of his life gives us the answer. Jesus Christ himself said, "I am come that they might have life, and that they might have it more abundantly" (John 10:10 NKJV). The abundant life he offers not only fills the God-void in a person's spirit, but also provides the power to eliminate depression and other emotional problems.

A very emotionally burdened man came to Jesus Christ one night (John 3:1–13), inquiring how he might come into a personal relationship with God. Jesus said, "I tell you the truth, no one can see the kingdom of God unless he is born again." Obviously puzzled by Christ's explanation, Nicodemus asked, "How can a man be born when he is old? . . . Surely he cannot enter a second time into his

A PERSON WITH CHRIST

A PERSON WITHOUT CHRIST

mother's womb to be born!" Jesus answered, "I tell you the truth, no one can enter the kingdom of God unless he is born of water and the Spirit." The context of this passage clearly indicates that Nicodemus needed a personal spiritual experience. Just as he had been born physically to enter this world, he had to be born spiritually to fulfill his destiny and prepare for the next world. This spiritual birth of power, created by individually receiving Jesus Christ as Lord and Savior, gives a person the external power he needs to cope with his emotional problems. This is particularly true in the case of depression.

Contrary to popular opinion, Jesus Christ is not automatically born within a person; otherwise a person would not have need for this spiritual birth. Instead (as illustrated in the next diagram) Jesus Christ is external to our spiritual nature, for we are born void of God. Through his Holy Spirit and the teaching of the Bible, Christ knocks at the door of our spiritual consciousness, saying, "If anyone hears my voice and opens the door, I will come in and eat with him, and he with me" (Revelation 3:20). This promise of Christ testifies that any individual conscious of his God-void and his rebellion against the will of God can invite the Lord into his life. Christ never forces his way into an individual's life, but responds only when invited. At that moment, the individual is spiritually made alive. This gives that person a consciousness for God and an increased capacity to cope with all the problems of life—including depression.

JESUS CHRIST'S EXPLANATION

In the Sermon on the Mount, Jesus Christ held forth two pathways to eternity: the "broad road" that leads to destruction and the "narrow road" that leads to life (see Matthew 7:13–14). Judging by the increasing number of miserable people today, it is obvious that the majority are on the broad road that leads to destruction—not only eternal destruction, but also mental, emotional, and physical self-destruction. This self-destruction is characterized by a person who leads a life spiritually void of God and reaps the results of decisions made by self, not by God.

When we pass the age of accountability and become conscious of right and wrong, we proceed on the broad road that leads to destruction. If our mental, emotional, and physical miseries make us conscious of our spiritual God-void, we may seek divine help. At that point in our lives, if we are confronted with the fact that Jesus Christ came into this world to die on the cross for our sins, we can personally receive Jesus as Lord and Savior.

The greatest expression of love the world has ever known is symbolized by the cross of Jesus Christ. On that cross God's own Son died for the sins of the whole world. Christ, who was God in human flesh and remained sinless during his thirty-three years of life, took on himself the sins of the whole world and died sacrificially that all people through him might be saved. For that reason he could say, "I am the way and the truth and the life. No one comes to the Father except through me" (John 14:6). The cross of Christ, then, becomes a bridge upon which those living on the broad road leading to destruction may travel to the wonderful road of life.

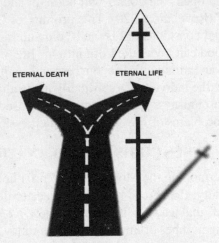

ETERNAL DEATH   ETERNAL LIFE

FOUR THINGS YOU MUST REALIZE

To fill the God-void in your life and become spiritually born again, you must realize four things:

(1) Your self-will, rebellion, and sin have separated you from God, maintaining the God-void within you. You and God

alone know the amount of your sin. It may be extensive, it may be moderate; it really doesn't matter. Your sin has separated you from God. You will never know lasting peace and happiness until your sins are forgiven.

(2) Jesus Christ died on the cross that you might be forgiven of your past sins. In God's economy "the wages of sin is death" (Romans 6:23). However, you do not have to die for yourself or your sins, for Christ has already done this for you.

(3) Jesus Christ rose again that you might be guided and empowered to live the new eternal life. "The gift of God is eternal life in Jesus Christ our Lord" (Romans 6:23). Jesus said, "Because I live, you also will live" (John 14:19). Jesus Christ's personal resurrection three days after his crucifixion is the cornerstone of Christian truth. He not only rose again to give you eternal life in heaven, but the abundant new life here and now. It is this life that will enable you to triumph over your weaknesses.

(4) You must personally receive him as Lord and Savior by inviting him into your life. Since willfulness caused you to be separated from God, increasing the God-void within you, it is imperative that you turn the controlling force of your life over to Jesus Christ. This must be done by personal invitation. Accepting him as your Savior and Lord occasions an exchange of roles. When you make him master of your life, your "self" becomes his servant. You still have to make decisions in life, but now your decisions are filtered through Christ. In a practical way it is no longer "What can I do about that?" but "Lord Jesus, what do you wish me to do about that?" No person who lives this latter way will experience a lifetime of misery. Similarly, no person who lives the other way will attain a lifetime of happiness.

THE BIG QUESTION

Have you ever personally invited Jesus Christ into your life? The best way to answer that question is to ask yourself which of the following two diagrams represents your life right now.

As you deliberate the answer, you should be prepared to pinpoint a time in your life when Jesus Christ was outside and you invited him in. If there has never been such a time, or you are not sure, I would urge you to invite him into your life right now. If you do not know how to pray, I suggest the following prayer:

A PERSON VOID OF GOD

A PERSON WITH GOD

Dear God, I admit that I am a sinner and need Jesus Christ in my life to become my Savior and Lord. This day I turn the control of my life over to You. Amen!

If you have sincerely uttered that prayer, you have the divine promise of God that "everyone who calls on the name of the Lord will be saved" (Acts 2:21). Let that promise dwell in your mind, because it is the best news you have ever heard. Today you have been *born again* (John 3:3–5). You have also been born into the family of God (John 1:12) and are guaranteed eternal life.

THE RESULTS OF THE CHRIST-CONTROLLED LIFE

The Christ-controlled life provides a spiritually dynamic power and corresponding assets that are almost beyond comprehension! Let the diagram above showing a person with God burn its way into your mind. Examine each of these key words, which signify your inheritance when you accept Christ. The Bible teaches that Jesus Christ has accomplished many things for you, but these six are particularly significant:

(1) *Pardon*—All your sins have been forgiven by the mercy of God through his Son, Jesus Christ. "If we confess our sins, he is faithful and just and will forgive us our sins and purify us from all unrighteousness" (1 John 1:9).

(2) *Peace*—Since your sins are forgiven, you now know the peace of a clear conscience before God. "Therefore, since we have been justified by faith, we have peace with God through our Lord Jesus Christ" (Romans 5:1).

(3) *Power*—A new power will gradually begin to control your life if you walk in the control of the Spirit of Christ. "Therefore, if anyone is in Christ, he is a new creation; the old has gone, the new has come" (2 Corinthians 5:17).

(4) *Joy*—Happiness is a transitory experience depending upon external events. Joy is an enduring experience that is contingent upon your relationship to God. As you continue to let Christ control your life, you will experience increasingly protracted periods of joy that are unrelated to the adversity of your circumstances (see Ephesians 5:19–20).

(5) *Purpose*—From the moment you receive Jesus Christ you have a whole new purpose for living. Before becoming a Christian, your purpose was to satisfy yourself. From this day on your purpose is to serve Jesus Christ. The apostle Paul said it in Acts 9:6 (NKJV): "Lord, what do You want me to do?" That mental attitude and prayer became the formula for his happy and successful Christian life. Christ said, "Seek first his kingdom and his righteousness, and all these things will be given to you as well" (Matthew 6:33). As you seek him, you will find that he provides adequate strength for every need.

(6) *Confidence*—As you nourish your new spiritual nature by reading, hearing, and studying the Bible, you will find a new assurance as confidence begins to grow in your life. You are now a child of God (1 John 5:10–15)!

If you sincerely prayed the prayer printed on page 88, you have become a child of God. As such, you enjoy the capacity for living a depression-free life. That does not guarantee you will, but you do possess the external source of power that will enable you to do so. Teaching you how to use this power to win over depression is the main purpose of this book. Although I have devoted an entire chapter to the causes of depression, we purposely reserved the *primary* causes until this point. My reason for doing so is very simple. Until an individual has access to the spiritual resources discussed in this chapter, he is incapable of coping with these primary causes of depression. From this point, we can proceed not only with a careful consideration of the real causes of depression, but also with the remedy that God has made available.

THE TRANSFORMATION OF A DEPRESSED DOCTOR

It is almost unbelievable the way God sends me real-life illustrations to help my readers whenever I am writing on a particular subject. Recently, two doctors and their wives dropped by my office. One of them, who I would estimate was about forty years of age or so, was carrying a copy of this book in its original printing. Before asking that I autograph it he told me this thrilling story and gave me permission to use it.

After being a physician for several years, during which he married and had three children, he was gradually overcome with a severe depression. In fact, recognizing that he was becoming suicidal, he agreed to be hospitalized. The year was 1984. After being treated for three weeks, he became convinced that the people that were working on him "really didn't know what they were doing." At the end of three weeks he got a pass to go home for a visit. Somehow that made him even more depressed. The next day he was going through a shopping mall and stopped at a bookstore. He told me, "The title of your book stood out from all the other books on the shelf—*How to Win Over Depression*." At that point in his life, he was not sure it was possible to win over that dread disease. He had tried everything the medical profession had to offer and was no better off.

Reading through the book he found that there was hope. He was particularly struck by my positive assertion: "I am confident that you or those you love do not have to be depressed." For the first time someone was offering him a way out. He read the whole book! As a non-Christian, he was also struck with the realization that my book offered help from a dimension he had never considered—the "spiritual side." He was used to trying the mental, emotional, and physical sides, but did not realize there was a spiritual dimension he had not tried. Reading on to the sixth chapter, he was impressed with the need to surrender his life and will to Jesus Christ, or as he said, "put Christ on the throne of my life. I was driving my car when I distinctly invited Christ in and surrendered my life to him. Nothing happened immediately. When I got back to the hospital, I watched a football game, and as I turned off the TV I noticed I felt different in my spirit. It was almost as if a great cloud was lifted off me. I began reading the Bible regularly, and the owner of the Christian bookstore got so well acquainted with me, he kind of discipled me in a warm and caring way. It was not long until it dawned on me, I was not only growing as a young Christian but I was experiencing permanent deliverance from my depression!" (Keep in mind, he was telling me this eleven years after the experience).

By this time tears were running down his wife's face as she said, "I have been married to two different men—the depressed man he was before his conversion and the man he is today!"

This story illustrates the fact that there is indeed a spiritual side to your nature through which God can change your whole life. It all begins by inviting Jesus Christ to come into your life as Lord and Savior. Or as my new friend said, it all began when "I put Christ on the throne of my life." And so it will for you!

You may say, "But I have met Christians who are depressed!" So have I. Becoming a Christian does not automatically keep you from being depressed. But it does give you the power of Christ in your life to help you to change your thinking pattern that will in turn enable you to win over depression. As my friend said, "The promise of God that has blessed my life is that he has given me 'the oil of joy for mourning and the garment of praise for the spirit of heaviness'" (Isaiah 61:1–3 NKJV). As we shall see, "thanksgiving living" is the mental key to overcoming depression.

Chapter 8

The Place of Anger in Depression

Depression always results from a specific cause. That the individual does not know the cause does not eliminate the fact of its existence. In his book, *The Psychology of Melancholy,* Dr. Mortimer Ostow says, "Generally, even in the case of individuals who are susceptible to depression some current insult is needed to trigger the depression process."[1]

Although we would like to blame depression on organic or psychological change in the human body, seventy-five to eighty percent of the time we are forced realistically to admit that it is the result of our reaction to an insult or disappointment or rejection. The first step in the chain reaction that produces depression is anger. Don't be surprised that you involuntarily reject such a proposal. I have consistently observed that most depressed persons cannot and do not think of themselves as angry people. A number of counselees with whom I have shared this have challenged me, but on further questioning and closer examination of their thought patterns prior to depression, we established the problem without exception.

Dr. Ostow adds,

Depression, at every phase of its development, includes a component of anger, whether visible or invisible, whether conscious or unconscious. This anger is directed against the individual who is expected to provide love but who disappoints. At different phases, the anger may arouse a wish to irritate, to hurt, or to destroy, depending upon the degree of pain which the patient suffers. Even the rebirth fantasy carries a component of anger, for it defiantly asserts that the patient will cure himself and that he does not require the assistance of the "parent" who disappointed him.[2]

Dr. Ostow further explains the problem of anger as follows:

Some parents regard and treat their children with severe hostility. In these instances the child becomes fixed into a childish pattern in his relation with his parents, and subsequently as an adult is apt to have to contend with a strong depressive tendency. Overt hostility of parent to child seems inhuman and perverse, and yet we know of numbers of such instances. . . .

If we study psychoanalytically patients who harbor hostility toward their children, we find that in each case the parent, as a child, had to contend with intense anger against his own parent or one of his own siblings; that he had contrived some defensive maneuver to contain that anger, such as reactive affection, loyalty, or subservience to the hated person; and that with the advent of the infant of the new generation the defense had collapsed and the individual was left once more to deal with this overwhelming anger. . . .

Hostility and rejection by the parent constitute a serious threat to the child. Feeling threatened, he clings more tightly, and this clinging includes both affectionate and hostile components. The intensity of these mixed situations tend in general to repeat themselves. The child may respond to any subsequent rejection with aggressive clinging. The child, when he becomes an adult, may attach himself to an unreliable, hostile partner. As an adult, he may provoke rejection by his partner. Or as a parent he may repeat the same pattern with his own child, rejecting the child and abusing it as he was rejected and abused.[3]

The conscious or subconscious anger of the abused child comes to the surface in adulthood. It often destroys a person's interpersonal relationships, particularly those most important to them, from their spouse to their children and their boss. Angry adults will show their hostility eventually, or as the sage has said, "anger will out." Some reveal it in violence to other adults, the more cowardly often turn to children, and those who internalize often become depressed. One of the sociological problems of our times is the penchant for those who were abused as children to abuse their own children. It seems to defy human logic for one would think that anyone who was abused as a child would be so sympathetic and understanding they would never repeat that crime against their own child. Instead, most law enforcement agencies report that the adult child abuser was himself abused as a child. The culprit is anger! That is why anger should be dealt with in all counselees, for if it is not confessed and forsaken it is like a walking volcano, always on the verge of eruption. I am convinced that anger is more powerful than love. Parents can love their child dearly, but if they have not forgiven the adult that abused them, that anger, when provoked, can explode into action that causes them to abuse the child they love. That is why child abusers show so much remorse after they calm down—they really love their child, but unresolved anger becomes all-powerful. (Fortunately the spiritual resources available to us, which will be revealed in this book, offer a more powerful remedy.)

The two most powerful human emotions are love and anger. Love is a health-producing emotion; anger a health-destroying emotion. It follows, then, that anger is the most negative and damaging emotion with which man has to cope.

Anger is a natural defense mechanism against insult, rejection, or injury. It explains why many depression-prone people are angry people or the product of angry homes where they were abused or rejected by their parents. Such anger is not only harmful emotionally, but physically and spiritually as well. I am convinced that the current age of depression is largely caused by the inability of people to cope with their anger. The rebellious, hostile people of the '60s and '70s have become the depression-prone people of the '80s and '90s.

The indulgence of children as a result of the false notions of behavioristic psychologists of a past generation has produced a generation of undisciplined, angry, rebellious, hostile, and bitter young people who go quite easily from anger to depression. When these individuals are counseled, they commonly indicate that before they became depressed something made them angry. It is most helpful for individuals to recognize the needless bitterness anger engenders.

THE HIGH COST OF ANGER

It would be impossible to estimate the immense cost of anger emotionally, physically, and spiritually.

Emotionally, the cost is seen in the needless bitterness it engenders. A *Reader's Digest* article explained the tragic deaths of four employees and the critical wounding of another. The assassin was a "Mr. Nice Guy" type, the kind of man who would make a pleasant neighbor. At forty-three years of age he seemingly "went berserk" and shot his fellow employees.

Investigation revealed that his bizarre behavior was not spontaneous. Eighteen months before the tragedy he was bypassed for promotion in favor of someone else. His wife acknowledged that "from that day on he gradually became a different man." It is not difficult to imagine the mental chain reaction he experienced. As he nursed his grudge and indulged his bitterness, mulling over the injustice of the occasion, he became so emotionally distraught that he took his .38 caliber revolver to work and shot five people. One common thread of identity united the victims: They were all in a position to have participated in the matter of his promotion. Today this man is kept behind bars, estranged from the family he loved. Four people met an untimely death, and one may be crippled for life all because of his hostility.

The physical cost of anger produces a tragic toll in human suffering that fills our hospitals. The human body can stand only so much stress, and nothing produces tension quite like anger. When we are young, our bodies can absorb some of these hostilities, but as we get older we lose that ability. Consequently the body breaks down in some of the vital areas, causing ulcers, high blood pressure, colitis, arthritis, heart trouble, headaches, kidney stones, gallstones, and a host of other illnesses.

One day I visited County Hospital in San Diego to call on a seventy-two-year-old minister hospitalized due to a severe case of glaucoma. He was basically a fine man who loved God and wanted to serve him, but like many Christians, he had never really dealt with his sin of anger. When I arrived in his room I was ill-prepared for the angry tirade that erupted in my direction. He proceeded unceremoniously to downgrade the medical profession in general and the doctors and nurses of County Hospital in particular. After a few moments he literally became livid with rage. Clasping him by the wrist, I shook him and exclaimed, "Paul, if you don't stop this, you're going to kill yourself!" Little did I realize that within two days he would drop dead of a heart attack, though he had never experienced one before and had not been confined to the hospital for that reason.

Several months after the funeral I used his case in a sermon illustration. After the service an ophthalmologist in our church said to me, "Just this week I read in a medical journal that protracted hostility is one of the leading causes of glaucoma."

As tragic as the emotional and physical results of anger may be, they can scarcely be compared with the terrible spiritual damage they create. Ephesians 4:30–32 explains it clearly: "And do not grieve the Holy Spirit of God, with whom you were sealed for the day of redemption. Get rid of all bitterness, rage and anger, brawling and slander, along with every form of malice. Be kind and compassionate to one to another, forgiving each other, just as in Christ God forgave you." If I were to ask, How does a person grieve the Holy Spirit of God? you would probably reply with a list of overt sins such as adultery or murder, but these verses make it clear that grieving the Holy Spirit takes place in the mind through anger.

It is impossible for a Christian to enjoy his spiritual resources if he grieves the Holy Spirit. In the previous chapter we saw that the Spirit of Christ, the Holy Spirit, comes into a person's life when invited. This gives an individual the capacity to overcome his or her weaknesses and cure such a malady as depression. But victory is not automatic! In order for a Christian to secure the victory, he or she must cooperate with the Holy Spirit. That means that the person must stop indulging in the mental sin of anger.

Anger is the sin that besets more Christians and probably causes more spiritual defeat than any other sin. It severely limits God's use of an individual's life. It grieves the Spirit of God and keeps the

Christian a spiritual pygmy throughout his life. It not only minimizes his usefulness to God and compounds his emotional maladies, but it can destroy what could have been an enjoyable love relationship with his own family.

GOD'S CURE FOR ANGER

The secular world proposes no meaningful cure for anger. A young man came in for counseling one day acknowledging that he had visited a psychiatrist on six occasions. The diagnosis given to him was, "I hate my mother." This hatred of his mother tied his stomach in knots, raised the hair on the back of his arm on occasion, and had created the initial wave of marital disharmony in his home. "If you have been to see a psychiatrist and he told you that your tensions were produced by hatred of your mother, why did you come to me?" I asked. The young man sadly replied, "He told me what my problem was, but he didn't tell me what to do about it."

We should not be surprised that the young man was not instructed how to overcome his anger, for without God's power in one's life, there is no cure. One psychiatrist in a *Reader's Digest* article offered this typically secular suggestion: An anger-prone person, he advised, would be wise to analytically chart what sets off his anger and accordingly avoid it. Escapism usually becomes the recourse of a person who refuses to rely on the power of God. In response to the above psychiatrist's suggestion, we may well counter, "What if anger is occasioned by your wife, your children, your job, your neighbors, or planet earth?" It is impossible for a person to avoid all sources of irritation.

A Christian publisher of many fine books sent me a manuscript on how to cope with anger and asked that I write a foreword to it. After reading it, I had to write my friend and decline his offer. Then I told him how disappointed I was that his editorial department would even think of offering such a book to the Christian community. It was filled with humanistic philosophy. The author told her women readers how to cope with a husband who repeatedly made them mad. Basically what she said was, get a rag doll and keep it in the back bedroom out of sight. Then when your husband makes you mad, just go back to the bedroom, close the door, take out your rag doll, and pound on the bed until you work out all your anger. That is raw humanism! A human attempt to solve a basically spiritual problem without God. Fortunately that publisher did not publish the book.

God offers a much better remedy. Consider the following six steps, which I have shared with hundreds of people, many of whom have experienced their first victory over anger by using this formula.

(1) *Admit that your anger is sin.* As long as you excuse anger, you are incurable! After twenty-five years in the counseling room I think I have heard just about all of them. One man complained, "I am a German choleric." Another Christian worker, whose anger had caused him to be dropped from a mission board, told me, "I come from a Syrian background; my father and mother are angry, my entire family is angry." Another man explained, "My father and mother had ulcers from being angry, my sister and brother had ulcers—how could I be anything but angry?" Although all of these people were seriously in error, I can appreciate their feeling because for the first thirty-six years of my life, I lamented, "I'm Scotch, French, and Irish; who wouldn't be angry?" All of this is subterfuge in a misguided attempt to cover up the fact that we have sinned. Until a person calls anger sin and stops trying to justify it, his plight is hopeless. Through the years it has been my privilege to help many angry people, but in the process I have failed to assist numerous others. I find one common thread winding through the files of those I could not help: They refused to admit they were angry people, but insisted on justifying their anger. Repeatedly people in the counseling room tell me, "If my husband would change, I wouldn't be angry," or "It's my wife that sets me off." They have not yet learned that victory in Christ is not contingent upon other people's behavior, but on Christ alone. Only by facing your anger as a sin will you ever cure it. That is the first giant step toward victory.

(2) *Confess your sin of anger to God.* Like any other sin, anger can be forgiven and cured. First John 1:9 promises that "If we confess our sins, he is faithful and just and will forgive us our sins and purify us from all unrighteousness." The sooner you recognize your anger and confess it, the sooner you will obtain victory over it.

(3) *Ask God to take away the habit pattern of anger.* First John 5:14–15 assures us that if we ask anything according to the will of God, he not only hears us but also answers our requests. Since we know it is not God's will that we be angry, we can be assured of victory if we ask him to take away the habit pattern. Since we have at our disposal the power of the Holy Spirit, we do not need to remain slaves of the habit of anger.

(4) *Give thanks for God's mercy, grace, and power.* We need to follow up our request for victory over the habit pattern of anger by thanking God for his mercy and forgiveness in the face of our failure. We must then thank him that we have within us his Holy Spirit, for by his power we can experience a reversal of this habit pattern.

(5) *Confess to any person you have wronged by your anger.* If your anger spilled out on someone else in verbal or physical abuse, be sure to go to them and apologize. The Bible tells us we are to "confess [our] sins to each other" (James 5:16). Don't leave your angry outburst unconfessed, or it will become a continuing cause of stumbling to another. Besides, humbling yourself by confessing it and asking the offended person to forgive you makes you less likely to lash out in anger at a later time.

(6) *Repeat this formula every time you are angry.* It would be idealistic to assume that invoking this formula only once would change a lifetime habit of anger. It is much more practical to face the fact that anger will occur even after your first use of the formula. The ultimate victory, however, comes with repetition. Quickly follow your sin with a

prayer of confession, asking God to change the habit pattern and give thanks by faith for what he is going to do in your life. As one man admitted after trying this formula for a few weeks, "I had to confess my anger the first day at least 1000 times, but the next day was better; I only had to do it 997 times. Now, however, anger is gradually becoming a thing of the past." In my opinion this man provides a practical case study for those who gain victory over anger. I have met no one who experienced an instant cure. Instead, with God's power, the cure comes by conscious and repetitive attention, combined with the gradual exercise of new mental habit patterns.

After speaking on this subject several years ago, I was asked by an elderly gentleman, "Do you think it is possible for a man who has been angry for seventy years to break the habit?" In response, strictly by faith, I replied, "God's power is available to you and can cure any habit." Two years later, while speaking in a nearby city, I spotted him and his wife in the audience. After the meeting he said, "I want to give you a progress report. God has cured my problem of anger. If you don't believe it, ask my wife." I could see by the expression on her face that she was ready to testify that he had experienced the life-changing power of God. Literally hundreds of other testimonials like this could validate that the power of the Holy Spirit of God is able to put love in the heart of any anger-prone person who is willing to let him. *When love replaces anger, depression will not occur.*

Chapter 9

Self-Pity and Depression

A t last we have come to the primary cause of depression. In spite of the causes listed previously, nothing produces depression faster or more deeply than self-pity. In fact, even when depression is triggered by a biological malfunction it is exacerbated by self-pity. "Why me?" is an understandable cry of those who develop some debilitating illness or disease, but even when justified it compounds the depression.

Whenever I confront a person with this cause for their depression, they invariably resist me, usually protesting, "I never feel sorry for myself!" or "That may be true most of the time, but my case is different." One lady angrily retorted, "I came to you for help, but I can see you don't understand my problem!" Some people even stalk out in a huff and slam the door. The truth, like surgery, hurts. There is simply no way to have a tumor removed without pain. The same is true emotionally. The moment we call the tumor of self-pity to the attention of a depressed person, he or she resists it. But that doesn't change anything! In fact, I never expect agreement on this point from one who is depressed. In their depressed condition, anything as ugly as self-pity is simply too much to bear. They would much rather receive sympathy, pills, or pious platitudes that place the responsibility on someone else.

I have repeatedly noted that nondepressed people seem to accept this diagnosis easily. Even individuals usually prone to depression, when not depressed, seldom argue. It is the depressed themselves who seem to rebel against it. Fortunately, upon reflection most people will acknowledge the problem and take steps to cure it. Of one thing I am certain: If the mental thinking pattern of self-pity is not arrested, the person is hopeless; the more he or she indulges in self-pitying thoughts, the deeper the depression becomes. Even medication or electric-shock therapy can only offer temporary periods of relief. If the mental thought patterns are not changed, the person soon returns to depression.

Various excuses are offered by the depressed who refuse to face self-pity as a possible cause for their miseries. The intellectual or highly educated often protest, "That's too simple! It must be more complex." Others refuse to approach a counselor who provides his counselees with such an analysis. One woman has suffered with depression for more than seven years, but she has steadfastly refused to see me. Her reason is quite simple. She has read the chapter on depression in my book *Spirit-Controlled Temperament,* where I briefly dealt with the problem. She tells her friends, "I know he would say that I'm feeling sorry for myself, and I know that isn't true. My problem is much deeper than that." I am convinced she could have known deliverance years ago if she had just faced the problem honestly.

RARE EXCEPTIONS

Except for *Spirit-Controlled Temperament,* I have not seen anything in print that places the primary blame for depression on self-pity. Since the book was published several years ago, hundreds of counselors, pastors, and formerly depressed individuals have indicated their agreement. In addition, I have expanded this theme before thousands of people in family seminars. Although some have taken issue with me at first, many letters in my files strongly confirm the principle.

Some time ago, I returned to a city in which I had directed a seminar the previous year. A woman conceded, "Last year I was so angry at your suggestion that self-pity was responsible for my depression that I stalked out of the seminar before it was over. But a friend bought your cassette tape on the subject and insisted I hear it. As I began tracing my thought patterns prior to the depression, I realized that I really was feeling sorry for myself. Honest confrontation of that fact has changed my life."

I do not enjoy telling depressed people that they are indulging in self-pity. In fact, on one occasion I felt downright unpatriotic. While holding a family conference in a midwestern city, I was requested by a pastor to counsel one of the women in his congregation. As she walked into the room, I remember thinking, "She is the thinnest woman I have ever seen." She had lost thirty-nine pounds during the previous six months and weighed only eighty-nine pounds. Her husband was an Air Force officer shot down over North Vietnam, officially reported as "missing in action."

As she sobbed out her story, I almost wept with her. For four years she had not known what to prepare for mentally. Was her husband alive or dead? Each day her three small sons would ask, "Mommy, do you think our daddy is alive?" Finally she broke down and sobbed, "I'd rather know he was dead than face this constant uncertainty!" If ever I was tempted to offer a person sympathy in the counseling room, it was at that moment with this woman. As a basic rule, I never sympathize with depressed people. Compassion, understanding, and help are appropriate, but these people have already pitied themselves excessively, thus generating their depression. What they need is help, which comes by gently getting them to see that they are indulging in self-pity.

When I asked this dear lady if she loved her husband, she replied, "Yes! He and my boys are the only things in life that are important to me." I then drew her attention to the fact that her previous statement indicated greater love for herself than for her husband. "Is mental certainty really more important to you than the possibility that your husband is alive?" She sat up straight and exclaimed, "O God, I've let myself get so upset that I'm not thinking straight anymore!" That woman changed her entire lifestyle by altering her mental attitude. Her circumstances did not change, for her husband remained an MIA. Instead of feeling sorry for herself, however, she began to give thanks that she did not know her husband was dead. Her genuine love for him soon took precedence over her love for herself, and she communicated that thought to her sons. As they asked questions about their father, she led them in prayer that wherever he was, he would be strong and look forward to seeing them all again.

The prospect of this goal lifted that entire family out of the slough of despondence and depression. By claiming God's grace and giving thanks in the face of the circumstances, they could face their uncertain future and get on with the rest of their lives.

THE DEPRESSION FORMULA

Seldom in life are we able to reduce an emotional problem to a formula, but in the case of depression it is possible. Consider the following:

Insult or Injury + Anger x Self-Pity = Depression or Rejection

The validity of that formula has been confirmed hundreds of times, both in and out of the counseling room. On a flight from Mobile to Atlanta I was pressed between two businessmen. Absorbed in writing this book, I nevertheless could sense that the fifty-year-old oil company executive seated by the window was reading my manuscript. Finally he apologized and said, "I wonder if you could explain something about depression to me. For the first twenty-two years of our marriage my wife was almost never depressed, but eight years ago, after the birth of our last child, she became seriously depressed. We have spent a fortune on doctors, psychiatrists, and electro-shock treatments, but she is getting worse. Now I find that I am becoming depressed because she is."

The obvious question was the right one as I asked, "Did your wife want to get pregnant eight years ago?"

"No," he replied, "she was very resentful all during the pregnancy and has never forgiven me for it."

I would have been very surprised if her depression had been caused by some mysterious birth problem or menopausal chemical imbalance. Consider the formula applied to that woman:

Unwanted Pregnancy + Resentment x Self-Pity = Depression

The fact that her depression didn't go away but got worse is evidence of the fact that it was self-pity, not a malfunction of the glands. The more she felt sorry for herself, the worse her depression became. Consider his identical formula:

Depressed Wife + Resentment x Self-Pity = Depression

One day as my wife and I were returning to San Diego from a seminar, a very personable flight attendant kept watching as I was working on this manuscript. Finally her curiosity got the best of her and she asked, "What are you writing so furiously?" When I told her it was a book entitled *How to Win Over Depression,* she spontaneously replied, "Hurry and finish it—I need to read it right now!" My response to this woman who looked like she didn't have a care in the world was, "How could you at twenty-two have anything to be depressed about?" Instantly her resentments spilled out. "This airline is so inconsiderate! We are shorthanded on this flight and they forgot to stock it properly, so we can't give halfway decent service." When I explained to her that resentment times self-pity equals depression, she said, "Oh, I'll be all right when I get on the beach where I can hear the waves lapping up on the shore. It seems to soothe my jangled nerves." At the risk of being considered obnoxious, I felt I should warn her that if she didn't stop indulging in self-pity, one of these days she would no longer be able to hear the roar of the waves over her mental bitterness. "But I can't quit," she blurted out. That is when I introduced her to Jesus Christ, who is able to straighten out our faulty thinking patterns.

Depression-inducing self-pity seems to be no respecter of persons. It ambushes intellectuals and nonintellectuals with equal treachery. One brilliant but depressed scholar I know holds a Ph.D. and has developed a world-renowned reputation. As a young man, he had offered great promise and was expected by those in his field to excel. Having a problem marriage, he drifted into serious patterns of hostility toward his wife. These, in turn, caused him to indulge in the habit pattern of self-pity, which demotivated him.

After years of such thinking, he came in for counseling. Having written few articles and never having finished a book, this brilliant man had wasted his creativity potential. Naturally he blamed his wife instead of himself. "If it hadn't been for that woman, I could have realized my potential." He spent so much time feeling sorry for himself that he had no mental space or emotional inspiration to be creative. Instead of constantly reproaching her for his lack of motivation, he ultimately had to face the fact that he was responsible.

Another illustration of the depression formula entered my office and sighed, "After eight months of marriage, I'm as frigid as an iceberg." This lovely young woman had married a handsome marine in our city. They had been madly in love, according to her report, and she had looked forward to their wedding with great joy. Depressed after only a few months of marriage, she lost all interest in her husband. It seems that this young woman had been accused of promiscuity by a stepmother when she was fourteen years old. Two of her older sisters were very loose in their morals prior to marriage, which had caused the family no end of shame. When the stepmother made her untrue accusation, the girl mentally promised herself, "I will be a virgin when I marry, no matter what." Unfortunately, when her handsome fiancé put the engagement ring on her finger and they set their wedding date, she let down her barriers, and they had intercourse. She admitted to enjoying it and practicing it several times before the wedding.

Her problems really began when she donned her beautiful white wedding gown for the first time. That was her first genuine reminder that she was entering marriage without her virginity. The more she thought about it, the angrier she became. Instead of blaming herself for giving in, she placed all the blame on her husband. Self-justification is a natural defense mechanism against self-condemnation, of course, so it was easier to blame him than share the responsibility. Before long, her hostility produced self-pity, and finally she became depressed. Her doctor prescribed medication that merely afforded temporary relief. The only hope for that young woman was to forgive her husband, forgive herself, and seek God's forgiveness for her sins. When she finally did that, she was not only able to rid herself of depression, but to experience a renewed love for her husband. Since that time they have effected a warm and meaningful relationship together.

YOU DON'T NEED A CHANGE OF CIRCUMSTANCES

Most people insist that a change in circumstances would begin an end to their depression. Unfortunately, that provides only temporary relief. If a change of circumstances does not convert one's thinking pattern, depression will recur. One woman, married four times, admitted that the best husband was really her first. After being depressed with four different men, she was finally willing to admit that *she* was the problem, not the husbands.

SELF-PITY IS A SIN

When stripped of its false facade of excuse making and self-justification, self-pity stands naked and exposed as a mental attitude sin. Those who would be most hesitant to commit an overt act of sin such as adultery or fornication seem to have no compunction against this mental sin.

Self-pity is really a denial of the biblical principle that "In all things God works for the good of those who love him, who have been called according to his purpose" (Romans 8:28). That verse does not state that all things are good, but that "in all things *God works*" for our good. There is a vast difference. God can use everything in our life for good, if for no other reason than to get us to look to him for guidance when we are faced with the frustrating problems of life. For that reason it is imperative that once a person has faced self-pity as sin, he must look to God for grace to face his circumstances. The sooner he builds up his faith by reading and studying the Word of God, and by the filling of the Holy Spirit, the sooner he will experience lasting deliverance.

Once you have received Jesus Christ, you become a child of God (John 1:12). As a member of the family of God, you have a heavenly Father who is not only abundantly able to care for your needs but is infinitely interested in every detail of your life. According to Jesus, he is the God who has numbered the hairs of our head and who sees the sparrow when it falls. Since he is the God who designs the beautiful lilies of the field, Jesus concludes, "If that is how God clothes the grass of the field, which is here today and tomorrow is thrown into the fire, will he not much more clothe you, O you of little faith?" (Matthew 6:30). A Christian should keep in focus the fact that God is interested in every facet of his life and is more than willing to give him victory over his problems.

TRIALS ARE NOT OVERWHELMING

Every human being faces trials. For some strange reason Christians develop the notion that because they are Christians they will escape from tribulation. That is just not true. Dr. Henry Brandt, a Christian psychologist, wrote an excellent book entitled *Christians Have Troubles Too*. In it he points out that God has not promised to save us from our problems but to supply our need as we go through them. The apostle Paul had also learned this, for he stated, "My God will meet all your needs according to his glorious riches in Christ Jesus" (Philippians 4:19). D. L. Moody labeled that verse "God's blank check" because it provides a supernatural provision for every human need.

Trials are never overwhelming; they just seem that way. First Corinthians 10:13 explains, "No temptation [trial] has seized you except what is common to man. And God is faithful; he will not let you be tempted beyond what you can bear. But when you are tempted, he will also provide a way out so that you can stand up under it." At any point in time, any Christian can undergo a common trial of life, but the child of God can face that trial with the absolute confidence that it will not be so overwhelming that he breaks under it. God knows your limitations. As evangelist Ken Poure says, "That is the guarantee that our trials are 'Father Filtered.'" In other words, every trial that comes into your life is filtered by the heavenly Father. He sees to it that the problem is not so large that it will crush you. Most Christians, however, are not content to accept the grace of God when they enter the furnace of trial. Instead, they demand immediate deliverance or request a path which bypasses all affliction.

Nobody takes pleasure in the testings of life, but James 1:2–3 prescribes, "Consider it pure joy . . . whenever you face trials of many kinds" for "the testing of your faith develops perseverance." This is the way we grow up spiritually and emotionally.

People are like steel: They are soft unless tested. Your tests in life are an essential part of your tempering process. As we have seen, you are never tested above your ability to endure. Oh, you may be tried beyond your desires, but God knows your mettle, he diagrams your future, and he knows exactly what you need. Therefore, the Word of God instructs us that instead of griping and groaning and feeling sorry for ourselves, which only produces depression, we are to "consider it pure joy."

One depressed woman spent most of her time in the counseling room dissecting her husband. Nothing he did seemed to please her. In an excessive expression of self-pity she exclaimed, "Why couldn't I have married a kind and gentle man like Mrs. K.'s husband down the street. He is considerate, thoughtful, and respectful to her as a woman." Knowing the counselee's husband as I did, fully aware that he was surly, inconsiderate, and unkind to everyone, I still had to offer an encouraging reply. In all honesty I could assert, "God's grace is sufficient for you." I then proceeded to explain that the greater her problem, the greater the grace. "The lady down the street does not have a sizable problem to live with, consequently, she does not merit much grace from God. But since you face such an enormous problem, you will be granted more grace to cope with it." Instantly the woman snapped, "I'd rather have the kind husband than the grace!"

Her response is not unusual, though refreshingly honest. Most people would rather avoid the trials of life than obtain the grace to face them.

It should be of great comfort to us that all problems are filtered by the Father. That is, before they ever come our way, he has measured whether or not we are able to endure them, guaranteeing that, with the testing, "he will also provide a way out." When confronting a testing experience, you must make a distinctive choice. You can either respond with anger and bitterness over the problem and then indulge in self-pity, which will induce depression, or you can look to God your heavenly Father, thank him by faith for his power and grace to pass through the trial, and then lean on his everlasting arms. You must make the decision. But of this you can be certain: Yielding to self-pity will assuredly lead to depression.

CRISES, TRIALS, AND STRESS

The way you face the crises and trials of life often determines your state of health. Doctors Thomas Holmes and Richard H. Rahe, psychiatrists at the University of Washington School of Medicine in Seattle, have actually worked out a system that shows how much stress each crisis in life creates. In an article in the *Chicago Tribune,* he explained that after twenty-five years of study he has compiled a list of forty-three of the most common stress-producing experiences of life.[1] His study has been a classic for over twenty-five years. It has been quoted in many books on pressure, tension, and related subjects. Dr. Holmes attributed a point score from 100 down to 11 according to the severity of the stress on an individual's emotions caused by the crisis. As you read his list, consider the fact that no human being can escape all of these crises (and hopefully, no human being is going to experience all of them!).

Crisis	Points	Your Score
Death of a spouse	100	_____
Divorce	73	_____
Marital separation	65	_____
Jail term	63	_____
Death of close family member	63	_____
Personal injury or illness	53	_____
Marriage	50	_____
Job firing	47	_____
Marital reconciliation	45	_____

Retirement	45	_____
Change in health of family member	44	_____
Pregnancy	40	_____
Sexual difficulties	39	_____
Gain of new family member	39	_____
Business readjustment	39	_____
Change in financial state	38	_____
Death of a close friend	37	_____
Change to different line of work	36	_____
Change in number of arguments with spouse	35	_____
Foreclosure of mortgage or loan	30	_____
Change in responsibilities at work	29	_____
Son or daughter leaving home	29	_____
Trouble with in-laws	29	_____
Outstanding personal achievement	28	_____
Wife begins or stops work	26	_____
Beginning or end of school	26	_____
Change in living conditions	25	_____
Change of personal habits	24	_____
Trouble with boss	23	_____
Change in work hours or conditions	20	_____
Change in residence	20	_____
Change in schools	20	_____
Change in recreation	19	_____
Change in church activities	19	_____
Change in social activities	18	_____
Change in sleeping habits	16	_____
Change in number of family gatherings	15	_____
Change in eating habits	15	_____
Vacation	13	_____
Christmas	12	_____
Minor violations of the law	11	_____
Total		_____

Dr. Holmes then established an illness predictor scale showing that there was a high risk potential of developing major illnesses within a two-year period after accumulating a certain number of stress points accordingly.

ILLNESS PREDICTOR SCALE

Low Risk	150–200
Medium Risk	225–300
High Risk	325–375

According to the above chart, there is a high degree of possibility that you will be physically ill if you collect as many as 300 or more points within a reasonably short time. For example, if a person loses his partner and out of loneliness rushes into a second marriage, he has accumulated 150 points. If his wife quit working (26 points), if he develops sexual difficulties in the new marriage (39 points) and experiences a job change (36 points) along with the natural change in social activities that a new spouse would cause (18 points), receives a minor traffic violation (11 points), and a disagreement or two with his new wife (35 points), all it would take is Christmas (12 points) or a vacation (13 points) to push him over the precipice of accumulated stress points that could induce illness.

Is it realistic to blame this illness on these crises or changes in one's lifestyle? Closer examination indicates that the real culprit is one's mental attitude toward these circumstances of life, not the trials or crises themselves. You have doubtless seen individuals go through similar experiences seemingly unscathed emotionally, whereas you have also seen others thrown into a despondent or despairing state of depression by only one of them. Consequently, we are confronted again with the fact that more important than the crises of life is the mental attitude with which we face them.

An interesting observation about Dr. Holmes' stress-producing experiences was made by my secretary. After laboriously putting all forty-one of these events and their ratings on a visual transparency to be used with my lectures, she said, "The one thing these experiences all have in common is change." If you read over the list, you will agree. Subconsciously most of us dislike change, but who can possibly avoid it? In fact, life would be rather dull and boring if we didn't experience change once in a while. It is not the change that produces the problem; the person with a good mental attitude can thrive on such change, but the person who gripes verbally or in his mind about the change and feels sorry for himself that it became necessary will have trouble. Some people have such a poor mental attitude that they can get depressed just by the thought of impending change.

The error of the depression-prone person is that his thought patterns are too inward. Everything in life is scrutinized from a self-centered point of view. For that reason the slightest insult, affront, or difficulty can send him into a state of depression. Only by recognizing self-pity as a sin and dealing with it forthrightly is he ever going to have lasting victory over this insidious habit that will destroy him spiritually, mentally, emotionally, and physically. The importance of mental attitude can be seen by studying the following chart showing the characteristics of the three kinds of depression. By following the progression from mental, physical, emotional, and spiritual, you can trace the effects of improper thoughts on your entire nature.

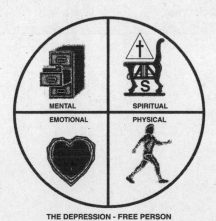

THE DEPRESSION - FREE PERSON

CHARACTERISTICS OF THE THREE KINDS OF DEPRESSION		
Discouragement (mild)	**Despondency** (serious)	**Despair** (severe)
Mental		
self-doubt	self-criticism	self-rejection
resentment	anger	bitterness
self-pity	self-pity	self-pity
Physical		
loss of appetite	apathy	withdrawal
sleeplessness	hypochondria	passivity
unkempt appearance	weepiness	catatonia
Emotional		
discontent	distress	hopelessness
sadness	sorrow	schizophrenia
irritability	loneliness	abandonment
Spiritual		
question God's will	angry at God's will	resents God's Word
displeased with God's will	rejects God's will	indifferent to God's Word
ungrateful, unbelieving	gripes about God's will	disbelieves God's Word

Chapter 10

How to Overcome Self-Pity

Self-pity is not only a sin, it is also a habit. The more it is indulged in, the easier it is for an individual to shift into this thinking pattern whenever disagreeable circumstances confront him. Most of the things we do in life are the result of habit. Certain instincts we received at birth through our temperament combined with environmental circumstances produce habit. The more we follow an established pattern, the more ingrained it becomes in our behavior. Habit is simply a form of what psychologists label "conditioned response."

We must constantly remind ourselves that we are not slaves to habit, even though most people think they are. Studies have proved that habits can be broken. One researcher concludes that any practice you indulge in for thirty-nine days becomes a habit; similarly, any activity you discontinue for thirty-nine days becomes a broken habit. While this may be true for such things as jogging, smoking, or drinking coffee, I seriously question the validity of that suggestion regarding self-pity, because you may go thirty-nine days without an occasion for self-pity. But it does highlight the fact that the modification of a thinking pattern over a protracted period of time can thwart one's self-pitying thought habits, which produce depression.

STEPS TO VICTORY OVER SELF-PITY

I have shared the following formula for overcoming self-pity with many depression-prone individuals. Those who have been willing to follow it have found great relief. Those who preferred to indulge in the "pleasure" of self-pity have not been helped. (As startling as it may seem, self-pity is a pleasurable mental exercise to many people, although the consequences of depression are not so pleasant.)

Face Self-Pity as Sin

"Do everything without complaining or arguing" (Philippians 2:14). Facing self-pity as a sin is the initial step toward victory over this cruel slave driver. This is probably the hardest step, for, humanly speaking, self-pity is so easy to justify. In the courtroom of your mind during times of distress you are the judge, jury, and prosecuting attorney. Perry Mason never had a more cooperative listening audience. But instead of commiserating with yourself and blaming other people for the insult, injury, rejection, or tragedy, face self-pity squarely as a giant mental sin that will destroy you.

Unless you severely judge self-pity as sin, you will never break the habit. The person who justifies self-pity is like the alcoholic who refuses to face his condition as an alcoholic. You cannot break any strong habit until you are willing to admit its evil control over you.

Never excuse self-pity! Humanly speaking, you will not find this easy to do. You may have been rejected by your parents or betrayed by a Judas whom you trusted; you may have a deplorable job with no apparent chance for advancement; or you may find yourself married to a very selfish, insensitive, and inconsiderate partner. You may even suffer from a serious physical impairment or be isolated from everyone you love. Surely human wisdom admits these and other such problems in life as just cause for self-pity. But be sure of this: Self-pity will create depression whether the cause is justified or imagined.

In addition, the sin of unbelief from which self-pity springs will keep you from drawing on the power of God's Holy Spirit at your time of need. Even though you are a child of God, when you quench or grieve the Holy Spirit by self-pity, you become as powerless as those who are not Christians. For that reason, the sooner you label the thinking pattern of self-pity as sin, the sooner you will take your first step toward recovery.

Confess self-pity as sin.

"If we confess our sins, he is faithful and just and will forgive us our sins, and purify us from all unrighteousness" (1 John 1:9). Our heavenly Father is a merciful God, ready to forgive whenever sinners confess their sins in the name of his Son, Jesus Christ. The word *confess* literally means to agree with God that what we are confessing is sin and should have no place in our thinking pattern. The sooner you confess the sin of self-pity, the sooner you take your second step toward curing this self-destroying habit.

Ask God for victory over self-pity.

"This is the confidence we have in approaching God: that if we ask anything according to his will, he hears us. And if we know that he hears us—whatever we ask—we know that we have what we asked of him" (1 John 5:14–15). Since God has already pronounced his anathema upon self-pity, we can be sure that if we desire victory, he will provide it. Remember also that the Christian commands resources for overcoming habits not shared by the non-Christian. For that reason I do not hesitate to point out that a Christian does not have to be a slave to this tyrannical habit.

Dr. Henry Brandt, while speaking on pastoral counseling, stated to a group of ministers in San Diego, "You can use your background as an excuse for present behavior only until you become a Christian. After that it is no longer a valid excuse for present behavior." When a person receives Jesus Christ, he inherits a new dimension of power created within to provide victory over old habit patterns (2 Corinthians 5:17). With all due respect to self-discipline and mental self-control, most people lack the strength of character within themselves to inhibit self-pitying thoughts. However, since the Spirit of Jesus Christ entering "the natural person" provides him or her with supernatural power through the Holy Spirit, that person is abundantly able to achieve victory. The apostle Paul announced for all of us, "I can do everything through Christ who gives me strength" (Philippians 4:13).

Thank God in the experience that produced self-pity.

"Give thanks in all circumstances, for this is God's will for you in Christ Jesus" (1 Thessalonians 5:18). Victory is dependent upon this next step! Unless by God's help and in obedience to his command you give thanks in the experience, your self-pity will return and reactivate your depression. It is important to realize that thanksgiving "in everything" is critical not only because it is required by God to be a Spirit-filled Christian, but also, as we shall see in a later chapter, it is emotionally therapeutic.

It is not always possible to thank God *for* the experience, but it is essential to thank God *in* the experience. If nothing else, you can thank God for his presence in your life while going through the circumstances—and by faith you can thank him for the victory that will eventually come.

To be profitable, prayer must include thanksgiving. The Bible admonishes, "Do not be anxious about anything, but in everything, by prayer and petition, *with thanksgiving,* present your requests to God. And the peace of God, which transcends all understanding, will guard your hearts and your minds in Christ Jesus" (Philippians 4:6–7, italics added).

The right kind of prayer always includes thanksgiving. If you really believe that God answers prayer and is able to work on your behalf, give thanks by faith, before there is any indication of what he will do. That kind of prayer is therapeutic. Prayer without thanksgiving will be detrimental and tend to make you depressed. Any time you come away from a period of prayer more depressed than when you started, examine your prayer for that missing ingredient—thanksgiving.

Several years ago, when a new car meant more to me than it does today, I learned a valuable lesson. Upon leaving a banquet, I started to open the door of the car for my wife, only to find that someone had backed into my one-month-old car, caving in one-fourth of the side.

For a moment my blood ran cold, my stomach sank, and rather ugly thoughts ran through my mind. But looking up into the sky, I said, "Praise the Lord!" Even though I didn't understand why it happened and it remains a mystery to this day, I wanted to be obedient to God, so I thanked him by faith, as he commanded in such circumstances. As a result I have never felt bad about the accident. That certainly is not the way I would have felt had I not given thanks.

That situation underscored the principle that one need not understand or even enjoy an experience to give thanks for it. But when faced with an unexpected circumstance in life, you create your own emotional state by either griping or giving thanks.

Ask to be filled with the Holy Spirit.

"If you then, though you are evil, know how to give good gifts to your children, how much more will your Father in heaven give the Holy Spirit to those who ask him!" (Luke 11:13).

Now that you are a clean vessel, having faced and confessed your sin, having asked God for removal of the habit pattern, and by faith having thanked him in the experience, you are in a spiritual position to be filled with the Holy Spirit. "How often should you ask to be filled with the Spirit?" is a question I am frequently asked. My answer is, "Every time you are conscious you are not filled." Ephesians 5:18 makes it clear that we should be continually in the process of being filled with his Spirit.

Repeat the formula whenever self-pity recurs.

Educators tell us that repetition is an aid to learning. I have found repetition to be an essential ingredient in gaining victory over habits. It is unrealistic to expect the mental habit of self-pity to vanish immediately, and thus it will take many applications of this formula to insure consistent victory. But the sooner you follow your self-pity with this formula, the sooner you will experience protracted periods of victory.

Do not expect your triumph over self-pity to be a miracle of God's grace without your cooperation. Many depressed people, even after admitting the cause for their depression, want God to take away the thinking pattern without any effort from them. On some occasions I have actually seen people get angry with God because he didn't miraculously subtract their thinking mechanism of self-pity. However, God does not do for us what, according to his Word, he expects us to do for ourselves.

Instead, he exhorts us to cooperate with the Holy Spirit, who enables us to do whatever he commands.

Victory over self-pity and thus over depression can be yours as a Christian, but only if you avail yourself of the spiritual resources that the Spirit-filled life provides. (For a thorough description of how to be filled with the Spirit, see my book, *Spirit-Controlled Temperament*.)

EVEN PRAYER DOESN'T HELP

You may find it strange that a high percentage of depressed people pray frequently. Their undesirable habits of self-pity and continual griping have alienated them even from their dearest friends. Their verbalized self-pity wears out the most persistent friendship until it seems that only God will pay any attention to them. The severely depressed or despondent person, of course, is apt to feel that even God has turned him off.

You may also be surprised to learn that all prayer is not good. In fact, much of what people call prayer is downright harmful because it is contrary to the will of God. Most depressed people use their prayer life to nurse their grudges and announce their self-pity. This is not only debilitating but spiritually harmful.

Moses, one of the great Old Testament saints, offered probably the poorest example of a prayer to be found in the Bible. Admittedly very displeased with the children of Israel for their griping, he turned his displeasure upon God and prayed,

> Why have you brought this trouble on your servant? What have I done to displease you that you put the burden of all these people on me? Did I conceive all these people? *Did I give them birth?* Why do you tell me to carry them in my arms, as a nurse carries

an infant, to the land you promised on oath to their forefathers? Where can I get meat for all these people? They keep wailing to me, "Give us meat to eat!" I cannot carry all these people by myself; the burden is too heavy for me. If this is how you are going to treat me, put me to death right now—if I have found favor in your eyes—and do not let me face my own ruin. (Numbers 11:11–15, italics added)

During the course of his prayer, which began in anger and progressed in self-pity, Moses became so depressed that he actually asked God to let him die. Poor Moses! Resenting the clamor of the people and their rebellion to his leadership, he disregarded God's promise to supernaturally supply all of his needs. He turned inward to self-pity. Count the personal pronouns, there are sixteen! Such prayer will always leave a person depressed.

A minister friend shared with me the results of a survey on prayer made while he was in college. A large number of depressed persons with a Christian background were separated into three categories. One group was offered counseling on a group and individual basis in methods of improving their mental attitude. The second group met together for prayer with an instructor who showed them how to pray properly. The third group was told to go home and pray. After several weeks almost fifty percent of those who were counseled had improved. Of those who prayed together on a weekly basis under the guidance of a biblically oriented instructor, eighty-five percent were helped. But of those who prayed privately without instruction, not one improved, and several showed deterioration. Upon investigation it was found that every uninstructed person had indulged in the sin of self-pity in his prayer life. No wonder their depression increased.

PHYSICIAN, HEAL THYSELF

In the introduction to this book I confessed that on October 7, 1969, I experienced the first real depression of my adult life. Since that time there have been three other occasions that provided me a personal opportunity to evaluate this formula for overcoming the self-pity that produces depression. Our growing church bought forty acres of property in the heart of San Diego to relocate our entire ministry of church, junior and senior high schools, college, and Institute for Creation Research. By faith we paid $500,000 for this land, which would have provided sixteen usable acres located where two freeways intersect, one of which has a traffic load of 105,000 cars per day—the ideal site in our city for a church. For three years I had eaten, slept, thought, and dreamed about that development. For months I tramped the streets, lining up adjoining property owners until we owned fifteen lots that would provide access to our land. Somehow local politics and the first wave of ecologic hysteria combined to oppose the project.

For two years we carried on a running battle with city hall. We spent thousands of dollars on lawyers' fees and an equal number of legal man-hours were donated by interested lawyers in the congregation. I had absolutely no doubt our plans would be approved. Naive as I was, the thought that our city fathers would be more interested in authorizing two hundred tax-generating condominiums to be built there instead of a church had never occurred to me. Consequently, when their vote flashed on the screen showing that our application for a zone variance was defeated, I was stunned.

People began milling around, but I could hardly move—I was numb to the bone! Eventually I mustered enough strength to leave as discreetly as possible. When I finally got away from everyone, I drove alone to the property. I didn't have the courage to visit the spot where my wife and I had knelt and claimed that property for God. Instead, I went out to a lovely vantage point overlooking the site and sat down in the dirt to think. Can you imagine the nature of my first thoughts? I must confess they weren't very pleasant. "Why, Lord? Why did you let this happen? What did I do wrong? I prayed over this place, I walked over it and claimed it, just as others did for theirs. Why did you let this happen? It worked for Abraham, for some of my minister friends; why hasn't it worked for me?"

I had lots of questions. And the more I griped, the worse I felt. After two hours I was so miserable I decided it was time to leave. When I climbed the hill we had wanted to cut down, I found my wife waiting to console me. Walking over to her car, I tried to thank her for coming and my voice wouldn't work. Try as I would, I couldn't speak. Finally I just walked away and went for a drive.

For two days I went through the worst siege of depression I have ever experienced. Finally it dawned on me that I had quenched the Holy Spirit and was walking in a very carnal state. The thought came to me, *Here you are, the author of a book with a chapter on how to cure depression, a preacher who challenges Christians not to become depressed—and you are depressed. Why don't you practice what you preach?* After confessing my sins of self-pity, doubt, griping, and questioning God, I began thanking him. I thanked him for his power and leading, and that though I didn't know what he was going to do, the problem wasn't really mine but his.

A thrilling thing happened that day. The depression lifted, my spirit began to rise, and a deep peace flooded my heart. During succeeding months, though actively engaged in the search for new property and knocking on every door of opportunity, I gained no more idea of God's plan for our church than I had on October 7. The thrilling part, however, is that I have not felt the slightest twinge of discouragement as long as I have given thanks by faith that God knew what he was doing, even if I didn't.

For the next two years I tried every conceivable method available to get that project approved. Nothing worked! Folks bent on preserving every known tree in San Diego County showed up at each hearing. Finally we tried selling the land, only to find that developers were afraid that if a church couldn't gain permission to build on four percent of the land, they would find it difficult to get approval for more. The only thing that was consistent was our $55,000 annual payments.

During that time I had three other bouts with depression. In each case self-pity set me up for defeat. Oh, I could justify it—hadn't I stepped out by faith? Didn't we need a new church? Our three morning services were filled to capacity, we didn't have enough parking space, and people were being turned away. All that kind of thinking did was make me depressed! Each time I recognized the depression and applied the formula given above, I got relief. My usual light heart and optimistic spirit returned, and I recaptured the excitement of what I consider the greatest vocation in the world—being a minister of the Gospel!

During the summer of 1970 the Lord lifted me out of my last period of depression over this problem. It was then I turned the situation over to him completely, deciding to quit trying to work it out myself and let him take care of it. Shortly after that he gave me the work of Family Life Seminars. This ministry of two-day seminars on family life has taken me to more than eighty cities in this country, and to over forty-six countries of the world. I have had the privilege of ministering to over one million people, who have been helped through the teaching of biblical principles for family life. Frankly, I've been too busy pastoring, traveling, speaking, and writing thirty-four books to indulge in self-pity. Consequently, I have never again been depressed.

Since God is always faithful, it occurs to me that you might like to hear what has happened with our church since I started thanking God by faith instead of griping in unbelief. On February 27, 1973, we bought a beautiful thirty-acre Catholic school and church with twenty-eight buildings, including dormitories, kitchen, recreation field, swimming pool, and an auditorium that seats 700 people. Competent builders say we couldn't duplicate it for three to five million dollars. Our cost? $1,325,000—the same price our other property plus development and parking costs would have been without a single building!

Now we have two churches, one in San Diego, and one in El Cajon, eighteen miles away, which more than doubles our effectiveness. The first Sunday we opened the new church for services, 397 people attended. Today that church has two morning services in its new 2,500-seat auditorium. As I walk through the lovely grounds overlooking the new administration building, dormitories, enormous gymnasium, and other facilities, I can thank God by sight. Obviously it was a sinful act of unbelief and a waste of my time to be depressed back in 1969 and 1970. God knows what he is doing with our lives, even when we don't. Happy is the Christian who can trust him by giving thanks even when everything looks black. That is the real key to depression-free living—faith in our loving heavenly Father's plan for our good. Faith that allows us to "give thanks in all circumstances, for this is God's will for you in Christ Jesus" (1 Thessalonians 5:18).

Chapter 11

Depression and Your Mind

The human mind is easily the world's most amazing mechanism. Yet we consistently waste its phenomenal potential, for scientists report that the average person never uses more than ten percent of his brain.

Dr. Gerhard Dirks, possessor of more patents (over fifty of them) for the IBM computer than any living man, told me, "I got most of my ideas for the computer by studying the human mind." And someone has observed, "If scientists could build a computer that equaled the feats of the human mind, it would take a structure the size of the Empire State Building to house it."

CONSCIOUS VS. SUBCONSCIOUS

The brain is divided into two main sections—the conscious and the subconscious. We have accumulated considerable knowledge about the conscious, but we know little about the subconscious. In the last few years careful studies have turned up some intriguing concepts. One theory suggests that our subconscious mind never forgets anything we have seen, felt, heard, tasted, or smelled. Of course, the trick is to remember at the right time! But you can be sure that your present likes, dislikes, feelings, and reactions are etched on the record of your subconscious mind, particularly those mental transcriptions made during the impressionable days of your youth.

Another recent discovery about the mind claims that you are influenced more by the subconscious than the conscious. Let me illustrate. Suppose you are fifteen pounds overweight and your conscious mind warns, "Don't eat that piece of fudge; it will make you gain weight." Do you eat it? That depends upon the reaction of your subconscious mind. If it responds, "But I have an unquenchable sweet tooth"; "I'm destined to be fat"; or "I'm too weak to resist," you will partake.

Now transfer that pattern to the problem of self-pity. Suppose some friend rejects, insults, or injures you. Your conscious mind will caution, "Now don't indulge in self-pity!" (particularly after reading this book), but if your subconscious mind by force of habit retorts, "Everyone treats you like dirt; you're always getting the raw end of the deal" or "You can't trust anyone" or "How could they do that to me after all I've done for them?" you will indulge in self-pity, which follows an unswerving path to depression.

Another important discovery related to the mind concerns the response of the subconscious to the imagination. In fact, the imagination, in my opinion, is the most powerful factor of the mind. Regardless of the vitality of your willpower, maintaining a negative image on the screen of your imagination will ultimately break down your will.

A friend of mine is an alcoholic, but for six years he had not touched a drop. One hot day an urgent thought flashed on the screen of his imagination: "An ice-cold glass of beer sure would taste good right now." His conscious mind responded, "Don't do it! You're an alcoholic." Because his imagination was visualizing the beer in living three-dimensional color, he talked himself into the assurance that after six years he had learned to control his problem. Within two hours he visited a bar, tried one drink, then another, and you can imagine the rest.

Whenever the will and the imagination come into conflict, the imagination wins. For this reason self-pity projected on the screen of the imagination is so devastatingly harmful!

Previously, we saw the influence your mind, will, and heart have on your actions. Your will determines what you put in your mind, which in turn activates your feelings and ultimately your conduct, forming a powerful chain reaction:

Will + Mind + Emotions = Actions

Your will can determine what new material you put into your mind, but it cannot govern your attitude toward the old material, nor can it fully regulate the mind. This is particularly true of the subconscious, which cannot be controlled by the will directly, but may be influenced through the imagination. The governor of your mind is the imagination. As the imagination goes, so goes the mind, both conscious and subconscious. For illustrative purposes, let us use a computer monitor to demonstrate the power of the imagination over both the subconscious and conscious mind.

THE NEGATIVE USE OF IMAGINATION

You can use your imagination either creatively or destructively. Most people, I'm afraid, employ their imagination destructively, for they picture themselves as ineffective, clumsy, fearful, and rejected. If this becomes the governor of their self-image and the inhibitor of their expectations, they may dwell upon the negative experience of the past and look negatively to the future. It is far better to make creative use of the imagination. Only by projecting wholesome and positive images on the screen of your imagination will you rise above the inadequate view of yourself that ensnares most people.

THE PERSISTENCE OF THE SUBCONSCIOUS

Whatever you place on the screen of your subconscious mind will govern your activities! The Bible says, "For as [a man] thinks in his heart, so is he" (Proverbs 23:7 NKJV). Your imaginative self-image determines how you feel and, as a result, how you work and act. The subconscious mind functions inexorably toward the fulfillment of whatever image you flash on the screen. For that reason you should become a very careful and skillful mental operator.

Exhaustive studies with obese people have brought to light some very interesting uses for creative imagery. Many overweight people who find it difficult to lose weight crave more food the longer they remain on a diet. Whenever they gaze upon sweets, though conscious of the effect these foods will have, they seem powerless to resist. In recent years we have discovered the culprit: the screen of the imagination. When overweight people project an image of themselves as obese or an appetizing image of their favorite delicacy, their subconscious mind draws them inexorably toward the fulfillment of that image. Even when their stomach is full, an impelling force entices them to eat. This problem can rarely be changed by the power of the will, but great success has been found in "thinking thin." If they consistently project on the screen of their imagination a picture of themselves as slender, their subconscious mind will abruptly reject foods that violate that image. Dieting becomes less painful because they gradually lose their craving for foods that conflict with their renewed mental image of themselves.

On several occasions I have suggested this to depressed counselees who were struggling with an obvious weight problem, and many have experienced positive results. I have found that the so-called "happy fat man" is a misnomer; he may be laughing on the outside, but he is grieving on the inside. He urgently needs to change the mental image he carries of himself. Only then will he attain lasting success with weight control.

One night in a local ice-cream parlor I saw this graphically illustrated when a woman entered apparently forty-five pounds lighter than when I had counseled her several months before. Rejecting the hot fudge sundae ordered by her friends, she casually requested a dish of plain strawberries. Later she remarked to me, "It's no sacrifice since I have learned to picture myself as thin. Sure, I want the hot fudge sundae, but not nearly as much as I want to be thin." As she spoke, my mind raced back to that day in the counseling room when she confessed to dieting unsuccessfully for almost twenty years. The change in her was not due to willpower, but to the discovery of an effective precept: *Utilize the energy of the imagination to insure desired behavior.* Remember, whatever you picture on the screen of your imagination will become the goal toward which your subconscious mind will irresistibly lead you. The Bible teaches us to cast down "imaginations, and every high thing that exalteth itself against the knowledge of God, and [bring] into captivity *every thought* to the obedience of Christ" (2 Corinthians 10:5 KJV).

THE POSITIVE USE OF IMAGINATION

THE GOOD USE OF IMAGINATION

This principle of controlling your mind, feelings, and actions by projecting only beneficial images on the imagination screen of your mind works admirably in the field of depression. People who have tried without success to rid themselves of depression by various therapeutic techniques have tried this method with gratifying results primarily because it deals with the problem, not the symptoms. Medication, counseling, electric-shock treatments, or other methods will only provide minimal results unless the individual also changes the image he projects on the screen of his imagination. Depressed people create a negative, self-pitying picture on the imagination, inevitably making them feel depressed. By creating a fresh, new image they will gradually modify their feeling and their behavior.

A lonely, middle-aged nurseryman came in for counseling after his wife had left him. "She just couldn't stand my long periods of depression any longer," he freely admitted. "I've tried everything, but nothing seems to work." The familiar pattern emerged through his story. Rejected and criticized by a perfectionist father, he felt completely inadequate and apprehensive, incapable of fulfilling his real capabilities.

Negative, self-pitying, critical mental images continually projected on the imagination screen of his mind. I challenged him to trust God for a new set of files for his mental computer screen. As we prayed together I gathered that he had never given God thanks for the qualities and gifts he did possess, and in his prayer he made particular mention of his spirit of ingratitude, but even before he got up off his knees, he thought of three things to be grateful for, and before he reached the door a slight trace of a smile appeared on his lips. Today, by his own testimony, "I have not been depressed in five years." His wife later explained to a friend why she was able to come back to him.

"He isn't the same morose, pessimistic critic I lived with for twenty-three years. He is actually fun to be around."

CREATIVE IMAGERY AND THE HOLY SPIRIT

The Holy Spirit certainly understood the function of the human mind when he inspired men to write the Bible. That is why he never instructed us to think about negative or undesirable things. Instead the Bible directs us to project only positive thoughts on the screen of our imagination.

Unlike the analyst who leads his patient to "talk out his frustrations" or "recall his childhood experiences" for the sake of digging up dirt or blaming others, the Bible instructs Christians to forget "what is behind" and "to press on toward the goal to win the prize for which God has called [us] heavenward in Christ Jesus" (Philippians 3:13–14).

Instead of dwelling on your own inadequacies or failings (real or imagined), "Your attitude should be the same as that of Christ Jesus" (Philippians 2:5). Do not indulge in self-pity because some friend has insulted, injured, or rejected you. The Bible reminds us: "Do not fret because of evil men" (Proverbs 24:19).

The importance of keeping one's mind clear of negative, harmful, and evil thoughts by replacing them with good, wholesome ideas is clearly reflected in Romans 12:2, which challenges Christians to be "transformed by the renewing of your mind." As the mind goes, so goes the behavior! Transformed conduct only follows in the wake of a renewed mind. In other words, exchange your natural (often negative) thinking patterns for the wisdom of God found in the Word of God. This principle is further illustrated in Romans 8:6: "The mind of sinful man is death; but the mind controlled by the Spirit is life and peace." A spiritually minded person will imaginatively project only those things that are pleasing to God. Consequently, he will feel and act in a manner acceptable to God. The Holy Spirit enables us to imagine creatively in those patterns that produce healthy emotions.

THE POWER OF SUGGESTION

Never underestimate the influence of suggestion on your mind. A suggestion is capable not only of motivating you, but also of activating the glands in your body. Consider, for instance, what happens when you visualize a delicious red apple. Merely picturing that apple on the screen of your imagination arouses your saliva glands until your mouth waters. If you think about it long enough, you can literally "taste that apple."

Did it ever occur to you that depression can be fashioned the same way? Recently a minister's wife drove me to the airport after I had spoken to a group of ministers on the subject of depression. Obviously quite engrossed in the subject, she asked me a question of interest to many women: "Isn't it quite common for women to experience depression when they go through their monthly period?" I responded, "Often it depends on whether they expect to be depressed." If a woman anticipates depression each month at this time, she will undoubtedly not be disappointed. This is not to minimize the physiological change within a woman's body. Premenstrual syndrome can certainly account for hormonal changes that can cause an increase in anxiety tendencies and a decrease in energy. But though most women do not like to admit it, those symptoms can be greatly exaggerated and compounded by the power of suggestion.

The minister's wife laughed and added candidly, "I have noticed that when my period comes at a time when I am excited about something else and my mind is occupied with other things, it doesn't have nearly the effect on me that it does at other times." A psychiatrist couldn't have stated it better. If a woman has been trained by her mother to expect debilitation or depression three or four days each month, she will experience it until she reorients her thinking pattern. However, if she has been taught that menstruation is part of God's fantastic design for her life, a symbol of womanhood and motherhood for which she can be grateful, it is less likely to leave her in an apathetic condition.

The same power of suggestion influences the severity of menopause. Many a woman expects to fall apart during her menopause. Rarely is such a woman disappointed! However, women I have met who were determined to face this stage of life as if it were just an ordinary facet of living would not permit themselves to be disabled by it—and they were not.

Your mental attitude is more important in such matters than your hormones and glands because your attitude controls them. Whatever you flash on the imagination screen of your mind will influence your life, starting with the subconscious mind and progressing to the conscious mind and to the function of the glands.

SIX THINGS THAT INFLUENCE YOUR SUBCONSCIOUS MIND

Your Imagination

As we have already illustrated, the imagination may be used negatively or positively to the glory of God. Your task is to direct it.

Goals

It is no accident that our age of emotional despair and depression is also a time of hopelessness. The younger generation, experiencing an alarming degree of depression, has in many cases given up on their homeland, society, culture, and humanity in general. The Bible warns us that "where there is no vision, the people perish" (Proverbs 29:18 KJV). It is not enough for the individual to create good mental images of himself, for he must in addition project worthy goals on the screen of his imagination that will lead him to witness the power of God effecting a change in his life. Because the human mind is a goal-oriented mechanism, it must be pursuing an explicit end or it will not function properly. If you do not project on the screen of your imagination a series of worthwhile, challenging goals, you will gradually develop the demotivating habit of projecting self-defeating, pessimistic goals that will depress you.

As you begin to set goals that reflect God's power in your life, you may be confronted with a typical dilemma: Most people think too small. The person of faith always thinks big. And why not? He or she is a child of the great God whose abundant power is always placed at his or her disposal. One of Christendom's mighty thinkers, the apostle Paul, communicated an essential truth in this regard: "My God will meet *all* your needs" (Philippians 4:19, italics added). Think big!

A survey of successful businesspeople indicated that ninety-five percent of them had drawn up a list of goals to guide them. Putting goals down in tangible form helps to etch them more deeply on the screen of our imagination and makes it easier to activate our subconscious mind toward their achievement. And once we have committed our goals to writing, we should make a habit of reading them every day for sixty days. Successful people are not usually smarter than others, they are more goal oriented. In fact, they usually have clear and definite goals. Unsuccessful people usually have none.

Spiritual Principles

The psalmist said, "I have hidden your word in my heart, that I might not sin against you" (Psalm 119:11). The best way to reverse negative thinking patterns is to memorize scriptural principles that produce happiness. Throughout this book you may have discovered that you are violating certain basic biblical precepts and thus have lost your inner joy. Jesus Christ said, "If you know these things [principles of God], happy are you if you do them" (John 13:17 NKJV). Happiness, then, is the result of *knowing the principles of God and doing them.*

As a pastor I have encouraged the members of our congregation on numerous occasions to keep four-by-six cards in the flyleaf of their Bibles, ready to write down those principles for living that particularly suit their needs. The Word of God is so filled with practical advice that every time you hear it faithfully taught you will discover principles that will meet your heart's special need. The more of them you program into your mind, the easier it is for your subconscious to direct your living habits into those principles that produce a happy life.

Memory

We already have mentioned that the human mind never forgets anything. Even though we may not consciously remember something, it can apparently have a spontaneous influence upon us. One woman indicated that she always became depressed when a particular hymn was sung in her church; on some occasions she even had to leave the church service weeping. Later she discovered through a relative that the piece was sung at her mother's funeral. A young girl at the time, she grieved sorely over the loss of her mother and thus, although not recalling the event on the conscious level, she subconsciously reacted each time she heard that hymn.

Often we are unaware that certain experiences strongly influence our behavior. For this reason we should guard our memory by walking in the Spirit on a consistent basis, for then our memory bank will remain pleasing to God. The individual who indulges in sensual thoughts develops a sensual memory and cultivates sensual appetites. The same is true regarding depression. The individual who dwells upon every distress, every rejection, every loss is naturally liable to depression.

Whenever the memory of such events comes to mind, develop the habit of "forgetting what is behind" (Philippians 3:13). Refuse to focus upon disagreeable experiences of the past, for they only become more deeply etched on the table of the mind and perpetuate the feelings of sadness or depression. As you consciously look forward to the future with the power and blessing of God, reprogram your mind by looking at difficulties through the eyes of faith, thus replacing negative or self-pitying thought patterns that will subconsciously depress you. When those negative thoughts come to mind, and they will, thank God for bringing you through that trial and "set your mind on things above."

Habits

Everyone knows that we are influenced by habits. Since anything you do on a consistent basis becomes easier each successive time, it is essential that you learn constructive thinking habits. The more you think positively about God's blessing in the future, the sooner you will maintain an affirmative mental pattern. Naturally, the converse is also true. In Romans 12:2 the apostle Paul discloses the secret to being "transformed" by "the renewing of your mind." As we renew our mind on the principles of God and create proper mental habits, the transformed way of life that God promises to every believer becomes a reality.

The Holy Spirit

One of the special functions of the Holy Spirit is to "remind you of everything [Jesus has] said to you" (John 14:26). For this reason it is important for the Christian to read and memorize the Word of God regularly so that the Holy Spirit can bring out of the memory bank those things that God has declared. The Holy Spirit will not bring to your mind anything that God has not said to you, for he relies upon the Word of God to program our minds through hearing, reading, meditating, studying, and memorizing the principles of God. From this storehouse of biblical principles the Holy Spirit can draw out his bountiful riches as we require them. In addition, learning biblical principles for living will remove the influence of harmful past memories and replace them with positive messages from God, thus reassuring the individual's heart toward the future and preparing him to face it.

The Holy Spirit wants to fill and enrich your life to instill in you a dynamic testimony of the abundant Christian life. For him to do so, you must cooperate by learning the Word of God and "keeping it." God blesses those who obey him, but knowledge always precedes obedience. The psalmist evidently had this in mind when he wrote in the psalm of the happy man, "[Happy] is the man . . . [whose] delight is in the law of the LORD [the Bible]. . . . He is like a tree planted by streams of water, which yields its fruit in season and whose leaf does not wither. Whatever he does prospers" (Psalm 1:1–3).

If you would live the abundant life mentally, like a tree whose roots lie near a river of water, then your mind must be refreshed daily with the water of life, the Word of God.

Chapter 12

Depression and Your Self-Image

A person's attitude toward himself has a profound
influence on his attitude toward God, his family, his friends,
his future, and many other significant areas of his life.
Bill Gothard

Every depressed person I have ever counseled has had a problem with self-acceptance. That really is not too profound a statement in view of the fact that almost every human being holds an inadequate image of himself. At some time in his life even the boldest and most self-confident individual battles self-rejection. Although most people regain their self-assurance, none is immune.

In the last several years, research has produced new concepts called "self-image psychology" that have proved more helpful to people than some of the ideas of humanistic psychology. Dr. Maxwell Maltz, an expert in this field, suggests that self-image psychology is the most important discovery of the century. It stems from the idea that each of us is controlled by the mental picture we develop of ourselves.

Two popular expressions from self-image psychology illustrate its basic thesis: "You are what you think you are" and "What other people think of you is not nearly as important as what you think of yourself." Everyone has some image of himself, either good or bad, but whatever that self-image, it affects our behavior, attitudes, productivity, and ultimately our success in life.

Thoughts produce feelings and feelings produce actions; consequently your self-image thoughts definitely affect your actions, negatively or positively.

One who maintains a self-confident image of himself will perform to his maximum ability, but the insecure person who lacks self-confidence will not. This explains why some talented people fail while other mediocre people often succeed.

A person's self-image is not formed by a single event or experience. Instead, it is the culmination of all of life's experiences. Naturally, many subconscious influences produce self-image, including the thousands of victories, failures, frustrations, humiliations, and successes we experience. The influence they have on our self-image depends in large measure on our natural temperament.

Temperament comprises the raw material a person is born with, creating the combination of traits passed on to him by his parents through the genes. It is probably the largest single factor that produces personality characteristics. As we will see in a later chapter, these temperament traits contain both strengths and weaknesses. Whatever your temperament, it will be influenced by your life experiences. If, for example, you were born happy-go-lucky or self-confident by temperament, you may be constrained to develop a defeatist's complex by excessively critical parents who always carped at you or accentuated your ineptitude or failure. Conversely, if you were born with a negative or retiring temperament and are prone to be indecisive and insecure, wise parents can help you avoid a defeatist's attitude by surrounding you with love, acceptance, and encouragement, particularly during the early years of life. Whatever the cause, your personal self-image governs your life! Consider the expression "You are what you think you are." If you think you are ugly or inept, you are. It doesn't matter what you actually are, for what really affects your productivity and actions is what you think you are. I know a young mother who always commands attention when she walks into a room. Both men and women take a second look at her. When I mentioned this to some associates recently, we all agreed that she was not necessarily a beautiful woman, but that something about her drew our attention. As I have come to know her, I find that she enjoys a tremendous amount of self-respect. She always looks her best wherever she goes; she is never overdressed but always looks attractive. She chooses her clothes and accessories with care and exudes the confidence that exemplifies a dynamic Christian. Neither haughty nor proud, she makes the best use of her assets. I know many of her female friends who are actually better-looking women, but they never command that attention. Why? They lack her self-image. It is interesting to note that her self-confidence was not generated by her family, for they have rejected her because of her Christian faith. Only her personal faith in Christ has bestowed upon her a confidence in his ability to enable her to be a dynamic, attractive woman. And she is!

The two most beautiful women I have ever counseled were severely depressed. To my dismay, neither woman accepted herself. As I looked into their lovely faces, faces that most women would covet, I was reminded that looks alone are irrelevant; how you *think* you look is critical. Neither of these women considered herself attractive, so what difference did it make that she was?

The younger of the two was frigid, the slightly older woman a nymphomaniac—yet both shared the same problem. One was so obsessed with the false notion of her inadequate appearance that she could not stand exposure of her body to the opposite sex. The other woman was so obsessed with the inadequacy of her appearance that she drove herself through a series of illicit affairs in an attempt to gain the acceptance she craved. Today both women are well-adjusted, effective Christians, powerful evidence to the stabilizing influence of Jesus Christ in this very needed area of a person's life. Their lives began to change when they recognized that God forgave and accepted them. That made it easier for them to accept themselves.

THE BIG MISTAKE

Most people make a singular mistake regarding self-image: They allow other people's opinions to influence their view of themselves. Quite to the contrary, what a person thinks of himself will affect what other people think of him. I have seen this illustrated many times while standing at an airline baggage counter. A porter will approach one individual and address him politely and with dignity, whereas he will speak to another with quiet disrespect. Through these contrasting treatments, I have judged that the man who exudes self-confidence and self-acceptance is extended respect by others. You can often observe similar episodes in a restaurant as the waiter approaches his customers.

Once we understand that we create this public image by our actions and by our impression of ourselves, we will realize the importance of self-acceptance, which determines whether we will act confidently or with great uncertainty. Be sure of this: If you lack confidence in yourself, so will everyone else.

Here are three good reasons why you should not let others' attitudes influence what you think of yourself:

(1) God values you and loves you because he created you. His attitude about you will never change.

(2) You cannot always judge what people think about you by their appearance or actions, for they may be concentrating on something else entirely. Many an insecure individual has spent a sleepless night wondering why so-and-so gave him a disapproving look. When he stopped to investigate, he found that poor so-and-so had not even consciously seen the one who was so wounded by the unknowing glance.

(3) What other people think of you is usually a reflection of your own self-image. If you feel inferior, you emote the feeling of inferiority, and consequently others will look upon you as inferior.

FOUR AREAS OF SELF-ACCEPTANCE

The Institute of Basic Youth Conflicts, directed by Bill Gothard, has probably helped more people learn the art of self-acceptance with God's help and power than any other such training program.

Most of those who attend his seminars are well educated in the mental, emotional, and physical areas of life. However, because most of them have been brainwashed by the atheistic, humanistic philosophers of our secular educational system, they noticeably lack spiritual knowledge or reserves. By recognizing the spiritual side of our nature as described in chapter 6 and by applying the biblical principles Mr. Gothard teaches, these individuals are able to gain self-acceptance and become mature, productive people.

In his seminars Bill Gothard describes four areas in which people must gain self-acceptance. (There are undoubtedly other areas, but these are the main ones.) Naturally, it follows that these are the very areas in which most people reject themselves: appearance, abilities, parentage, and environment.

Appearance

It has been my observation that almost everyone rejects his or her appearance. Twelve Hollywood actors and actresses were asked the question, "If you could change something about your facial features, what would it be?" The answers ranged anywhere from four to twelve items per person. As incredible as it may seem, these people, admired by millions as the most beautiful or handsome in our society, obviously did not accept themselves. Again we are confronted with this fact: It is not so important what we are, but what we *think* we are.

Rejection of one's appearance is an intensely spiritual problem. Since God is our Creator, we tend to blame him for our condition. This subconscious and sometimes conscious resentment toward God will keep us from becoming mature Christians. Through the years I have been able to help hundreds of people who lacked the assurance of their salvation to gain that precious emotional blessing. In almost every case I discovered that they lacked assurance in the beginning primarily because they did not like their appearance. According to their standard, they were either too tall, too short, too fat, or too thin. In addition to prescribing the daily reading of 1 John for at least one month, I required them to look in the mirror every day and thank

God for the way they were made. Only by the removal of this resentment toward God for the way they were created could the door be opened for their much needed self-acceptance.

Abilities

Except for a very rare number of gifted individuals, most people develop an inadequate view of their abilities, especially when they tend to compare themselves with others. Whether running with a football, riding a motorcycle, or passing a geometry exam, we compete as a way of life. Sooner or later everyone finds someone better than himself, and this may trigger the problem. We regularly tend to make unfair comparisons of our abilities with those of someone else. Just because someone hits sixty home runs a year does not mean that he is a mature person. Many mature and adequate people cannot hit one home run, but they make excellent husbands, fathers, teachers, and people. It is far better to accept the fact that our talents or abilities are conferred by God and that our responsibility in life is to serve and glorify him (see Revelation 4:11). Fulfillment, happiness, and self-acceptance are best found in doing the will of God for one's life.

I truly believe that the most self-fulfilling use of our talents appears in successfully raising children. Since God's first commandment was to be fruitful and multiply and replenish the earth, it follows that the successful fulfillment of that commandment will become a very self-rewarding experience. It must be understood, however, that God was not merely referring to the biological function of begetting children. He had in mind a much longer range view—that of raising those children to be God-conscious Christian young people, taught by their parents the principles of God and capable of teaching these principles to their own children.

After forty years of dealing with people I do not find that vocational triumphs provide lasting self-acceptance. Instead, many individuals would willingly relinquish the fortune earned during their lifetime if they could reclaim the failure experienced by the son or daughter who was neglected as a child. On the other hand, I know hundreds of happy, contented Christians who feel enriched because their children are a source of pride and satisfaction to them.

Don't think that you must wait until you become a grandparent, however, to achieve this self-recognition. It can be achieved also by spiritual productivity. Those who invest themselves in service for Christ by personally sharing their faith with others usually do not have a lasting problem with self-acceptance. Worthwhile productivity is a great cure-all for self-rejection. That is one reason teenagers are prone to reject themselves—they haven't had time yet to be productive.

Parentage

Anyone who is ashamed of his parents will have a serious problem with self-acceptance. Too many young people today hate their parents and bring on themselves the curse of God and the tragic results of harbored animosity. Admittedly, some parents can be decidedly inhuman to their children. As a pastor, I have been called into some unbelievable situations.

Some time ago, I had all I could do to control myself while watching a young mother abuse her young son, who looked to be about eighteen months old. While waiting in line at an airline counter, I observed this mother in her midtwenties rush up to the agent, highly distressed because she was about to miss her plane. At her side was her pajama-clad boy, who, sensing her anxiety, was trying to cling to her side. First she pushed him away with her suitcase, and finally in her exasperation she put her foot in his stomach and shoved him out of the way. The boy fell whimpering to the tile floor as the mother walked off. My final glimpse was of a boy frantically trying to catch up with a fleeing woman, crying as if his heart would break.

It doesn't take a psychiatrist to diagnose what that child will be like as a teenager if he is continually subjected to that kind of treatment. He will certainly become a rebel, always seeking acceptance from others because he has none for himself. His clinging tendency because of continual rejection will give way to malignant bitterness that may cause him either to reject women and fall a victim to the sin of homosexuality or to cruelly abuse his wife and daughters.

Nothing destroys like bitterness, particularly when it is aimed at one's parents. Having dealt with hundreds of bitter people, I am convinced that failure to rid oneself of that bitterness will destroy the normal love relationships in life. Only by confessing this spirit of anger and hostility as described in chapter 8 will the individual experience relief. The Bible teaches us, "Refrain from anger and turn from wrath; do not fret—it leads only to evil" (Psalm 37:8).

Aside from the spiritual dangers of harboring anger toward one's parents, there is another tragic result. For years I have noted that young people who hate their parents either grow up to be just like them or marry a partner similar to them. Those who study the function of the brain now explain that such a strange phenomenon originates with the subconscious mind, which always works toward the fulfillment of whatever image we throw upon the screen of our imagination. For example, I have noticed that the young woman raised by an alcoholic father tends to marry an alcoholic. The reason is simple. Thousands of times during her youth a girl has visualized a mental picture of her drunken father and pledged, "I will never marry a man like that!" But her subconscious mind brings her inexorably to the fulfillment of her negative thoughts of disgust or hatred for her father. The same thing happens to the young man whose cruel, angry father mistreated him. Although he insists he will never act like his father, he does. When the child I saw mistreated in the airport grows up and marries, he will probably unite with a woman much like his mother, because all through life his resentment toward her will cause him to project on the screen of his imagination that bitter image with the promise, "I will never marry a woman like her." But he will!

All of the previously mentioned tragedies can be avoided if people would recognize the importance of permitting only those thoughts on the screen of their imagination that are pleasing to God. We cannot always control what thoughts flash onto our imagination screen, but we can regulate those that linger. Those persistent, recurring thoughts activate the subconscious mind, which in turn creates feelings that motivate actions.

Instead of projecting negative images, visualize positive ones. If the young woman had envisioned a wholesome young man embodying Christian principles, instead of her alcoholic father, she would have married that kind of man. Anything else would have violated her mental image. In fact, I know one young woman, the product of an alcoholic father, who rejected a fine Christian lad to marry a man who turned out to be an alcoholic. Why? She fixed upon the wrong kind of mental image in her imagination.

Environment

Although highly exaggerated by behaviorists of a past generation, our environment does create a profound effect on our self-acceptance. If a person is embarrassed by his home and family, he will be miserable. In addition, his attitude of shame or rejection will severely mar his self-image out of proportion to the actual circumstances.

To understand that mental attitude toward one's circumstances is far more significant than the material or physical circumstance itself, consider the classic story of the teenage girl who was ashamed of her mother because her mother's hands were terribly disfigured by burns. When her father noticed how she avoided being seen in public with her mother, he explained to her in detail how the disfigurement had occurred. When the girl was a baby, her mother had rescued her from falling into an open fireplace. In the process the mother's hands were marred for life. The girl was so ashamed for the heartache she had caused her mother by her selfish attitude that she went to her, took those scarred hands into her own, kissed them, and said through her tears, "Mother, I love you. Can you ever forgive me for the way I have treated you? I don't know how to thank you for all your kindness and love." From then on she was proud to be seen with her mother, and the ugly hands became a badge of honor. What made the difference? Those hands remained just as grotesque as before, but now the daughter's mental attitude toward them had changed.

Some young people have been victimized into a poor self-image by the false notion that second-class people come from second-class living conditions. The products of the inner city afford good examples. Those who are raised there are often trained to think less of themselves because of their environment. There is nothing new about inner cities; we have always had them. They are simply larger today because of our increased population and more conspicuous because of recent national attention. During high school I lived in what would be considered the inner city, but it didn't affect me negatively, because no one informed me how terrible it was. I was naive enough to think it was pretty good, so my mental attitude remained positive about my home environment.

History books are filled with stories of men who have risen from Illinois log cabins to occupy the White House and from dark inner cities to become exemplary educators. I once read a survey that claimed that the majority of history's successful men have risen above an unfortunate or inadequate environment. The key to a positive attitude toward your environment involves your acceptance of it. At least give thanks for the surroundings that provided you with the life from which to emerge to a better environment, and be grateful for the valuable lessons learned in the process of emerging.

Let us pause here long enough to emphasize that all four areas that influence self-image are affected by a proper spiritual attitude. If you really believe God loves you and has produced you for a special reason, as the Bible teaches, then you can accept with thanksgiving your appearance, abilities, parentage, and environment. Once you accept these by faith in God and his Word, you will find it is easy to accept yourself. But if you reject one or more of these areas, you will suffer the miseries that accompany self-rejection.

THE TRAGIC RESULTS OF REJECTION

It would be impossible in a small book like this to investigate all the results of self-rejection, for they affect literally everything in a person's life. However, I will offer eight critical consequences of importance.

Depression

Resentment that follows the rejection of appearance, abilities, parentage, or environment soon turns into self-pity, which invariably produces depression. This depression will increase in intensity as you age unless you learn to accept these areas as instruments of God, which he wants to use in your life for his glory. Changes in your environment or life circumstances may provide temporary periods of relief, but unless you modify your thinking pattern of self-pity, you will be chained by the emotional slavery of depression.

Lack of Personal Faith in God

It is impossible to develop a vital and personal faith in God until you learn to accept yourself. Your rejection of God's design of your body and his endowment of talents, parents, and environment are not conducive to the submissive spirit (see Ephesians 5:21) that is required in a happy, productive Christian. Only by giving thanks by faith for your appearance, talent, parents, and environment can you clear the way for a vital relationship to him, which is absolutely essential in ridding yourself of depression.

Doubtless you have heard people criticize themselves openly. But Christians should know better than to censure themselves. When they do, they not only advertise their personal mistakes but the inadequate view they have of themselves. Bill Gothard wisely reminds us all that as imperfect as we are, "God is not finished with us yet." As children of God, we are still being molded and fashioned for his divine purposes. Instead of rejecting ourselves, according to the Bible, we must present ourselves to him and anticipate by faith his ultimate use of our lives. Such a spiritual viewpoint will produce a mental attitude conducive to productivity, which in turn will assist in producing self-acceptance.

Rebellion

Self-rejection for any reason will kindle the fire of rebellion in your heart toward God and others, whether parents, boss, life partner, or anyone in authority over you.

We live in a rebellious society. We should not be surprised that we also live in an unhappy society. Think of it! Although we dwell in the lap of luxury with conveniences thought impossible twenty-five years ago, many Americans are bitter, hostile, and for the most part miserable. This is the typical result of people who reject themselves, for they are prone to lash out at everything and everyone around them.

Withdrawal

When a person rejects himself, he finds it difficult to enjoy other people. He tends to be supersensitive to others' attitudes toward his appearance, capabilities, parental background, or environment. Therefore he withdraws so as to avoid conflict and the unhappy feelings it creates. As he retreats, he muses increasingly upon his own needs, feelings, and thoughts. Since he doesn't like himself anyway, he becomes more unhappy.

Overemphasis on Material Things

The rejection of one's self creates an inordinate drive for materialism. This may be characterized by narcissism, an overemphasis on clothes, or the amassing of material goods—none of which produces happiness. It is extremely difficult to convince a young person that the attainment of material possessions does not foster happiness. I can name at least fifteen men worth well over a million dollars who have not found their money a source of happiness. And in some cases wealth has actually destroyed the happiness they enjoyed in less affluent days.

Jesus Christ said, "But seek first his kingdom and his righteousness, and all these things will be given to you as well" (Matthew 6:33). By way of contrast to my previous statement, I am familiar with other millionaires who are extremely happy. Their money, however, did not bring them happiness. Their primary objective was to serve God, and their material possessions followed in the wake of loyal service.

Negativism and "failuritis"

We frequently hear the popular maxim, "Know thyself." Such advice is dangerous to the person who rejects himself, for in practical terms he interprets it to mean "Know your negative self." He recollects the past as an amalgamation of failure, affront, insult, and abuse to which he has been subjected. He concludes, "Nothing ever works for me; nothing ever succeeds. I must be doomed to failure!" Since the subconscious mind tends to bring us to the fulfillment of whatever we place on the screen of our imagination, such thinking inevitably produces failure, not because he lacks the potential of success, but because he expects to fail.

"Imitationitis"

The person who rejects himself not only compares himself to others but often tries to imitate others. This can be a most harmful practice. Dr. Maxwell Maltz advises, "Remember this, and remember this every day: you will never be happy if you spend your life trying to be someone else. God created you as a unique individual. You have within you an authentic greatness all your own. Use it; don't waste it! You waste it when you try to be someone else for the simple reason you are not someone else."[1]

Limiting God's Use of Your Life

The sad result of self-rejection is that you keep yourself from being used of God, who has fashioned a plan for every life. Maximum happiness is achieved in fulfilling that plan, but maximum misery follows in resisting that plan. By rejecting yourself, you not only refrain from using your own natural talents, but you hinder God from injecting his miracle powers into your life. A life of faith is an exciting life! Most people never experience that kind of living because instead of accepting Jesus Christ's statement, "I have come that they may have life, and have it to the full" (John 10:10), they reject themselves and short-circuit the power of God by their unbelief. You will never experience the abundant life until you realize by faith that God is able to bless even you!

WHY MOST PEOPLE TEND TO REJECT THEMSELVES

Anything as universal as self-rejection should have some common causes. Consider the following possibilities:

(1) *Little people in a big world.* We all start out the same way: little people incapable of any productivity. Whether it is a young boy trying to help his father overhaul the family car only to be frustrated with the feeling that his wise father can fix anything whereas he cannot, or the little girl whose clever, experienced mother can bake a cake from scratch while she doesn't know her way around the kitchen, we all share the same problem. Everyone wants to achieve, but we lack the patience to gain the time, training, and experience commensurate with the task.

(2) *Childish ridicule.* No child can grow up without being ridiculed by his peers. For many children, however, such ridicule may teach them to find fault with themselves.

(3) *Being more conscious of one's own mistakes than the mistakes of others.* It has long fascinated me that some perfectionists tend to admire people who are far less capable than themselves. A perfectionist often feels like David did when he said, "My sin is always before me" (Psalm 51:3). This person is, therefore, much more readily confronted with his failures than those of others. In actuality, he becomes far too obsessed with his own faults.

(4) *Critical parents, relatives, teachers, and friends.* Constant criticism is always harmful. Everyone seeks and needs praise, particularly from those he loves most. Unfortunately, the parent who lacks self-esteem often will be overly critical of his children, almost as though he tries to boost his own feelings of importance by calling attention to their clumsiness and inadequacy. This criticism is regarded by a child as rejection. If his parents reject him, it is easy for him to reject himself.

THE HALLMARKS OF SELF-ACCEPTANCE

Mature people are not perfect people, but those who have learned to accept themselves for who they are. That includes both their strengths and weaknesses. They will then try to effect some kind of program to overcome those weaknesses. Without their realizing it, this kind of self-acceptance will manifest itself subconsciously in their actions and reactions. As they gradually develop in their spiritual life, they will mature emotionally. Such maturity will be a walking fulfillment of the first two commandments as defined by Jesus Christ; they contain the hallmarks of true self-acceptance. "'Love the Lord your God with all your heart and with all your soul and with all your strength and with all your mind'; and 'Love your neighbor as yourself'" (Luke 10:27).

In addition to these two hallmarks of the person who accepts himself or herself, there are at least five others. It will be profitable to look briefly at each of them.

He will love and serve God.

Such an individual will become a submitted Christian, yielded to the will of God. He will not be confused about his identity or constantly driven by ambition to succeed. Instead, his concern with his relationship to God and pleasing him will overshadow any attempts to gratify himself.

She will love and accept other people.

A mature person can love others and share life's successes with them. The Bible teaches that we should rejoice with those who rejoice and weep with those who weep. Whereas a mature person will be able to do both, a selfish person can only weep with those who weep (see Romans 12:15). If your neighbor wins a new Cadillac in a drawing, can you honestly rejoice with him? The selfish, immature person will mutter, "Why doesn't something like that ever happen to me?" If the neighbor's wife has died, however, it is not difficult to weep with him without wishing for a similar misfortune.

A truly mature person will love and accept others for themselves and rejoice in their success.

He will love and accept himself.

Do not be afraid to love yourself. Christians may be deluded into thinking that any form of self-love is sin, but Jesus did not say, "Do not love yourself." He said, "Love your neighbor as yourself" (Matthew 22:39), aware that self-love in proper perspective is actually essential. Everyone loves himself to some degree, even though harboring thoughts of self-deprecation. However, people too often love themselves more than God or others. Jesus gives ample room for self-love so long as it appears third on your list of priorities.

Proper self-acceptance may be substantiated by the manner in which a person accepts compliments about his work or appearance. Instead of self-consciously brushing the compliment aside or apologizing for himself, a mature person graciously acknowledges the word of praise. The person who rejects himself becomes flustered and embarrassed, usually extending his embarrassment by uttering something foolish and unnecessary.

She will exercise responsibility.

A fully mature person is trustworthy, always taking full responsibility for her actions. This is particularly noticeable if something has gone wrong. A self-accepting person will not blame other people for the mistake, for she recognizes that her security and self-acceptance are not contingent on a single experience in life. She is more interested in learning from mistakes than in fixing blame for them. Such maturity is a requirement of good leadership.

He is emotionally expressive.

A mature person has freedom not only to laugh and to cry if the occasion warrants, but also to respond emotionally to those around him. His joy is not dependent upon people or circumstances, but radiates from within. Ephesians 5:18–21 declares that the Spirit-filled person will have a song in his heart, a thankful spirit, and a submissive attitude. Such an individual will never be depressed.

She maintains creative flexibility.

A mature person will readily bend when necessary and readjust her program or schedule when the occasion demands. She is not so intent on having her own way that she becomes insensitive to the needs of others. Many have cheated themselves out of profitable experiences by their resentment toward circumstances over which they have no control. The mature person will be sufficiently relaxed and positive so that when adverse circumstances arise, her creative mind will produce an effective alternative.

He evaluates rebuke, insult, and criticism.

A mature person does not feel threatened when someone corrects him or proposes a better method. Instead, he is appreciative of other people's suggestions and willingly explores better methods for attaining his goals.

HOW TO IMPROVE YOUR SELF-IMAGE

Since developing a good self-image is so important to overcoming depression, it is worth taking the time to consider workable methods for improvement.

Develop a personal relationship with God.

Not only is it essential to fill the God-void in yourself by having a personal relationship with him through his Son Jesus Christ, but it is essential to accept yourself. After filling the God-void in you by receiving Jesus Christ through personal invitation, develop a vital relationship to God in learning about him as he manifests himself in his Word. From the first chapter in the Bible, God began to reveal himself to Adam, Noah, Abraham, and others by the use of different names (the word *name* literally means "nature"). Consequently, each time God revealed a new name for himself in the Old Testament, he disclosed a new aspect of his nature that was needed by his children at that point. Like Abraham, the more we learn about God, the more we grow to love him, and the easier it becomes to trust ourselves to him.

There is only one way to learn about God: Read, hear, study, meditate, and memorize what he teaches about himself in the Bible. Non-Christians, ignorant of God, have a strong problem with self-rejection. Only by gaining knowledge of God as revealed in his Word can one develop the ability to accept oneself. As Colossians 3:16–17 enjoins us, "Let the word of Christ dwell in you richly as you teach and admonish one another with all wisdom, and as you sing psalms, hymns and spiritual songs with gratitude in your hearts to God. And whatever you do, whether in word or deed, do all in the name of the Lord Jesus, giving thanks to God the Father through him." If the Word of God dwells in you richly, you will naturally find peace toward God, yourself, and others.

Accept yourself as a creation of God.

The Bible tells us that we are "fearfully and wonderfully made" (Psalm 139:14). Since God formed you for his own purposes, you must accept yourself for the fulfillment of these purposes. By looking to him for guidance, power, and instruction, you link yourself with the omnipotent power of God. If you are a Christian, learn to accept yourself by starting to thank him for who you are as a member of his divine family.

The importance of this step in self-acceptance can be illustrated in the life of a young woman who spoke to me after a seminar. Approximately twenty-two years of age, she sported dowdy-looking corduroy trousers and long, stringy hair. Indicating that she had an irrepressible habit of itching her scalp on one side of her head until she was bald in that spot, she swept back a portion of her tresses to reveal the bald spot. She then related that her father had sent her to the best dermatologist in the city, but he could find nothing organically wrong. She had taken several kinds of tranquilizers and spent a few sessions with psychiatrists, but nothing seemed to improve her condition. When I probed for the problem of self-acceptance, she hung her head and acknowledged that she did not like her appearance. I immediately suggested two courses of action: First, look yourself squarely in the mirror and thank God for your appearance (she really wasn't unattractive but obviously thought she was); second, visit a beauty parlor and have your hair styled in such a way that it protects the bald spot and prevents you from itching your scalp without ruining the cut. Within six weeks I received word from her that little hairs had begun to grow on the bald spot. This young woman had so convinced herself she was unsightly that she had subconsciously proceeded to destroy her natural attractiveness by rubbing herself bald and dressing in a most uncomplimentary manner.

Appearance is quite often an index of self-acceptance. If people feel inadequate, slovenly, and downcast, they will wear clothes that exhibit those feelings. If, however, they possess an adequate supply of self-acceptance, they will dress commensurate with their vocation, environment, and resources. I am inclined to believe that some of the fashions worn by high school and college students may perpetuate their actual feelings of self-rejection. What they interpret to be a broadside at the establishment could be little more than an expression of inadequacy and self-rejection. Naturally, it is dangerous to generalize here, for some prefer casual clothes because they are more comfortable, but it should not be forgotten that we gain a certain psychological comfort in being properly dressed when the occasion calls for it. It can be healthy when a person's tastes in style change with age and maturity. In fact, it may signal self-acceptance.

Learn how to cope with guilt feelings.

Self-rejecting people often become discouraged with themselves because of minor blunders, and their frustration can be out of proportion to the failure. They seem to forget that everyone fails personally, socially, and even spiritually, at times. Unfortunately, psychology has done its best to explain away guilt by blaming it on religion rather than administering a remedy for it.

Some years ago a doctor treating me for laryngitis took advantage of my inoperative voice to inform me rather pointedly that in his opinion ministers had "done more harm to more people than any other known profession." He went on to explain that during his internship in a mental institution, he found that "ninety-five percent of the patients were there because of religiously induced guilt complexes." "Doctor, you couldn't be more in error," I whispered. "People feel guilty because they *are* guilty!" The Bible teaches what modern psychology tends to reject: Human beings are not conscience-free animals who can sin with impunity. They are living souls whose consciences either "accuse or defend" them (Romans 2:15).

To enjoy good mental health and self-acceptance, the conscience must not be ignored! Instead of expecting a psychiatrist to explain away one's pangs of conscience, an individual needs to face his sins and appropriate God's forgiveness. For that reason God has sent the *good news* that "Christ Jesus came into the world to save sinners" (1 Timothy 1:15).

The New Testament is filled with this good news that we can receive forgiveness from God and deliverance from the tyranny of our guilty conscience. But forgiveness begins with personal acknowledgment of sin, for the Bible teaches that "all have sinned and fall short of the glory of God" (Romans 3:23). Having confessed our sin, we need to accept God's judgment upon that sin in his own Son on Calvary's cross and to recognize that "the blood of Jesus, his Son, purifies us from all sin" (1 John 1:7). This verse means that God actually "keeps on cleansing us from our sin."

Having once gained pardon for our sin, we must thank God by faith for that forgiveness. The sense of release from the tyranny of a guilty conscience will motivate us to desire a life more pleasing to God. When, however, we again fall short of the standard of God, we can once more avail ourselves of his forgiveness.

A clear conscience is essential to adequate self-acceptance, but it is a gift of God, *not* a work of man. Perfectionists in particular struggle with a giant conscience, which bullies them unmercifully because they fail to live up to their own standards. They need to learn that if God, who is perfect, can forgive their sins, certainly they, who throughout life "fall short of the glory of God," can forgive themselves.

Praise and thank God for your successes.

It is never healthy to let one's mind linger on negative matters, for such rumination fosters griping and self-pity, which in turn produces depression. Instead, thank God for his blessings. I have found this particularly helpful in marriage counseling when a husband or wife indicates a loss of love for the other spouse. I encourage them to list ten things about their spouse that they value and then thank God verbally each day for these ten attributes and refuse the temptation to think negatively. It is amazing to watch the renewal of love, even in those who have convinced themselves that it is impossible to regain that original romantic response.

Several years ago in a counseling situation, I met a very beautiful but insecure, frigid, and tense wife. It quickly became obvious to me that this woman had nourished the sin of self-rejection even before she married her dynamic, perfectionist husband. Every night when he came home from work, he treated her with cold contempt and disdain because nothing she did pleased him. And like most men, he did not understand a woman's ability to read a man's spirit. Her failure to satisfy him and her painful consciousness of his rejection severely compounded her self-rejection. And the more she rejected herself, the less motivated she became to attempt to please him. Her situation turned into a vicious cycle.

When I counseled with her husband, he was amazed when I explained that he was the key to his wife's condition. I then urged him to select ten positive qualities he found in his wife and thank God for them twice every day, in the morning and on the way home from work. Before long he reported that she became more affectionate and showed signs of self-respect and motivation, all of which signaled improved self-acceptance. Recently I asked him if he had memorized his list by this time. He replied with a smile, "I not only have it memorized, but I'm finding new things in her to be grateful for every day."

Thanksgiving begets thanksgiving. Once you develop a thinking pattern of thanksgiving for the Lord, yourself, loved ones, family, job, and so forth, you will find it easy to be grateful. Unless struck by some rare illness, thankful people cannot become depressed.

Face the future with excited anticipation.

Each of you reading this book has a future, but more important than the details of that future is your attitude toward it. In fact, many authorities stress that your expectations for the future help to create your future.

The Christian has no cause to dread the future. Repeatedly Jesus admonished his disciples for the benefit of all succeeding generations of Christians, "Take heart! I have overcome the world" (John 16:33) and "Go. . . . I am with you always, to the very end of the age" (Matthew 28:19–20). Since Jesus Christ is with us now and will accompany us in the future, we have no adequate reason to dread what it may hold.

Happy is the Christian who develops the habit of greeting each day with an attitude of expectation, eager to appropriate God's blessing and provision. Recently I shared a motel room with a Spirit-filled minister friend who is well known for his spontaneous spirit of rejoicing and praise. Our alarm went off at 6:10 A.M. Though the sun was shrouded by a bleak and wintry cloud layer, my friend shut off the alarm and exclaimed aloud, "Good morning, world! Thank you, Jesus for this new and exciting day!" I couldn't help but conclude that he had captured what the psalmist meant when he said, "This is the day the LORD has made; let us rejoice and be glad in it" (Psalm 118:24). People who approach life daily with this mental attitude rarely face the problem of depression.

Chapter 13

Depression and Your Temperament

The world has not lacked theories of human behavior to explain why we act the way we do. The ancients emphasized inherited traits as the cause for a person's actions. Freud and his followers blamed environment and childhood experiences for a person's behavior. Actually, both contribute to our conduct, but our inherited temperament influences us most. My book, *Spirit-Controlled Temperament,* was the first of five books I have written on human temperament. I am more convinced of its validity today than when I first took up writing thirty years ago. To me, the ancient theory of the four temperaments is the best explanation of human behavior ever devised.

It all begins at conception. People inherit from their parents and grandparents their entire nature, including the color of their hair and eyes, body structure, talents, and, of course, their temperament. That temperament acts as the most powerful single influence on their behavior, for it is the cause of a person's spontaneous actions and reactions. Occasionally some of the students of modern psychology try to accentuate the significance of "learned behavior," but as a parent, I find that suggestion rather puzzling. Our four children were all raised in the same basic home environment and were subjected to the same training principles, but they are as different as night and day! Something dissimilar in their inherited ingredients must have caused that. Our boys' closet was always a case in point. One side was orderly and neat, the other like the aftermath of a tornado. Our girls were equally different. One loved to dress in "grubbies" and to this day prefers casual clothes for everyday wear. The other girl, before she was three years old, showed a strong preference for dress-up styles and coordinated outfits. Those and a host of other differences appeared in their lives long before we had time to teach such things.

When this book was originally written, our first grandchild was nine months old. Before she could crawl, I detected the same traits of strong will and dogged determination I have observed in both her parents. The reason should be obvious! She inherited certain temperament traits that spark her actions and reactions. Now, she is twenty-three, a college graduate and a strong natural leader. Her traits are not taught, they were inherited.

Made up of the traits we inherit at conception, temperament is influenced later by childhood training, education, life experiences, environment, and both human and spiritual motivation.

Psychiatrists today seem more open to the fact that temperament, or as some call it, personality traits, are indeed inherited. Then, when I wrote my early books on temperament, Doctors DePaulo and Ablow, in *How to Cope With Depression,* made it clear they accept this ancient theory. They write,

> Psychiatrists, too, believe personality is stable. It is described in terms of traits—tendencies people demonstrate over and over again to respond to situations in particular ways. Thus, a person who has the characteristic of quickly revealing his or her feelings about situations is considered to be something of an extrovert. A person who is initially quiet and only slowly reveals himself or herself is considered an introvert.
>
> While most people believe that life experiences shape personality, some aspects of personality appear to be inherited. Studies have been done of twins separated after birth and reared apart. The data show that, in spite of different environments, twins still have more personality traits in common than would be expected by chance.

Many traits will be more or less securely rooted in people by the time they reach 30. By then, even with most of life's successes and failures still ahead, an individual responds pretty much as he or she will always respond. People are not textbook examples, however. They vary on a continuous spectrum of personality traits. While there may be living examples of the stereotyped extrovert and introvert, most men and women fall between the extremes.

Ancient physicians believed that a person's temperament was enduring and predetermined. In the opinion of Hippocrates and Galen, two fathers of medicine, personality was decided by the interaction of four bodily fluids—blood, phlegm, yellow bile, and black bile. Depending on which predominated, a person would be either passionate, sluggish, irritable, or depressed, respectively.[1]

Doctors no longer consider bodily fluids the cause of temperament. Today it is known that temperament is in the genes at the time of conception.

THE FOUR BASIC TEMPERAMENTS

Currently, the best explanation of human behavior is the ancient theory of the four temperaments, which was proposed by Hippocrates 2,400 years ago and has been upgraded by many through the years. The writer in Proverbs 30:11–14 saw four distinct kinds of people five hundred years before Hippocrates was born. Hippocrates gave names to these four basic temperaments: the sanguine super-extrovert salesperson, the choleric extrovert—a strong-willed leader, the melancholy introvert perfectionist, and the phlegmatic super-introvert passivist. Although variations have been suggested, this theory is disseminated today in a form very similar to the original. Perhaps the key addition is that no one fits perfectly into *one* of Hippocrates' molds, for people tend to represent a blend of two or more of these temperaments. This seems a reasonable corollary: Since children show physical characteristics of both their mother and father, why not a mixture of their parents' temperaments?

Most people tend to be predominantly one temperament with slight traits of another. It is not uncommon for a person to be eighty percent sanguine and twenty percent phlegmatic or seventy percent choleric and thirty percent melancholic. There is no end of variations and percentages these traits may produce; one man I tested proved to be about sixty percent sanguine, twenty percent melancholic and twenty percent phlegmatic.

TEMPERAMENT AND TRANSFORMED TEMPERAMENTS

The analysis of human temperament is one of the most fascinating subjects I have ever studied. And although it is tempting to launch into a comprehensive discussion of it here, in the interest of space I am forced to resist. Instead, for a full presentation of the subject I suggest you read my books entitled *Spirit-Controlled Temperament; Transformed Temperament; Why You Act the Way You Do; I Love You, But Why Are We So Different?; Understanding the Male Temperament;* and *Your Temperament: Discover Its Potential.* In this book we will touch on the subject of temperament only as it relates to the problem of depression.

The Sanguine and Depression

The sanguine temperament breeds warm, friendly, and outgoing people who draw others to themselves like a magnet. They are good talkers, happy-go-lucky optimists, the "life of the party." Though generous and compassionate, responsive to their surroundings and to the moods or feelings of others, like the other temperaments, they feature some natural weaknesses. They are often weak willed, emotionally unstable and explosive, restless and egotistical. Voted "most likely to succeed" in their youth, they rarely measure up to expectations, due to lack of self-discipline. They have great difficulty following through on details and are almost never quiet. Beneath their bold exterior, they are often insecure and fearful. Sanguines make good salespeople, speakers, actors, and sometimes leaders.

Sanguines are rarely depressed when in the company of others. They are such response-oriented people that the sight of another individual usually lifts their spirits and brings a smile to their faces. Whatever periods of depression they do experience almost invariably commence when they are alone.

The most pleasant characteristic of sanguines is their ability to enjoy the present. They do not look back on unhappy experiences in their past, and they never worry about the future. A delightful sanguine friend of mine affords a classic example. While traveling across the country with me, he commented on the many people who approached me for counseling due to depression. Spontaneously he exclaimed, "You know, I've never had much trouble with depression; I guess it's because God has been so good to me. Actually, I can't remember ever having any real problems or difficulties in my life." His statement really astonished me, for I knew the man well. I was forced to recall that he failed to finish high school until he was almost forty years of age because he ran away from home to join the Merchant Marines. While in the service he married, and after two children were born, one of them died of a rather strange and rare disease. This caused great bitterness on the part of his wife, which plunged her into deep depression. His happy-go-lucky spirit so embittered her that one night he awakened at 3:00 A.M. to see his wife poised over him with a butcher knife at his throat. After several unhappy years, she divorced him and remarried. At the time my friend made his statement, he had been single for six years. Only a sanguine could recollect that type of life and state, "I've never really had any problems in life." But there would be much less depression if all temperaments could think that way.

Many undisciplined sanguines experience depression during the fourth or fifth decade of life. Their lack of discipline and weakness of will has usually made them rather unproductive, much to their own chagrin and disappointment. They are also prone to obesity by this time because of their inability to refuse fattening desserts and other delicacies. This lowers their self-esteem and heightens their tendency toward depression. Although they usually go through the motions of responding happily to other people, their tendency toward mild depression will increase. One writer likened them to Peter Pan—they wish never to grow up. Although they are well liked because of their magnetic and fun personalities, they frequently are undependable and without real substance of character.

As these charming sanguines who often act like overgrown children become aware of their own shallowness, their insecurities are heightened. They become defensive, sensitive to slights or criticism, and almost obsessed with others' opinions of them. It is not uncommon for them to become depressed at this point by engaging in self-pity. They may even blame their parents for indulging them so much in childhood that they never developed self-discipline, but it is very difficult for them to blame themselves, confess their sin, and seek the filling of the Holy Spirit for the strength of character they so desperately need. If they do not face their problem realistically and learn to walk in the Spirit, they will fluctuate up and down between depression and happiness for a time until, in some childlike way, they make the mental adjustment and then go through life fixed in a playful position far beneath their level of potential.

Spirit-filled sanguines are different! The Holy Spirit not only convicts them of their self-pitying thought patterns as sin, but guides them to those areas of productivity that make it easier for them to accept and appreciate themselves. When sanguines are filled with the Spirit, like the apostle Peter in the Book of Acts, they become productive and effective people, untroubled by depression.

The Choleric and Depression

The choleric temperament produces practical activists. They are strong-willed, natural leaders, and very optimistic. Their minds are filled with ideas, projects, or objectives, and cholerics usually see them through. Like the sanguines, cholerics are extroverts, but not nearly so intense. Although very productive in life, they reflect serious natural weaknesses. They are self-sufficient, impetuous, and hot tempered, and they tend to be harsh or cruel. In fact, no one can be as cutting and sarcastic as a choleric. They make good supervisors, generals, builders, crusaders, politicians, or organizers but are not usually able to do precise detail work.

Cholerics rarely become depressed, primarily because their active, goal-conscious minds keep them so motivated that they may pursue several different activities or projects simultaneously. If one of them proves baffling or frustrating, cholerics' disappointment is short-lived and they quickly pursue a fresh challenge. Cholerics are happy when busy, and thus they have little time to be depressed. Their primary frustration in life is that there are not enough hours in the day to engage in their endless supply of goals and objectives.

The rejection or insults that often set other temperaments off into periods of depression rarely faze cholerics. They are so thick-skinned, self-sufficient, and independent by nature that they seldom feel the need for other people. Instead of feeling sorry for themselves when they are alone, they spend the time originating new plans.

They are the most underdeveloped emotionally of all the temperaments. For that reason they usually experience very slight mood changes. Although they quickly become angry, they rarely indulge in self-pity. Instead, they explode all over everyone else. Because they are so insensitive to others' opinions, they are not vulnerable to depression occasioned by other people. If a choleric ever battles depression, it will come as a result of frustration or retreat.

By the time cholerics have reached the fourth or fifth decade of life, their activity-prone brain can often create a mental activity syndrome that makes their thoughts cancel or short-circuit each other much like an overloaded switchboard. This tendency was noted in the chapter on the causes of depression. As Christians, cholerics must learn to rest in the Lord and commit their way to him. An indomitable will and spirit of self-sufficiency often cause them to be useless, unproductive Christians because they insist on doing everything in the flesh instead of in the Spirit. If they do successfully promote Christian activities, their pride makes them spiritually myopic, and they fail to discern their carnal motivation.

The peace of the Holy Spirit that passes all understanding can modulate their thinking pattern, causing them to concentrate on the Lord first and then on the task. They must learn that God's program does not depend on them; rather, they need to depend on God. They must further recognize that fulfilling the work of God is not enough; they must do it in the power of the Spirit. As the Bible says, "Not by might nor by power, but by my Spirit, says the LORD Almighty" (Zechariah 4:6). The apostle Paul, possibly the best illustration of a

Spirit-filled choleric used of God, had learned this well, for he said, "when I am weak, then am I strong" (2 Corinthians 12:10).

Flesh-filled choleric Christians can become depressed until they realize this principle, because they get frustrated by the lack of spiritual results from their hard-driving, fleshly efforts. Instead of blaming themselves for their carnal, self-willed spirit, they may swell up in self-pity and withdraw from church activities. This carnal spirit is often easily discerned by others in the congregation, and thus cholerics may be bypassed when officers are elected. "I don't understand," they complain. "Isn't my hard work sufficient proof of my devotion to Christ?" Happy is the choleric who learns with James to say, "If it is the Lord's will, we will live and do this or that" (James 4:15). If they seek the priorities of the will of God through the leading of the Holy Spirit in their lives, cholerics will not only be more productive but also more composed. Once they comprehend that walking in the Spirit is the secret to spiritual productivity, they will gain consistency in their Christian life.

Another period of life during which cholerics are vulnerable to depression is retirement. Though they usually do not retire until age seventy or later, they must program into their thinking some added form of productivity or they may give way to depression.

A former business executive was forced to retire at sixty-five. Within six months he went, in a state of depression, to see his pastor. It did not take the minister long to perceive that the unproductive inactivity of retirement was the culprit of this man's depression. In addition, of course, the executive was indulging in the sin of self-pity and mentally lamenting, "My life is over; the period of my productivity is past; I am no longer good for anything." The pastor was leading a very dynamic church much in need of a businessperson to coordinate and direct the business affairs. He challenged this man to be a $1.00 a year Christian worker. Today that church rates among the most efficient in the nation, and the energetic choleric business manager is thoroughly enjoying his "retirement."

The ability of the Holy Spirit to literally transform a choleric tendency toward depression is illustrated superbly in the life of the apostle Paul. If ever a man was an illustration of choleric temperament, it was Saul of Tarsus before he became a Christian. After his conversion, his indomitable choleric will directed by the Holy Spirit surged forward throughout the book of Acts. His response to confinement offers a classic illustration of depressing circumstances overcome through the invasion of the spiritual nature by the Holy Spirit. Confined to the cold, clammy Mamertine Prison in Rome for preaching the Gospel, he manifested not one sign of self-pity. Instead, this dynamic Christian took advantage of the opportunity to share his faith personally with every new Roman soldier assigned to guard him. So many of these men were converted that he addressed the church of Rome, "All the saints send you greetings, especially those who belong to Caesar's household" (Philippians 4:22). In addition, from this prison he penned the prison letters, including the letter of joy called Philippians, in which he stated, "I have learned the secret of being content in any and every situation" (Philippians 4:11). Spirit-filled cholerics will never become depressed.

The Melancholy and Depression

The richest of all temperaments is the melancholy. Rich not only in gifts and aesthetic appreciation, a melancholy has the capacity to experience the entire spectrum of emotional mood fluctuations. In addition, he or she is rich in emotional weaknesses, particularly in the tendency to be depressed. Some of the world's greatest geniuses have been gifted melancholies who squandered their talent in the slough of despondency, becoming apathetic and unproductive. This is so evident that the ancients frequently used the words *melancholy* and *depression* interchangeably.

Melancholics are usually the most talented of all temperaments. Natural perfectionists, very sensitive and appreciative of the fine arts, they are analytical and self-sacrificing. As a rule they are not outgoing by nature and rarely push themselves forward, but they make very faithful friends. However, they tend to be moody, critical, pessimistic, and self-centered. Many of the world's great artists, composers, philosophers, inventors, and theoreticians have been melancholies.

Dr. Ed Diener, a University of Illinois psychologist, has spent much of his life researching what makes people happy. Interestingly enough, he discovered that more people in the U.S. were "content" than any other country in the world. Many factors enter into that result, of course, but then he added that even contentment "can be overridden by temperament." That should not be surprising. Temperament is probably the most powerful factor in any person's makeup. As we have seen, it influences all our spontaneous actions and reactions. Temperament alone could account for why few sanguines or phlegmatics become depressed for any length of time. It could also explain why melancholies and cholerics have a greater problem with depression than other temperament types. It has been my observation that the severely depressed usually have a high percentage of melancholy temperament, and what is not melancholy is usually choleric. That, of course, is not a new revelation. Hippocrates, the father of modern medicine, is credited with naming the four temperaments and used the word *melancholy* to describe the temperament most prone to *melancholia,* as they called it 2400 years ago. We are prone to call it *depression.*

Mental Attitude Is Everything

Although everyone is vulnerable to his or her own mental thinking pattern, none is more responsive than the melancholy. Among other creative gifts, melancholies harbor the great ability to suggest images to the screen of their imaginations—probably in living color with surround sound. Because melancholies are moody by nature, they may regard their moods as spontaneous, but it has been learned that most moods result directly from thinking patterns. If melancholies guard their thought processes and refuse to indulge in the mental sins of anger, resentment, self-persecution, and self-pity, they will not yield to their predisposition toward depression.

The powerful influence of the mind on our moods can easily be illustrated by an experience I had with my sons when they were younger. One Sunday night as they were going to bed, we reminded them, as millions of children are faithfully reminded by loving parents, "Don't forget—tomorrow you have to get up early and go to school." In unison they sang, "Do we *have* to go to school tomorrow?" Assuring them that this was a necessary part of their lives and accepting their grumbling with customary parental longsuffering, I sent them off to sleep. Needless to say, Monday morning they woke up in a sour mood. I sincerely hated to foist them off on their schoolteacher that day.

The next week, the same boys were lying in the same bed at night. As I tucked them in I admonished, "Don't forget, you've got to get up early tomorrow because we're heading for Disneyland!" You can imagine the happy chorus that greeted my announcement. The next morning both boys bolted out of bed, excited and expectant, as they anticipated the thrilling trip ahead. As I sat at the breakfast table that morning, I contemplated the difference in moods within just one week. Their metabolism seemed to function better, their eyes were clearer, their faces shinier, the whole world looked better *because they reflected an improved mental attitude*. The melancholy who recognizes the power of the subconscious mind to influence moods will seek the power of the Holy Spirit to orient his or her thinking patterns positively.

It is hard to select one period in life that melancholies find more depressing than another. Usually their depressions become apparent in early childhood; unless melancholies are spiritually motivated by the power of God, these depressions tend to follow them all their lives. Because they are supersensitive and self-centered, they read things into every activity, at times becoming almost obsessed with the idea that people don't like them or that they are laughing at them.

One day, the business manager of Christian Heritage College, my wife (who was the registrar), and I were having lunch together in a restaurant. Suddenly a melancholy, gaunt-faced young man appeared at our table and asked, "Pardon me, but may I ask you folks if you were laughing at me?" Naturally we were shocked into silence. Finally I explained, "Young man, I don't think we've ever seen you before." With that he excused himself and walked away. Reflecting on the incident, we concluded that during our laughter and conversation we must have looked in his direction, which gave that troubled young man the impression that we were laughing at his expense. Equally as substantial are many of the depression-causing events in the life of the average melancholy.

Melancholy Perfectionists

Melancholies often are easily depressed because they are perfectionists. Most people could profit by having more perfectionist tendencies, but true perfectionists are made miserable by them. In the first place, they measure themselves by their own arbitrary standards of perfection and get discouraged with themselves when they fall short of those standards. The fact that their standards are usually so high that neither they nor anyone else could live by them rarely occurs to them. Instead, they insist that their criteria for perfection is "realistic."

In addition to being perfectionistic, melancholies are also very conscientious and pride themselves on being "dependable" and "accurate." Naturally, all of their friends fall short of this standard, so it is not uncommon for melancholies to become depressed about themselves and their associates. Very rigid and inflexible, melancholies find it difficult to tolerate the slightest deviation from what they consider to be the "measure of excellence."

Such perfection-prone melancholies can love their children dearly while at the same time be depressed by them. Children are notoriously disorganized and unpredictable; they follow their own schedule and insist on acting like children. A rigid melancholy parent finds it difficult to cope with such unpredictability and, consequently, may experience depression, often over parenting skills. Sometimes a melancholy mother may become ambivalent toward her own children, loving them intensely, while at the same time being filled with anger and bitterness toward them. The carefree, happy-go-lucky little tike who insists on trekking across the clean kitchen with his wet boots can be a source of irritation to any mother, particularly to a melancholy. Before she was married, she probably could not retire for the night until her shoes were lined up and the bathroom was in perfect order. Children automatically change that, but perfectionists find it difficult to cope with such change; consequently, depression is their outlet. They become angry at the lack of perfection in others and indulge in self-pity because they are the only ones striving for lofty goals. Such thought patterns invariably produce depression.

In fairness to melancholy people, they are as critical of themselves as they are of others. Consequently, they tend to develop an inadequate view of themselves. From early childhood they construct a disparaging self-image on the screen of their imagination. As they get older, unlike some of the other temperaments who learn to accept themselves, melancholies tend to reject themselves even more. Consequently their periods of depression increase. If they were permitted to verbalize their criticisms in childhood, they are apt to be verbally critical in adulthood. Each time they indulge in oral criticism, they only imbed the spirit of criticism more deeply in their mind, and critics are never happy people!

One day I had an opportunity to see this principle in action. As I submitted to an airport examination before boarding a plane, the security officer began to criticize the individuals who flew on that airline as "slovenly, inconsiderate, disorganized, and ungrateful people." I took it just about as long as I could, but finally, looking at him with a big smile (I find you can say almost anything if you smile) I observed, "You must be an unhappy man!" He looked at me rather startled and replied, "Why do you say that?" "Because you're so critical. I've never met a happy person who is a critical person." After inspecting my baggage, he said, "Thank you, sir, I needed that." To my amazement he turned to the next customer and said, "Hello, how are you? So glad to have you on our airline." I don't know how long he will profit by that experience, but I am certain that he has the capability of making himself happy or miserable in direct proportion to the way in which he thinks and talks to people.

Not only are melancholy people rigid perfectionists and conscientious individuals, but they possess a low threshold of anxiety and tension. The American way of life is not conducive to happiness for such people. We live in an overly active, choleric society, as Dr. Paul Tournier verifies in a chapter on temperament in his book entitled *The Healing of Persons*. It seems that Western civilization, where the Gospel of Christ has had its most profound influence, reflects a highly choleric population. This would be characteristic of the Teutonic or Nordic race, whose people tend to represent a high percentage of choleric temperament. Such individuals settled in Scandinavia, Germany, parts of France, Ireland, and England, the very countries producing most of the American settlers. Although it would be difficult to prove, it would seem that the most courageous, hearty, and choleric members of Europe came over to settle this country. Consequently, their progeny would include a high level of choleric, very active citizens, which may account for our industrialized, fast-moving, high-pressure environment. Such an atmosphere is not the best for a melancholy, for he is not interested in achieving massive production, but perfection and quality. It is not uncommon to hear a melancholy professional person complain, "We just don't have time to be accurate anymore."

This may explain why so many of the youth culture today "drop out" of the mainstream of society. Rejecting its mad pace and witnessing its lack of perfection through the eyes of idealism, they seek a more passive culture. This may also be one reason some of them speak favorably about a governmental system that has totally enslaved people into passivity in contrast to the free enterprise system, which they think has enslaved people to activity.

I have repeatedly observed that many of the young people who have "copped out" of our society are very sensitive, gifted, idealistic young people indulging in escape rather than making an honest attempt to alter society. Dr. Tournier notes that some of the Indian or Oriental cultures place a higher priority on the mystic or passive individual. And it may be why some of them are vulnerable to the New Age cults or ecosystem teachings of mother earth or the worship of mother Gaia. By contrast, in the Western world, the dynamic, productive choleric seems to be the hero. Whatever its cause, the frantic pace we live in today contributes heavily to the melancholy's tendency toward depression.

Self-Sacrificial and Persecution-Prone

Two characteristics of melancholies that short-circuit each other are their natural desire to be self-sacrificing and their self-persecution tendency. Unless they are careful, this conflict will likely make martyrs out of them. Ordinarily they choose the most difficult and trying location to ply their vocations. When others seem to be more successful or gain more renown, instead of facing realistically the fact that they have chosen the path of self-sacrifice, they indulge in self-pity because their journey winds uphill and leads through arduous circumstances.

The determination of melancholies to gripe and criticize merely compounds their negative thinking and ultimately brings them to despair. For that reason 1 Thessalonians 5:18 can come to their rescue! If they painstakingly and consistently follow its formula, they will rarely become depressed. *"Give thanks in all circumstances,* for this is God's will for you in Christ Jesus" (italics added).

Melancholy Creativity

Fortunately for melancholies, they possess an unusual creative ability to project all kinds of images on the screen of their imaginations. Once they fully realize that their feelings are the direct result of constructing wholesome mental images of themselves and their circumstances, they are well on the road to recovery and prevention of future bouts of depression. Melancholy people risk depression primarily because of the continual misuse of their creative imagination. That is, on the imagination screen of their mind they project negativism, self-pity, criticism, complaining, helplessness, and despair. Once they realize that their creative suggestions starting with thanksgiving can either work for or against them, they can carefully project only those images that are pleasing to God. Such thoughts will lift their spirits, stabilize their moods, and help them to avoid depression.

The Phlegmatic and Depression

The easygoing, never-get-upset "nice guy" is the phlegmatic. In addition to featuring a calm and likable disposition, phlegmatics are cheerful folks who work well with other people. They are efficient, conservative, dependable, and witty with a practical turn of mind. Since they are quite introverted, as a rule, their weaknesses, like their strengths, are not as readily perceptible as those of other temperaments. Their most obvious weakness is lack of motivation. They can ignore work graciously and are prone to be stubborn, stingy, and indecisive. Their ability to look at life through the eyes of a spectator may generate a tendency to avoid "getting involved" with anything. Phlegmatics make good diplomats since they are natural peacemakers. Many are teachers, doctors, scientists, comedians, and magazine and book editors. When externally motivated, they make very capable leaders.

As a general rule, phlegmatic people are not easily depressed. Their unique sense of humor signals a happy outlook on life, and rarely do they reflect much mood fluctuation. It is possible to know a phlegmatic all his life and never see him truly angry, for no matter what the occasion, he tends to mentally excuse the person who has offended, injured, or rejected him. His ability to adjust to unpleasant circumstances is unbelievable to the other three temperaments, which find it easy to gripe or criticize mentally and verbally.

If phlegmatics ever do experience depression, it is usually aimed at their own lack of aggressiveness. Many times their practical, capable mind devises a suitable plan of action for a given set of circumstances, but because of their passive inclination or their fear of being criticized by others, they keep it to themselves. Consequently, driven by family or other group pressure, they may find themselves pursuing a plan inferior to their own. This can produce irritation which, when followed by self-pity, will make phlegmatics depressed. Fortunately, their depression is short-lived most of the time, for in a brief time one of those amazingly interesting characters called a human being comes along to amuse and entertain him.

At one critical period in life phlegmatics are most vulnerable to depression. During the fifth or sixth decade, they often become aware that the other temperaments have passed them by vocationally, spiritually, and in every other way. While they were passively watching the game of life as a spectator, their more aggressive friends were stepping through the doors of opportunity. Their security-mindedness has kept them from daring adventures in life, and thus their existence may seem rather stale during this period. If they indulge in self-pity, they will definitely become depressed.

Instead of blaming their fear or indolence, the phlegmatic finds it much easier to reproach "society" or "the breaks" or "my luck." Such a person should learn from the Lord Jesus early in life to attempt great things for God, for Christ said, "According to your faith will it be done to you" (Matthew 9:29).

Marital Frustration—Phlegmatic Depression

Phlegmatics usually make good marriage partners. They are relatively easy to live with, and even though they are quite selfish, they usually give in during controversy because they "just don't like turmoil." But capitulating against one's will can lead to bitterness and often results in self-pity followed by depression. The only lasting remedy for a phlegmatic (or any temperament) is to walk in the Spirit and learn to submit "to one another out of reverence for Christ" (Ephesians 5:21). Phlegmatics must learn to surrender their rights to God and their partner and genuinely seek their partner's happiness. When people enter marriage for what they can "get out of it," they will always be disappointed. However, when they determine to insure their partner's happiness, their own is guaranteed. Paul said, "A man reaps what he sows." I have yet to find a miserable, unhappy partner who genuinely set out to bring joy into the life of his or her spouse.

Surrender in marriage, when discharged in the right spirit, has an amazing effect on a partner, improving objectivity, removing competition, and inspiring the desire to reciprocate kindness. Many times it has the effect of "heaping coals of fire" (see Romans 12:20) on a spouse's head, for after getting his own way in a given situation, the spouse may be so overcome by guilt that he will be less aggressive or demanding the next time. But the crucial question is: Does the one surrendering do so joyfully or in self-pity? The answer determines whether or not the surrender is followed by depression.

A phlegmatic person must be unusually vigilant at this point, for he or she too frequently avoids conflict by giving in—while at the same time resenting it mentally. Self-pitying thoughts generally follow in the wake of resentment, and the consequent depression will subvert joy, even for the most phlegmatic.

Opposites Attract Each Other

Family Life Seminar audiences laugh uproariously at some of my illustrations of opposites attracting each other in marriage. Their merriment is cut short, however, when they discover the grim truth that one's weaknesses inevitably collide with a partner's strengths in the test tube of marriage. Unless couples learn to work toward adjusting to their partner's traits and habits, they are headed for conflict.

The captivating strengths that you found so alluring in your fiancé before marriage may be effaced by the disagreeable appearance of corresponding weaknesses afterward. Somehow that problem was not anticipated. You may have sensed that your partner's strengths corresponded to your weaknesses, which was what attracted you in the first place, but satisfaction gives place to alarm when you discover that your partner's weaknesses relate to an area of your strength. Ah, there's the rub! It is so easy to look contemptuously and disdainfully upon another person's weakness when it falls in an area of your strength!

When Opposites Detract

Although it is usually dangerous to generalize about people, I have repeatedly observed that like temperaments do not marry. Of the 328 couples whose marital knots I have tied, to my knowledge, none were temperament twins. This is particularly true of phlegmatics, who generally marry cholerics. But such a union can produce its own unique predisposition to depression.

If the choleric is the wife, the phlegmatic husband may face depression because he "can't stand that woman always pressuring" him! What seemed before marriage to be the woman's "dynamic leadership and practicality" becomes bossy, domineering autocracy after marriage. By contrast, the choleric wife discovers that the "kind, gentle, patient" boyfriend melts into a "weak, unmotivated, unchallenging, humdrum" husband. The harassed phlegmatic husband will rarely stand up for his convictions against his more forceful mate, and he then experiences depression because of his failure to "assert his manhood" and also because of his self-pitying thought patterns. Just recently a phlegmatic husband called to get a handle on "how to survive a marriage" to a choleric wife who is bossy, manipulative, and always demands her way.

The offended and often criticized phlegmatic wife of a choleric often indulges in self-pity because she can do nothing to please her husband. She is "too slow, too unmotivated, and too unchallenging." His vented wrath strips her of any positive self-image she brought into the marriage, and by the time his sarcastic outbursts have left her battered and bowed a few times, she adds "depression" to her list of undesirable characteristics.

In his book, *The Pursuit of Happiness,* psychologist David Myers stated that "the least happy people are those who have unhappy marriages. Happiest are those who married 'their best friend.'" Then he adds, "If you can say that [you are married to your best friend], chances are you'll describe not just your marriage but your whole life as happy."[2] I could not agree more! For if your marriage is unhappy, your whole life is miserable.

A happy marriage does not just happen—it takes commitment, faith, love, and personal sacrifice. Few couples start their marriage as best friends; that usually takes several years to develop. I have found that becoming "best friends" is so important in marriage that I dedicated an entire chapter to that subject in my book, *I Love You, But Why Are We So Different?,* showing that totally opposite temperaments can become best friends. For many, their opposite temperaments cause conflict that produces unhappiness and depression. When two depressed people live together, they have the ultimate formula for human misery. I am happy to say there is much hope for such people if they will let God have his way in their lives and learn his principles on how to treat each other.

THE REMEDY FOR TEMPERAMENT WEAKNESS

God has a thrilling plan for overcoming all temperament weaknesses—even depression. In Ephesians 5:18 he designates being continually "filled with the Spirit" as his remedy. As I will point out in a future chapter, the filling of the Holy Spirit produces three great emotional characteristics:

1. A song in your heart (Eph. 5:19)
2. A thankful mental attitude (Eph. 5: 20)
3. A submissive spirit (Eph. 5:21)

It is impossible to be depressed when you realize all three of these emotions. The filling of the Spirit, then, is the obvious remedy for emotional depression.

IS ALL DEPRESSION CAUSED BY SELF-PITY?

Almost every time I speak on depression, someone with a sad look on his face asks, "Aren't there any exceptions? Surely some depression must be caused organically." We have been so conditioned to blaming our behavior on other people or our physical condition that we hesitate to take responsibility for our actions.

As I have already indicated, doctors suggest that somewhere between fifteen and twenty-five percent of cases of depression are responsive to medication. Therefore they conclude that those cases were organic or physically induced. What they don't say is how many of those physical malfunctions were brought on by self-pity, or how many depressions that originally began due to an improperly functioning thyroid gland or other physical problem were made much worse by self-pity or negative thoughts. No one knows. I have a hunch the answer is many. Most depressed people want to blame their glands, body chemistry, and a host of other causes for depression, but those that get well the fastest direct attention to their thought processes or mental attitudes—not just their glands. The following diagram will illustrate the point.

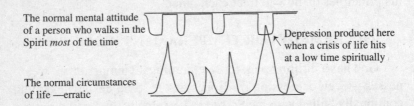

The normal mental attitude of a person who walks in the Spirit *most* of the time

Depression produced here when a crisis of life hits at a low time spiritually

The normal circumstances of life —erratic

The previous diagram clarifies the importance of maintaining good mental attitudes at all times. We cannot control the circumstances of life, but by the power of the Holy Spirit we can govern our mental attitude. In this diagram the individual indulged in a poor mental attitude three times because of spiritual neglect, sickness, a monthly period or mood cycle, hormone change, sin, or other reasons. During the first two mental-attitude sin periods nothing happened to trigger self-pity, but notice the third. On that occasion, one of those unpredictable circumstances for which life is famous collided with the improper thinking pattern. The predictable result was depression.

When a Christian walks in the Spirit, he or she will maintain the proper mental attitude that enables a response of praise and thanksgiving toward the negative circumstances of life. Remember, God has promised not to permit negative circumstances above our ability to cope with them. He is, of course, presupposing that we maintain the proper mental attitude.

WHAT IS THE RIGHT MENTAL ATTITUDE?

Several components make up the right mental attitude. Consider them carefully to see if you possess them.

(1) Complete commitment to the will and way of God (Romans 6:11–13; 12:1–2).

(2) Knowledge of the principles of God (Romans 12:2). No one will ever know all of the principles of God for living, but you can daily refresh your mind with them by reading and studying the Word of God.

(3) Faith (Romans 14:23; Hebrews 11:6). It is impossible to enlist the dynamic dimensions of God into your life without faith. If your faith is weak, don't wait for some miracle to make it strong. The following steps will strengthen your faith.

    a. Hear, read, and study the Bible (Romans 10:17).

    b. Pray for increased faith (1 Corinthians 12:31).

    c. Walk in the Spirit (Galations 5:22, 23).

    d. Experience faith (Romans 1:17).

Each time you trust God for something, it is easier to trust him the next time.

Chapter 14

Grief Is Not the Same as Depression

When my dear friend Frank Glena died at age seventy-nine after a nine-month illness, as I have already mentioned, his wife died of grief just three days later. She had lost all desire to live, and the emotional strain on her aged body was more than she could handle. She refused to eat or see her doctor and discontinued her usual medication. Her death was, in a real sense, a form of suicide made possible by her own poor health and a refusal to avail herself of the promises of God. She truly wanted to die. She is an example of how the early stages of grief have many of the same characteristics as depression—but they are not always synonymous.

Most people going through severe grief do not die. They may want to for a time, but few grief-ridden souls actually commit suicide. They may indeed experience many of the symptoms of depression, such as loss of appetite, hopelessness, slowing of most bodily functions, and even a desire to avoid people. But eventually, if they change their thinking pattern, they do recover, and many go on and live long and productive lives.

Few things in life are as devastating as the loss of a cherished mate. In the stress rating scale of Doctors Thomas Holmes and Richard H. Rahe, already referred to in chapter 9, these doctors found the most devastating emotional experience a person can have on this earth is the sudden unexpected loss of a mate. For that reason they ascribed 100 points to such a loss. What I find instructive is that the next most emotionally traumatic event in life was a divorce, to which they ascribed 73 points. The next was a "marital separation," which they scored 65. No wonder a *Newsweek* article on happiness cited the results of a survey where they found that the "happiest people are those who are married to their best friend." Conversely, "the least happy people were those with an unhappy marriage."[1] This simply points out that the most important thing in a married person's life is to have a good marriage. No wonder there is an enormous amount of grief that follows the sudden cutoff of that relationship through death or divorce. If a person still has his or her mate, even the loss of a child is not nearly so devastating because they still have someone with whom they can share their life and loss.

The principal differences between depression and grief are time and hope. Eventually, grief passes. Just as a broken leg takes two to six months to heal, broken emotions need time to heal themselves. Eventually the grieving mate, after experiencing feelings and thoughts of utter despair, begins to think of other people, obligations, duties, and future events. Life does go on, even though the one with whom they have shared much of their life is no longer with them. And most people do begin to heal and start making plans for the future.

CHRISTIANS HANDLE GRIEF DIFFERENTLY

Grief is normal. To suggest otherwise will only add unnecessary guilt to a sorrowing person's very real grief. The idea that Christians never experience grief is not only ridiculous and harmful, it is unscriptural. Some of the great saints of the Bible experienced grief. The classic illustration is Job, one of the greatest men of God who ever lived. Job let his understandable grief at the loss of his family turn into depression by self-indulgence and pity. But God forgave him, and he went on to live a long and fruitful life. I don't pretend that I would not experience great grief and sorrow if God in his wisdom saw fit to suddenly take my wife and best friend of over forty years from me. I experienced enormous grief when I was ten years old; my father suddenly died of a heart attack. It took many weeks for me to regain my normal emotions. For two years I was never far from tears.

But I never shall forget the Christian hope the pastor administered into our grieving hearts at my father's graveside service. Based on my father's faith in and acceptance of Christ some eight years before, the man of God read the Christian's hope passage that shows that we can be confident of seeing our loved ones again after death. This immortal passage of Scripture gave enormous comfort to my grieving heart.

> Brothers, we do not want you to be ignorant about those who fall asleep, or to grieve like the rest of men, who have no hope. We believe that Jesus died and rose again and so we believe that God will bring with Jesus those who have fallen asleep in him. According to the Lord's own word, we tell you that we who are still alive, who are left till the coming of the Lord, will certainly not precede those who have fallen asleep. For the Lord himself will come down from heaven, with a loud command, with the voice of the archangel and with the trumpet call of God, and the dead in Christ will rise first. After that, we who are still alive and are left will be caught up together with them in the clouds to meet the Lord in the air. And so we will be with the Lord forever. Therefore encourage each other with these words. (1 Thessalonians 4:13–18)

DON'T GRIEVE AS DO THE HOPELESS

Notice in verse 13 that it is all right for Christians to grieve. But we should not grieve "as others who have no hope," for our loss of a loved one is only temporary. The Bible teaches that because he lives, we too shall live (see John 14:19). By contrast, the unsaved have no such hope. Those who do not put their faith in Christ during this life die without hope, meaning the confident expectation that they will ever see their loved ones again. I have seen well-meaning people play games with themselves and others at the time of death. They suggest in essence that "because he lived a good life we are sure we shall meet him again in heaven someday." That is definitely not what the Bible teaches. Verse 14 makes it clear that if "we believe that Jesus died and rose again" we will see our loved ones again. That is not the wild expectation (or hope) of man, it is what the apostle Paul called "the Lord's own word" (v. 15).

I cannot tell you the hope that promise brought into my boyish heart after my father's death. I did indeed miss my father desperately, but it was a great boost to the healing process to know that one day Jesus Christ would return to this earth, my father would arise, and we would see him again.

Those who die without faith of course have no such assurance, consequently they grieve "as the hopeless." *Hope* in the Bible is not the kind of hope we are familiar with today, that is, "I hope you will come to see me." Biblical hope is the confident expectation of a future event based on the word of God himself. Christians don't just *wish* they will see their loved ones again. We have a confident expectation that is as certain as the promises of God that we and our dead loved ones will live again. Actually, that is what the Gospel and the coming of Christ into this world is all about.

No wonder the apostle concluded this marvelous passage with the words, "Therefore, *encourage* each other with these words" (v. 18, italics added). This whole teaching was not only to instruct his readers about their relation to the future life and those who had died already, but to produce *hope* or *confidence* in the wonderful future God has prepared for those who put their faith in him.

I saw that in action when I conducted the funeral of a deacon in my congregation. After thirty-nine heart attacks my friend Charles succumbed at the age of fifty-eight. He and his devoted wife Olivia were dedicated Christians and well aware that he could go to be with the Lord at any time. Her sister, Esther, who was not a Christian, traveled across the country for the funeral. After explaining from the previously mentioned Scripture where Charles was now and that we would see him again when Jesus returned for his church, we concluded the service with a song on the Resurrection. Afterwards, as the two ladies were walking to the funeral car, Esther began to weep uncontrollably and the wife, Olivia, put her arm around her and said, "Esther, don't take on so, I will see Charles again!" But Esther wept all the harder, for she had no such assurance.

Now that is Christian hope in action. It comforts the broken-hearted believer in the midst of loss. We also have other promises: "Never will I leave you; never will I forsake you" (Hebrews 13:5) and "My God will meet all your needs according to his glorious riches in Christ Jesus" (Philippians 4:19). Does God know our needs? Most assuredly!

Christians may sorrow when they lose a loved one or experience some other calamity in life, but their sorrow cannot compare to that of the unsaved who have no hope in this life or the one to come.

HOW ABOUT YOU?

Nothing brings us human beings to the point of considering eternity better than a discussion of the inevitable experience of life—death. That is why I must ask you which of the two women mentioned previously would you be most like in the moment of the death of a loved one? The woman of faith or the woman of unbelief? If you don't know, it is probably the woman of unbelief. May I suggest that you pray that prayer I mentioned in chapter 6 when offering God's cure for depression? Call on the name of the Lord, so that you can experience eternal life and that same assurance that Olivia and Charles and all Christians possess. "If you confess with your mouth, 'Jesus is Lord,' and believe in your heart that God raised him from the dead, you will be saved." Now all you must do is act upon that faith and call on the name of the Lord to be saved. I would suggest that if you are unsaved or if you are not sure that you have received Jesus Christ, that you pray a sincere prayer something like this:

Dear Lord, I am a sinner. I believe that you died for my sins, and I want to invite you into my heart so that I may have my sins forgiven and receive eternal life. I surrender my life to you for whatever you want me to do. In Jesus' name I pray, Amen.

Now it is important for you to read and study the Bible. I suggest that you read the little epistle of 1 John every day for thirty days to gain the assurance of your salvation. Then read the gospel of John several times until you know both of these passages very well. After that, allow fifteen to thirty minutes a day to read from the New Testament until you have read it several times.

It is also important for you to find a Bible-teaching church where you can experience good Christian fellowship and where you can grow in your spiritual life.

GRIEF OVERCOME BY A CHANGE OF MIND

I wish that I could say all Christians triumph over grief. The fact is, I have counseled many Christians whose grief has led to serious depression. Not because they did not have the assurance they would see their loved one again or because the Holy Spirit was not in their life to comfort them as he promised. Their grief was protracted long after the normal grieving process because they rebelled at God and continually asked him, "Why have you taken my spouse?"

Questioning the God who has promised that "in all things God works together for the good of those who love him" will always lead to depression. I will be the first to admit that God sometimes does things we do not understand or like. But questioning him leads to self-pity, and we already know that self-pity produces depression.

Somewhere in the grieving process the child of God has to commit that lost child or mate or problem to our loving heavenly Father and begin to thank him, not for the problem, but for who God is and what he can do for us in the midst of our problem (see 1 Thessalonians 5:18).

Grieving Christians should read the little book of Philippians through each day during their grieving process and remind themselves that the apostle Paul was in prison for preaching the Gospel when he wrote that book. We can give thanks, by faith, if we want to. If we do, the grief will begin to lift. If we don't, it will continue and eventually will drift into depression.

The choice is yours!

My mentor in the field of counseling was Dr. Henry Brandt, the Christian psychologist and counselor who for many years taught biblical principles for use in helping people in trouble. During his long life he has walked through "the valley of the shadow of death" with two of his three wives. His first wife died after twenty-three years of marriage. His second wife died of a heart attack after only five years of marriage. Both times I called to comfort him, only to be comforted and challenged by him. For he said, "Now I have an opportunity to prove that the principles I have been preaching through the years really work when tested on the anvil of life—even my own." In both experiences he had found "God's grace is sufficient" (see 2 Corinthians 12:9).

And so will you if you commit your loss and heartache to him and thank him that you will see your loved one again. Such a change of mind will not bring your loved one back, but it will begin to lift your grief, guaranteeing you will not drift into depression.

Chapter 15

Depression and the Occult

My wife is not predisposed to depression by nature, but maintains a very radiant and vibrant personality. One night furnished a distinct exception! On arriving home from work, I found her lethargic, rather somber, and somewhat depressed. The evening meal was not started, nothing seemed to interest her, and I noticed that she sighed heavily. After watching her for a few minutes, I commented, "You're not yourself tonight, dear. What's the matter?"

She looked at me and replied, "I don't know. For some reason I just feel depressed."

"What have you been doing this afternoon?"

"Since bringing the children home at 3:30," she answered, "I've been reading, and gradually this feeling of depression came over me." She handed me a copy of one of the current best-sellers regarding the occult, Satanism, and demon possession.

At that point I realized that this book on depression should contain a brief chapter on the emotional effects of reading about the occult. The book she had been pursuing was written by a Christian in a sincere attempt to help other people avoid involvement with the occult. Browsing through the book, I noted that the author gave his own personal experience and many of the intimate details concerning the occult movement and Satan's kingdom of darkness. Frankly, Christians need to know very little about the occult other than that it is sinful, detrimental, harmful, and something to keep at arm's length.

THE OCCULT FAD

Ever since his first rebellion against God, Satan has repeatedly attempted to destroy humankind. Primitive cultures have always inclined toward black magic, witchcraft, and other forms of the occult, and these practices have invariably had a detrimental effect on the people. Missionaries tell in gruesome detail how association with evil spirits or sophisticated methods of communication with demons produces depression and other forms of human misery. Questions asked at my Family Life Seminars frequently relate to demonism and the occult. I have seen enough to convince me that all depression is not the result of demon possession or oppression, but all contact with demons or evil spirits produces oppression, which is depressing. An individual may consult mystics, Ouija boards, knocking tables, tea-leaf readers, or palmists in any major city, but almost invariably within a few hours or possibly days he will be engulfed by a spirit of depression.

A harmful side effect in today's occult fad finds people tending to blame exorcism or demonism for their behavior. An angry individual would much rather take the irresponsible course by saying, "The devil made me do it!" than admit he is a hostile person. At times depression leads people to dabble in demonism. Their self-induced misery through protracted periods of self-pity causes them to grope for an easy release of spirit rather than an honest confrontation with the thinking pattern that has brought them down to this slough of despondency. Some resort to drugs or liquor, but mediums, mystics, and necromancers are also readily available as quick solutions. We are familiar with seriously depressed persons, grieving over the loss of a loved one, who have resorted to mediums to once again hear the voice of the departed. But invariably the latter end is worse than the first. Such panaceas may give short-term relief, but they compound the problem of depression.

A *Campus Life* magazine article quoted Roberta Blankenship, an eighteen-year-old college freshman, who described her experiences as a witch. When asked what common denominator she noticed in those who took up witchcraft, she replied, "First, they all share a deep dissatisfaction with life the way it is—many of these are rather emotional people—and there's always something important missing at home."[1] Referring to her own emotional state while being a witch, she admitted, "My depression was almost unbearable."[2] Evidently her periods of depression increased until even witchcraft gave her no satisfaction. "My messed-up world wasn't changing. My home was still full of hate; I had no close friends. In fact, I attempted suicide."[3]

If the truth were known, many modern suicides could probably be attributed to satanically induced depression. An individual who is prone to depression mistakenly thinks witchcraft or the occult offers relief. He soons finds that his depression is amplified. Then in complete frustration he sees no hope and erroneously concludes that suicide is the only way out.

Hal Lindsey in his best-selling book, *Satan Is Alive and Well on Planet Earth,* states,

> After Satan had used Judas for his purpose, he then used the power of guilt to drive Judas to self-destruction (Matt. 27:5–10). The demon-possessed boy in Matthew 17:14–15 had a strong tendency toward self-destruction. He threw himself into fire and then into water. This was the result of the demon attempting to inflict harm or self-destruction upon the child.[4]

DELIVERANCE FROM DEMON-INSPIRED DEPRESSION

We can be assured of deliverance from Satan! But that deliverance always occurs on God's terms, not man's or Satan's. If you have entertained the occult, demonism, or any other form of satanic communication or worship, you need to break all relationship with it immediately and turn to Christ. If you are not a Christian, receive Jesus as your Lord and Savior and then ask to be filled with the Holy Spirit. In the article about Roberta Blankenship quoted above, she excitedly related her thrilling release from Satan's power.

I found Jesus Christ. He led me out of my darkness. The Bible, much to my surprise, had the *authoritative* answers to my problems. I invited Christ into my life personally, and things really began to change. My hatred vanished, and an unexplainable love began to grow for the people I had hated. *Because I stopped pitying myself, I was ready to reach out and help people.* I found in Christ a Friend I could totally trust ... Someone who really cared about me with no selfish motives. I reached the end of my loneliness and unhappiness and reached out to Him. And I discovered that Jesus is still the great Healer ... not physically, in my case, but emotionally. He healed my wracked up emotions.[5] (italics added)

The deliverance Jesus Christ imparted to young Roberta, he wants to give to you. The joy that results from the Spirit-filled life is the only lasting solution (Ephesians 5:18–21).

Once having received Jesus Christ as your personal Lord and Savior, you need only be filled with his Holy Spirit daily and walk in his Spirit (Galatians 5:16–24) to rid yourself of the evil effects of occultism. Remember, God never makes his commandments impossible or difficult. Since he enjoins us to be filled with the Holy Spirit, it naturally follows that he has made it simple. If you have examined your heart, confessed all known sin, and are totally and unconditionally yielded to God, then ask to be filled with the Spirit and expect a consistent change in your emotions. The best way to speed the therapy is to read long passages from the Word of God. In fact, begin by a repetitious reading of the book of Philippians. I have counseled hundreds of depression-prone people to read the entire book of Philippians every morning for thirty to sixty days. The truths in that little book will change your outlook on life!

THE PERFECT OBSESSION

During the years I have taught the Bible, I have been requested many times to teach on Satan, demons, and the occult, and some of my friends have suggested that I did not address myself to such subjects often enough. As a rule, I have consistently refused to do so because I find it very harmful for Christians to spend much time thinking about Satan. All of the mystically minded people I know who talk repeatedly about Satanism and demons are sad, morbid people. If they understood the function of the human mind, they would realize why. As we have already noted, whatever you project on the imagination screen of your mind will influence your emotions. If you think repeatedly about Satan's devices and ways, you will naturally become depressed. However, if you consciously project the image of the Lord Jesus Christ and the blessings he has brought into your life, your spirit will be lifted. As a reminder of this the Bible charges, "Your attitude should be the same as that of Christ Jesus" (Philippians 2:5); "Let us fix our eyes on Jesus, the author and perfecter of our faith" (Hebrews 12:2). When we look to Jesus, he lifts our emotions. Therefore, I suggest that you develop the mental hygiene of projecting thoughts about him on the screen of your mind and avoid thinking about Satan. Anything that continually occupies your mind becomes an obsession and will exercise undue control over you. Never blunder into the pitfall of studying and thinking continually about Satan. A Christian should only be obsessed with Jesus Christ and being continually filled with the Holy Spirit.

Rather than becoming disturbed and even demoralized with the idea that "Satan is going to get me," the Christian can develop emotional and mental maturity through preoccupation with the concept, "My God will meet all [my] needs" (Philippians 4:19). After all, he has promised, "The one who is in you is greater than the one who is in the world" (1 John 4:4). Let your obsession be with Jesus Christ; then you will defeat Satan every time.

THE CHRISTIAN'S ARMOR

We are taught in the Word of God to "resist the devil, and he will flee from you" (James 4:7). Our means of resistance is clearly outlined in Ephesians 6, where we are introduced to the whole armor of God. Note especially that the pieces of armor provide adequate defense for everything but retreat:

> Therefore, put on the full armor of God, so that when the day of evil comes, you may be able to stand your ground, and after you

have done everything, to stand. Stand firm then, with the belt of truth buckled around your waist, with the breastplate of right-eousness in place, and with your feet fitted with the readiness that comes from the gospel of peace. In addition to all this, take up the shield of faith, with which you can extinguish all the flaming arrows of the evil one. Take the helmet of salvation, and the sword of the Spirit, which is the word of God. And pray in the Spirit on all occasions with all kinds of prayers and requests. With this in mind, be alert and always keep on praying for all the saints. (Ephesians 6:13–18)

All the pieces of the Christian's armor in his spiritual warfare are conferred upon him through the Word of God. For this reason it is as essential to read God's Word daily for spiritual nutrition as it is to take in a daily supply of physical food. Anemic Christians whose minds steadily consume the carnal food of television, movies, pornography, and materialism are no match for the devil. They can worry about him, study his methods, become conversant with his program—and still be defeated by him.

By contrast, the Christian who lets the "attitude of Christ" become his armor by daily Bible reading and obedience to its teach-ings will valiantly triumph over Satan—through the victory that comes only from Christ Jesus. Whenever a Christian sins or is pierced by Satan's dart, he must not concede to his adversary. Rather the Christian must recognize that defeat is imminent if he or she fails to appropriate the spiritual armor of the Word of God.

If you are prone to depression or if you find that reading mate-rial on the occult has a depressing influence upon you, I offer this suggestion: The next time you are tempted to read an article or a book concerning Satan or the occult, squelch the desire and read Philippians, Ephesians, 1 John, and the Sermon on the Mount. Your spirit will be uplifted and your emotional life strengthened.

Chapter 16

Depression and Music

Music has a far greater effect on human emotions than most people realize, for it can invigorate, lift the spirits, depress, and in some cases aggravate. Not only can it create moods, but it can also perpetuate or dispel them.

To discern the power of music over people, watch them during a parade. Their mood changes with the various tunes played by each of the marching bands. In fact, the body tends to sway or pulsate rhythmically in direct proportion to the music, whether folksy or patriotic, lilting or frenzied.

Until modern methods of communication made it possible to be exposed to every kind of music in the world, each culture seemed to gravitate to its own style of music. To a large extent, the finest musical forms were found in the Western civilizations. In fact, the art of music was not really developed to any high degree of proficiency in other countries because of the detrimental influence of the various religions on their respective cultures.

Happy music was limited almost exclusively to Western civilizations, primarily because until recent years, Christianity and Judaism have exercised the largest single influence on Western culture, including its music. Paganism, the chief influence on music in other parts of the world, has always been dominated by the dirge or the chant. Such music heavily utilizes the minor or mournful keys.

In the Old Testament, when people experienced an exhilarating relationship with God, they broke forth into singing. The New Testament similarly indicates that the first characteristic or evidence of the

Holy Spirit in the life of a Christian is a song in the heart and praise through melody (Ephesians 5:18–20). As a result, Christianity has contributed to the world some of its greatest music and musical forms, designed by God as an instrument of blessing to our emotions.

In a previous chapter we demonstrated that our emotions are influenced by our mind. Music furnishes an exception to that rule, for like medication or drugs, it is able to influence the emotions while bypassing the mind. For that reason, just as you regulate the kind of medication or drugs your family uses, it is important that you govern the kind of music you and your family hear.

MUSIC AFFECTS YOUR MOODS

In this age of depression, modern music often tends to be depressing, either because the people who write the music are depressed and the music reflects their mood, or because the music itself is depressing. Quite often both are true. Some blame Satan for this detrimental use of music in an attempt to demoralize people. I am inclined to consider it as the natural result of eliminating Jesus Christ from one's life and culture.

It is worth inserting here that the problem is much worse today than when I wrote the preceding words twenty years ago. The drug culture has introduced an even more depressing lament to much modern music and the mood becomes contagious to the listener. Some artists have even admitted they have written songs under the influence of drugs or in some cases were inspired by demons. Unfortunately, many parents let their kids pick out their own music and have no idea what the lyrics are inciting their children to do. Some of the worst offenders are rap writers who flat out challenge young people to rebel against their parents, the authorities, and God. They also challenge them to break every moral law of God. Not only will such music incite young people to even greater rebellion, it can lead them to serious depression. Many of the 30,000 people who commit suicide each year are into rock, heavy metal, or other music that has a depressing effect on their emotions.

If you examine carefully the words of many popular tunes, you will find them filled with complaint, lamentation, and rebellion.

Gloom and disaster seem to constitute the foreboding element in much modern music. The last thing a depressed person needs is to hear this kind of music! But strangely enough, because of his depressed mood he may indeed gravitate to that music.

The once-happy music of the West, because of the atheistic control of the communications media, is rapidly degenerating into the same depressing tunes I have heard in India, Africa, and China. Unless a musician is filled with the Holy Spirit, he is often prone to create morbid, pessimistic, negative music that features a detrimental beat or tune. We need a return to happy music today.

As I drove away from Forest Lawn Cemetery in Los Angeles one day, I was amazed to find myself singing. It had just been my privilege to participate in the funeral service for a very dear friend and teacher who had been a significant spiritual blessing in my life. My first reaction to the spontaneous song I felt was one of guilt, because traditionally we are supposed to be sad after leaving the funeral of a loved one. Upon reflection, I found that my mood echoed the "Hallelujah Chorus" sung at the close of the service. At his request, that jubilant song declaring the Christian's triumphant victory over death had supplanted traditional sadness with joy.

The capability of music to affect our moods has been well established. When King Saul of Israel was tormented by an evil spirit (probably a spirit of depression), he called for David, the sweet psalmist of Israel, to come and play on his harp. The beautiful strains of the harp in the hands of a spiritual instrumentalist had a lifting effect on Saul's mood (see 1 Samuel 16:23).

MUSIC IN THE HOME

Every home should be filled with music, but not just *any* kind of music. Wholesome, inspiring background music has a tendency to reduce minor sources of irritation and unpleasant noises around the home. In addition, it will lift the mood of children and adults. Because Sunday morning often seems to foment a degree of irritation and conflict in many Christian homes as the family dashes through breakfast, scurries to finish last-minute chores, and finally heads discordantly for Sunday school, the wise parent, aware of the hectic scramble that

Sunday morning occasions, but also conscious of the soothing effect of music, lets the radio or stereo fill the house with strains of praise and exaltation. No one awakening to "A Mighty Fortress Is Our God" or "Jesus Shall Reign" can growl through breakfast!

Someone who has made a thorough study of the influence of music on the home suggests that we play rousing music in the morning, active music in the afternoon, and restive music in the evening. I am convinced that one of the best ways a Christian family can counteract the nearly universal tendency of young people to favor hard rock or mournful ballads, which are usually detrimental to their emotional development, is to provide them with a creative alternative. Only in so doing will we create in them a wholesome appetite for good music.

If you or someone in your family is susceptible to depression, select your music carefully. Make sure that whatever the music or instrument, it has a joyous, lifting effect on your emotions. Don't let your circumstances determine the music, and reject music that matches your mood. Instead provide yourself with music that will exercise a positive influence on you and your household. Many times I have urged depressed counselees to select five or ten "happy" or "praise" CDs or cassettes when they are in a good mood, so they can put them on when they are feeling down. If they wait until they become depressed to pick out their music, they either don't bother to play music at all, or they select something that is so morbid or depressing they end up feeling worse.

It would be hard to find a more difficult place for singing than a prison cell. Yet the apostle Paul, together with Silas, his traveling companion, used such an occasion to elevate their spirits by singing.

Acts 16 relates their imprisonment for preaching the Gospel and casting out an evil spirit from a young girl. They were not only confined to a jail cell but severely beaten and left with their hands and feet in stocks. Instead of complaining to God and feeling sorry for themselves, they began to sing and to praise him. As a result they were in a spiritual frame of mind to be instruments of God in leading the first Europeans to a saving knowledge of Jesus Christ, which maintained and even further elevated their high spirits.

The Bible teaches that a heart free of guilt and at one with God produces a spontaneous and joyous hymn of thanksgiving. A life and heart void of God has a tendency to produce and respond to dissonent, sorrowful music. The writer of Proverbs 29:6 explains that "a righteous one can sing and be glad," and throughout the Bible we find that a person's relationship to God and knowledge of his wonderful ways and works produces singing.

Consider the following: "Sing to the LORD; for he has done glorious things; let this be known to all the earth" (Isaiah 12:5). "Sing for joy, O heavens, for the LORD has done this; Shout aloud, O earth beneath. Burst into song, you mountains, you forests and all your trees, for the LORD has redeemed Jacob, he displays his glory in Israel" (Isaiah 44:23).

The great singer of Israel exclaimed,

Shout for joy to the LORD, all the earth.
>   Worship the LORD with gladness;
>   come before him with joyful songs.
Know that the LORD is God.
>   It is he who made us, and we are his;
>   we are his people, the sheep of his pasture.
Enter his gates with thanksgiving and his courts with praise;
>   give thanks to him and praise his name.
For the LORD is good and his love endures forever;
>   his faithfulness continues through all generations.

(Psalm 100)

The emotional aftermath of joyous, lifting music is highly beneficial, similar to the results of thankful thinking and conversation. The proper kind of music will greatly assist your feelings of well-being and help you avoid the tendency to depression. Just as depression feeds depression, so joy feeds joy. Music can help create the right kind of mental attitude that, when followed by the right kind of thought patterns, will help you avoid depression.

Chapter 17

Ten Steps to Victory Over Depression

No one enjoys depression, though probably everyone has fallen victim to it during his or her lifetime. Some experience it more than others, depending on how much self-pity they have indulged in.

By this time we have established the fact that it is not usually a consequence of "body chemistry," "other people," or "the pressures of life," but our own mental attitude toward those pressures that induces depression.

It has been my purpose in this book to show that most depression is unnecessary and can be avoided! This chapter contains the ten steps you can take to escape the problem. Hundreds of people have tried these steps and have testified to their reliability.

If you or someone you love has a problem with depression, this chapter may change your life. Several years ago I spoke in Detroit to a group of ministers in preparation for conducting a Family Life Seminar two months later. During the break a Presbyterian minister asked me, "Can I give you a hug?" I was a little embarrassed but stifled my resistance tendencies and let him hug me. Then he said, "Your book, *How to Win Over Depression,* changed my life, especially the chapter, 'Ten Steps for Overcoming Depression.' I had been depressed a majority of the time for over ten years and was thinking of giving up the ministry when my counselor gave me your book. He suggested I read this chapter every night before retiring, which I did! Then I went off to sleep thinking and praying about each of your ten steps. Soon I had them memorized and now they are a way of life. It was just like a dark cloud was lifted off my mind and spirit. Today I am happier than I have been in years, and God is richly blessing my ministry."

I'll give a hug anytime for a report like that! For it not only illustrates that there is a cure for depression, it shows that incorporating what you learn into your life is what makes that cure possible. I would hope all those who have experienced depression for any length of time would read this chapter several times, memorize each of the ten steps, and incorporate them into their daily life. You will enjoy the results!

A twenty-four-year-old woman who came in for counseling acknowledged many years of depression. During the preceding four years she had undergone thirty electric-shock treatments for the malady—and was nothing bettered. In fact, her problem was compounded by a loss of memory. She had lost at least two years of her life in sanitariums due to depression.

Looking into the face of this young woman, I couldn't help thinking how her case was so typical of the severely depressed. To begin with, she was predominantly melancholy in temperament; consequently she was negative, sensitive, and overly occupied with herself. In addition, she had lost all hope for the future. The product of a broken home, she was literally unwanted by either parent or her brothers and sisters.

The first step in Beth's remarkable recovery was taken when she accepted Jesus Christ as her personal Lord and Savior. He provided the assurance of love and forgiveness she had always longed for. He also provided her with the power to overcome her thought patterns of resentment and self-pity. By gaining the ability from him to forgive her parents, she removed the root of bitterness that had immobilized her for years.

Three months after her conversion she discontinued the drugs prescribed by her psychiatrist and experienced the best emotional stability of her life. She revisited her psychiatrist at my suggestion because she felt guilty at not formally terminating her treatments. He was overjoyed at the change in his patient and immediately jumped to the conclusion that his combination of drug therapy and psychotherapy had finally brought her relief. When she informed him that she had become a Christian and that Christ had brought a whole new way of life to her, he must have felt threatened, for he immediately lashed out at her in a most unprofessional manner. He warned her, "It will not last! Christianity is only a crutch; you will be back here in a few weeks worse off than you were before." She informed him that she was no longer taking his drugs and was sleeping better than ever. He berated both her faith and her intelligence.

Fortunately, Beth drove straight to my office. All she needed was some biblical reassurance to the reality of her experience. We once again reviewed the steps to overcoming depression that had already helped her. Gradually her confidence and joy returned, and she left my office to continue living that abundant Christian life the Lord has promised to all his children who meet his conditions. If her experience with Christ is only a "crutch," it must be a pretty good one, because it has been over twelve years since she has been depressed, in spite of the fact that she was rejected by her family for becoming a Christian. About five years after the publication of the original version of this book, I met Beth and three friends at Hume Lake Christian Camp, where I was the Bible teacher for the adult conference that week. I was elated to see her in such a radiant frame of mind. When I asked what she was doing for a living, I was amazed at her reply. She had become the supervisor of a highly technical department of one of the largest hospitals in the city where MRI testing and other sophisticated exams were administered. Not bad for a former mental patient in another hospital—with little hope of recovery.

FOUNDATION STONES OF THE CHRISTIAN LIFE

Your depression, or that of someone you love, that has caused you to read this book is probably not nearly as severe as was Beth's. But the steps to victory over depression that I shall soon reveal have proven so effective for her and others that I am confident they will prove equally beneficial to you if you use them. But these ten steps can only be used by Christians. So, before reading them, see if you are really entitled to use them by examining the foundation stones of the Christian life.

Accept Jesus Christ as your Savior.

With all due respect to the powers of your mind and will, you do not have the capacity to avoid depression without help from God. One of the tragic blunders of modern psychology, success motivation, and other humanistic forms of self-improvement lies in their presumption that people do not need God's help to lift them out of depression. Jesus Christ said, "Apart from me you can do nothing" (John 15:5), and this is particularly true of depression. If you anticipate victory over depression on a lasting basis, you must begin by inviting Jesus Christ into your life. Once you have done that (see chapter 6), you will then possess the divine resources of God to enable you to take the ten steps for victory over depression. If you are not sure you have had such an experience, I would counsel you first of all to slip to your knees and personally invite him into your life. Be assured of the promise, "Everyone who calls on the name of the Lord will be saved" (Rom. 10:13).

Walk in the Spirit daily.

Accepting Jesus Christ as your personal Savior and walking in the Spirit on a day-to-day basis are not identical experiences. The latter, of course, is made possible by the first. The steps for being filled by the Spirit, considered in chapter 9, should be followed carefully.

The most important step in being filled with the Spirit is the total commitment of your life to Christ. The self-life always causes depression. It may not at first—self-will can be exhilarating on the short-term—but when the fruits of decisions made by self-will are ready for harvesting, they can be very bitter. Making Christ Lord of your life each day enables you to not only avoid selfish decisions, but self-pity, self-indulgence, self-centeredness, and the many other natural expressions of selfishness.

Who Controls Your Life?

It is not difficult to determine whether or not your life is committed to Christ at any given time. Just ask yourself, "Who is in control of my life right now?" The following diagram of the throne symbolizes our free will. Only one person can sit as Lord on the throne of your life at one time—you or Jesus Christ. The "S" on the throne of a carnal Christian represents self. Christ is in this person's life but is not allowed to control it. Such living, which unfortunately is all too common, constitutes a miserable state of existence. Christians who remain at the helm of their lives become unproductive and unattractive. Nothing about their lives exemplifies the change that Christ brings, for their self-directed program and egocentric perspective belie their position as new creatures in Christ Jesus. Some would even dare to ask God's blessing upon their selfish designs, but this doesn't exempt them from misery and emptiness.

The Christ-controlled life steadily wins over depression. Jesus Christ, by his Holy Spirit, sits on the throne of this person's life, directing all thoughts, feelings, and actions.

Life embraces an endless number of decisions, large and small. Where shall I live? What shall I pursue as a life vocation? Whom shall I marry? Either you or Jesus Christ will make these decisions. The life of faith and commitment to Christ places all decisions in his hands. The Bible teaches, "In all your ways acknowledge him, and he will make your paths straight" (Proverbs 3:6).

The following illustration describes that decision-making process with the following diagram and dots, each dot representing a decision in life.

Carnal Christians run their own lives and make their own decisions, whereas Christ-controlled Christians turn their lives over to Jesus Christ by prayerfully asking, "Lord Jesus, how do you want me to handle this situation?" "Do you want me to take this job opportunity?" "How do you want me to respond to my wife, or husband, or children, or boss, or neighbors?"

The practical differences in the two lifestyles are clearly listed in the preceding diagram. The self-controlled life is miserable. The

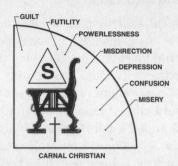

Christ-controlled life is dynamic! One propagates disarray and confusion, inducing self to stagger from crisis to crisis. The Christ-controlled life guarantees peace and confidence, thus avoiding many crises (because this life is supernaturally directed), yet confidently facing those inescapable crises that do come. This believer is confident that his director will abundantly supply every need.

I had just come in from water skiing on San Diego Bay with my sons when we met a college student named Bill. He began to tell me what Christ meant to him personally and how Christ was controlling his entire life. Since I hadn't seen him in church for several weeks, I asked which church he was attending regularly. (I have found that Christians cannot walk in the Spirit very long unless they go *regularly* to a Bible-teaching church where they can feed their mind, heart, and spirit on the Word of God.)

He replied, "Oh, I haven't been going anywhere lately."

"What do you do on Sunday mornings, Bill?"

He said honestly, "I sleep in."

"But I thought you were letting Jesus Christ control your life now."

Rather peevishly he retorted, "I don't have to go to church to be a good Christian."

"No," I said, "but if Jesus Christ is in control of your life at 9:30 on Sunday morning, what do you think he would have you do?"

Then his subtle self-indulgent thought processes came to the fore. "Sunday is the only day I have to sleep in. I work and study hard all week long, and I think I deserve one day to relax and do my thing." When I confronted him with the fact that his excuse contained five personal pronouns and totally excluded Jesus Christ, he suddenly realized that he had never consulted Christ about his Sunday morning decision.

I had the advantage in that conversation because I already knew what Jesus Christ's decision would be. Hebrews 10:25 says, "Let us not give up meeting together, as some are in the habit of doing, but let us encourage one another—and all the more as you see the Day approaching."

When confronted with any decision in life, prayerfully ask, "Lord Jesus, what do you want me to do about this?" Usually a verse of Scripture or a biblical principle will pop into your mind and cast light on the subject. If you act in that light, you will make a proper decision; if you don't, you will once again be thrown into the den of error. Never ask, "What do I want to do about this?" True spiritual maturity, the product of time spent in the Word and continuous walking in the Spirit, manifests itself when Christ's will and your will are synonymous.

Depression-prone people should scrutinize their thought processes to see if they are controlled by Jesus Christ. His control does not tolerate self-pitying thoughts, and consequently Christ-controlled living is depression-free living.

The Results of the Spirit-Filled Life

Though everyone wants the results of the Spirit-filled life, few people experience them. I have never met anyone who predetermined to make himself miserable, but most people do! By running their own lives selfishly, they create inordinate distress.

In this regard, Ephesians 5:18–21 becomes a crucial passage for Christians. It should be memorized and contemplated daily. After commanding us to be continually filled (or controlled) by the Holy Spirit, it specifies the results. Note them carefully:

Verse 19—a song in your heart
Verse 20—a thankful attitude

Verse 21—a submissive spirit

You will never find a miserable person with a song in his heart, a thankful attitude, and a submissive spirit! Nor will you find a happy person without them. And isn't happiness what *everyone* wants out of life? Unfortunately, people try to achieve their happiness through the mental, emotional, or physical areas of life. But it cannot be found there. Only by turning one's life and all of its decisions over to Christ can one ever gain lasting happiness!

Forgive those who sin against you.

It is impossible to walk in the Spirit for a protracted period of time while refusing to obey Christ's command to forgive those who sin against us (see Matthew 6:12). Depression-prone individuals are frequently conscious of a loved one or relative who rejected or injured them earlier in life. Until they forgive that person, they will never know lasting victory over depression. In fact, they will never develop spiritual maturity, either. Jesus said, "For if you forgive men when they sin against you, your heavenly Father will also forgive you. *But if you do not forgive men their sins, your Father will not forgive your sins"* (Matthew 6:14–15, italics added).

The unforgiving spirit of a carnal Christian is harmful spiritually, mentally, emotionally, and physically. You have doubtless heard the expression, "He burns me up!" Little does a person realize that the bitterness festering in his mind will destroy his relationship with God and others.

An unforgiving attitude is rarely limited to one person. Like cancer in the body, it is a mental disease that feeds on itself until it severs the expression of love and other wholesome emotions. In addition, it makes an invalid of its subject, who becomes prey to every gust of passion. Bitterness tends to expand and intensify through the years until even little things arouse the person's rancorous spirit. I have found that a bitter, unforgiving thought pattern toward someone you hate will even minimize or limit your expressions of love for someone you love.

If you would sincerely rid yourself of depression, ask yourself, "Is there anyone in life I have never forgiven?" If so, confess that sin to God immediately and ask him to take away that habit pattern. If the individual is aware of your resentment or bitterness, apologize personally, if possible, or by mail. Admittedly, this is a very difficult gesture, but it is essential for emotional stability.

A Christian couple came in for marriage counseling with several surface problems but no deep-rooted difficulties that I could find. In talking to the man, who seemed to be the primary source of friction in the home, I found that years before, he had suffered a tragic experience with a business partner and had steadfastly harbored this affront and indulged in bitterness throughout the years. His resentful thinking pattern was not only a sin, but was also a mental habit pattern that spoiled his relationship with other people, including his wife. This bitterness was probably a major reason why the man had never become a mature and effective Christian. Finally recognizing his problem, he made an appointment with the man and asked his forgiveness. To his amazement, he found that eighteen months previously this man had become a Christian and had likewise been convicted about the matter. Today they arc reasonably good friends, and a major source of irritation in the marriage of this couple has been removed. The elimination of that root of bitterness has improved his entire thinking pattern and strengthened his spiritual and emotional life to such a degree that business associates notice the change in him.

All causes of bitterness need not be real but in some cases may be imagined. One deeply depressed young woman came to me after an unhappy courtship explosion. As the author of the breakup she concluded that she lacked a normal attitude toward the opposite sex. Sensing that it was abnormal to be so cold and indifferent to marriage she came in for help. I understood enough about her background to know that she was raised by a divorced mother who sacrificed everything for her daughter during her childhood. When the girl was twelve her mother remarried a fine Christian man who adopted her as his own child and tried his best to raise her properly as a daughter.

This nineteen-year-old girl was consumed with a spirit of bitterness toward her loving and devoted mother "because she smothered and dominated my every decision." Unfortunately, the mother blamed herself for the breakup of her first marriage, had bent over backward to make it up to the daughter, and consequently had become overprotective. (A parent raising children alone must realize that God is able to supply the needs of a child raised with only one parent in the home.) Some bright-eyed college sophomore with a psychology book under his arm informed this girl that she was overly dependent upon her mother. As a result, she built up an artificial case of resentment until it spilled over and stifled her normal emotions toward others. Only by confessing her sins of resentment and ingratitude to God and by writing a letter of apology to her mother was she able to be restored spiritually, emotionally, and mentally.

Someone has sagely remarked, "Forgive or perish." The human mind is so constructed that if we protract bitterness and hatred toward someone, these negative emotions will ultimately destroy us.

Renew your mind daily.

As we have already seen, the way to consistently transform your life is to renew your mind with the Word of God. The way of this world is so contrary to the ways of God that it is nearly impossible to find any spiritual help in the secular world. Except for Christian radio, TV, and literature, the media are almost devoid of anything that is spiritually uplifting. Often, other forms of communication can be spiritually harmful. Therefore, just as you nourish your body on a daily basis, you should feed your mind those things that will contribute to your spiritual development. All such wisdom comes from God and is found in his library of divine truth called the Holy Bible. Only by reading, studying, meditating on, memorizing, and hearing his wisdom will you become the mature Christian that God wants you to be, established in the faith and competent to overcome tendencies toward depression.

Practice creative imagery daily through prayer.

In chapter 12 we examined the importance of daily fashioning a wholesome image of yourself and your goals on the screen of your imagination. Like breathing, this practice should become a way of life.

THE TEN STEPS

Now you are ready to take the ten steps to victory!

Accept yourself as a creature of God.

Thank God that you are an object of his love and that he made you as you are. Make a special point of thanking him for whatever part of your nature or looks you are apt to regret. Since it is impossible to change, and since God controls our genes at conception, it is an act of disobedience to resent those areas of your life that cannot be changed. Thank him for what you are and trust him to gradually make you the person he wants you to be.

Accept God's forgiveness for your sins.

If you find sin in your life, of course, confess it. But whenever you examine yourself on the screen of your imagination, don't be surprised if you focus upon the mistakes and sins of the past. The more perfectionist and conscientious you are, the more natural that is. Once having confessed your sin, be sure to thank God for his forgiveness. Accepting God's forgiveness would mean that you see yourself as clothed in the righteousness of Jesus, not in the raggedness of your sins. "He who overcomes will ... be dressed in white. I will never blot out his name from the book of life, but will acknowledge his name before my Father and his angels" (Revelation 3:5).

Superimpose God onto your self-image.

Thank God for his presence in your life in a real and practical way, reminding yourself as did the apostle Paul, "I *can* do all things *through Christ* who strengthens me" (Philippians 4:13 NKJV, italics added).

Visualize yourself as God is shaping you.

Resist the temptation to see yourself in the light of failures past, but envision yourself as growing and maturing as both you and God desire you to be. One mother confined to a small home with three preschool children found this practice helpful in learning to control her temper. For some time she had viewed herself on the screen of her imagination as an ill-tempered, irrational mother gradually losing control of herself because of the heavy demands of her children. The more she saw herself in such a light, the more she acted this way. By visualizing herself daily as Christ would have her become, she gradually learned to respond more patiently and graciously in obedience to the Spirit's control of her life. Naturally, the more patience she actuated, the more she reinforced the positive image on the screen of her imagination. This in turn made it easier for her to be controlled and patient. The Bible tells us, "Your attitude should be the same as that of Christ Jesus" (Philippians 2:5). Think of yourself as a reflection of the mind of Christ. How would he treat children under those circumstances? Or how would he respond to an irate boss or a demanding, domineering parent? See yourself reacting as Christ would and you will find yourself gradually sustaining that reaction.

Visualize by faith your basic life goals and write them down.

By noting your objectives and writing them down, you activate your subconscious mind to remind you of those things needing to be done to fulfill your goals. By praying about them in faith, you also summon the power of God on your behalf, which makes it possible to achieve the impossible.

Always be positive.

There is no place in the Christian's life for negativism. Linked as we are with the divine power of God, we should never anticipate anything but success. Avoid the complainer, the griper, and the critic; most of all, avoid imitating them. The personnel director of a large corporation who had learned the powerful influence of negativism on people explained to me why he selected one particular man over another for a special job assignment. I knew both men and volunteered my surprise at his selection, for I felt that the man he passed over was the more effective employee. He responded, "I never hire a top echelon executive until I first interview his wife.

Although I am aware of the tremendous capabilities of our mutual friend, I am also conscious of the excessive griping habits to which his wife is given. I therefore conclude that she would have a harmful, demotivating influence on his work. I chose the other man because I judged that the margin between them would easily be bridged by the supportive role of his wife."

Negativism, pessimism, griping, criticism, and gossip are not only harmful but also contagious. In fact, you reinforce them in your own mind every time you verbalize them. Keep your conversation *and* your mind positive at all times. Listen to the most powerful instruction on this subject in Scripture: "Finally, brothers, whatever is true, whatever is noble, whatever is just, whatever is pure, whatever is lovely, whatever is admirable—if anything is excellent or praiseworthy—think about such things" (Philippians 4:8).

Anticipate the superabundant life God has in store for you.

God has fashioned a complete plan for your life, but it is flexible. It includes God's "good, pleasing, and perfect will." Romans 12:2 says, "Do not conform any longer to the pattern of this world, but be transformed by the renewing of your mind. Then you will be able to test and approve what God's will is—his good, pleasing, and perfect will."

Man's needs	**Man's Desire**
"My God shall supply all your need"	"That your joy may be full"

God's Abundance
Exceeding abundantly above
all you can ask or think.

"According to your faith be it unto you."

We read in Philippians 4:19, "And my God will meet all your needs according to his glorious riches in Christ Jesus." Concerning his desire to supply your wholesome, God-honoring wants, John 16:24 promises, "Until now you have not asked anything in my name. Ask and you will receive, and your joy will be complete." In addition, he desires to shower you with "immeasurably more" than you could ever ask or think (Ephesians 3:20).

Most Christians spend their lives on the left-hand portion of the chart, asking God to supply their needs. I rarely *ask* him to supply my need because he has already promised to do that. Years ago I found in John 16:24 that God loves to make me happy by supplying those things that I want and providing these wants in accord with his basic plan for my life. In more recent years, I have found that God is a Father who enjoys giving to his children. In fact, Jesus Christ compared an earthly father with the heavenly Father when he said, "If you, then, though you are evil, know how to give good gifts to your children, *how much more* will your Father in heaven give good gifts to those that ask him?" (Matthew 7:11).

One day after a wonderful Christmas at our home, it dawned on me that being a parent is both thrilling and satisfying. We have always received much pleasure and enjoyment in giving to our children, even in excess of their wants. Most parents are like that. We don't give because they deserve it, because most children today already possess more than they deserve. Rather, we parents give to our children purely because we love them. If that is true of us, how much more is it true of God! He wants to give us "immeasurably more than all we ask or imagine" (Ephesians 3:20)! Never limit God by unbelief, but anticipate that he will perform something supernatural in your life. Remember, "According to your faith it will be done to you" (Matthew 9:29). Your success does not depend on your opportunity or ability, but on your faith. If your faith is weak, ask God to grant you more faith that you in turn may anticipate the power of a supernatural and superabundant God working in your life.

Seek first the kingdom of God.

Matthew 6:33 makes it clear that Christians can make no allowance for greed or selfish motives in our lives. Although we may seek employment or material gain, we can never let it become our primary objective. Instead, our first objective should be to seek the kingdom of God and his righteousness. Any time our quest for material gain runs contrary to the kingdom of God or his righteousness, it is wrong for us. Even if we were successful in achieving some degree of prosperity while doing something contrary to the will of God, it would not be a lasting source of enjoyment. Remember, it is essential that we be obedient to God. In establishing our priorities, consider the first commandment: "Love the Lord your God with all your heart and with all your soul and with all your mind and with all your strength" (Mark 12:30). We can judge our sincere love for God by whether or not we serve him. If our first objective is to earn a living and to stockpile this world's goods, then we not only demonstrate our greed, but also a lack of sufficient love for God. If we give God his rightful place in our hearts, express it in our attitudes toward things, he will bless us with the items we need and other provisions "immeasurably more than all we ask or imagine."

Give yourself to God to serve people.

The most rewarding and gratifying experiences in life come in serving people. This service will be emotionally therapeutic. Depressed people are inclined to spend too much time thinking about themselves. Serving God by helping people forces you to think about someone besides yourself. I am personally convinced that God has oriented the human psyche in such a way that unless a person befriends or ministers to others, he or she cannot be satisfied personally. The rewards of such service are not only beneficial for eternity, but also helpful in this life.

One seriously depressed woman decided that she had never really helped anyone since her children went off to school. Although she had taught Sunday school in her earlier years, the births of her three children directed her energies elsewhere. When she was free during the day, she considered it essential to "rest up," but finally she was overcome by depression. As we talked, she realized it was time for her to recognize that God could use her as a means of reaching her neighbors for Christ, so she started a women's Bible class on Wednesdays. Several weeks later she had become a very dynamic, outgoing woman. While casually visiting with her at a social activity, I smilingly inquired, "How is your depression lately?" I shall never forget her response. She laughed aloud, and with a twinkle in her eye said, "I don't have time to be depressed anymore!" The fact that several of her neighbors had found Christ and two families were spared a disastrous breakup in their marriages due to her Bible study had given her a whole new purpose for living and a sense of self-esteem.

The Bible teaches, "Give, and it will be given to you. A good measure, pressed down, shaken together and running over, will be poured into your lap. For with the measure you use, it will be measured to you" (Luke 6:38). Scripture also promises, "Whoever finds his life will lose it, and whoever loses his life for my sake will find it" (Matthew 10:39). If you would really live free from depression, stop hoarding your life and give it away.

Give thanks in all circumstances.

"Give thanks in all circumstances, for this is God's will for you in Christ Jesus" (1 Thessalonians 5:18). That verse offers an absolute guarantee against emotional depression! For several years in family conferences before thousands of people I have announced, "I can give you a money-back guarantee that will keep you from ever being depressed again. It is found in 1 Thessalonians 5:18." So far I have not encountered a single exception. There is just no way a healthy person filled with the Holy Spirit, rendering thanks *in* everything, can become depressed.

In recent years I have noted a new emphasis upon this matter of giving thanks that has injected lasting joy into the lives of millions of Christians. It is reflected in teaching, preaching, and music, until it becomes a way of life. There are two ways of appropriate thanksgiving: consciously by sight or consciously by faith. Consider them individually:

(1) *Give thanks consciously by sight.* The Bible repeatedly advises gratitude as the ideal mental attitude. A grateful person is a happy person. Counting our many blessings to see what God has already done in our lives develops an optimistic faith to trust him for the future.

Depressed people are usually ungrateful people who in turn become unhappy people. I have found it therapeutic to ask such people to list those things for which they are grateful and review this record once or twice a day, thanking God in prayer for these blessings. The results are absolutely amazing. Some counselees have been so morose and unappreciative that I have actually had to help them work up their list. But once it was made, they began to catch the spirit of praise and discover far more to be grateful for than they had realized. Rehearsing objects of thanksgiving consistently for one week revitalized their mental attitudes and dispelled their feelings of sorrow and despondence.

(2) *Give thanks consciously by faith.* At times in life it is impossible to understand God's dealings with us, usually because we lack his divine perspective. God sees not only the present circumstances but also the end result, extending his provision on a long-term, permanent basis. Unfortunately, we are usually more concerned with the immediate and, consequently, when circumstances annoy or displease us, we are prone to gripe mentally rather than "give thanks in everything." For that reason it is essential that we learn to give thanks by faith.

We have already seen that our computerlike mind will reject the impossible. Humanly speaking, giving thanks "in everything" is unreasonable and inconceivable, a violation of logic. For that reason we must learn to program God into the situation and recognize by faith that he has a plan, including even the most unhappy circumstances, which work for our long-range good. Therefore, as an expression of our faith and confidence in his love and ability to act in our behalf, we should "give thanks in all circumstances, for this is God's will for [us] in Christ Jesus."

THANKSGIVING AS A HABIT

Just as we form bad habits, we may also create good habits. Most of us brush our teeth every day, not because we enjoy the process, but because we recognize its value. Consequently we have developed the habit. By the same token we can create the good habit of giving thanks in everything in obedience to the will of God. Refusal to be obedient in this regard can make you depressed at almost a moment's notice, because the unexpected circumstances of life are bound to strike at the most inopportune time. If you react negatively, you will experience emotional depression and become spiritually useless to God at that precise moment.

Lest you think these are idle words and not genuine experience, let me share with you my own predicament that occured as I was first writing this section. In twenty-five years I had never missed a preaching assignment, although I have had some close calls. At 11:50 this particular morning I had just completed a pastor's seminar in Amarillo, Texas. Seated on a 727, I was expecting to arrive in Dallas at 2:20 and catch a 3:00 flight to Atlanta, Georgia, where I was to begin a Family Life Seminar at 7:00 P.M. At 12:55, as we were taxiing out to the run-up area, I watched as the pilot suddenly turned the plane around and headed back to the departure gate. A few moments later I saw him deplane and talk with a mechanic, who began taking the cover off one of the engines. Subsequently, a thirty-minute delay was announced. A few minutes later, the mechanic brought a piece of cable out of the engine, held it up, and gave the pilot a message. Within a few seconds a flight attendant announced that a defective part would have to be replaced and that the flight was canceled.

Walking inside the terminal, I practiced what I have written. "Praise the Lord." God knew that the next flight from Amarillo to Dallas arrived eleven minutes after the departure of the Dallas to Atlanta flight. When this information was confirmed, I asked him for guidance and then called an air charter service at another airport. The pilot assured me that for $200 I could be flown privately to Dallas and arrive on time. Although I thoroughly enjoyed the flight, we landed just as my Delta flight lifted off the runway at Love Field. "Now what am I going to do?" I knew the choice was mine. I could grumble, be miserable, or praise the Lord and just let him take care of the details. So I decided to take the biblical course, and there I sat, where I finished this chapter.

At that point, the director of Family Life Seminars had me paged. After I informed him that I could not get into Atlanta until 9:30 that night, fifteen minutes *after* the seminar concluded, he asked, "What am I going to do?"

I replied, "Why not praise the Lord?"

I settled back in to wait for my plane. As I wrote, I was fully conscious that some of those gathered for our seminar would become rather irate at the news of my delay, but I knew that our heavenly Father was able to provide for their needs in ways I did not have any way of foreseeing. Of one thing I was certain: I had done the will of God to the best of my ability, I had faced uncontrollable circumstances with joy, and I could therefore sit back without worry or agitation, trusting him to work out the details. I was convinced that he had something in mind in this experience that I knew nothing about.

As I walked by the ticket counter and heard the angry passengers berating the ticket agent, I couldn't help but think, "Why can't everyone learn the secret of living by faith, that they too might 'in everything give thanks'?"

One thing I saw demonstrated that day, and I believe it even now: Shrill lamentations and prayers of protestation, which would reflect my natural temperament tendency, will not help a bit. At a time like this a succinct biblical principle encourages me: "My times are in your hands" (Psalm 31:15). Even in this very frustrating situation, I knew I could trust God to know what was and is best for me. At the time I could not understand the delay and the suspended engagement, but God graciously revealed part of his plan to me the following day.

By the time I arrived in Atlanta and went to my hotel that night, I was dog tired. Ron James, the manager of my seminars at that time, told me he had brought along two of Dr. Henry Brandt's films on family living, so he showed them the first night to our seminar audience. The next day a very happy woman spoke to me during the break and told me that her husband had attended this seminar, even though he never attended church. It seems he was more impressed with psychologists than ministers. Consequently he enjoyed Dr. Brandt's messages thoroughly. What thrilled his wife most, however, was that he told her on the way home, "During the prayer time at the end of the second film I invited Christ into my life." Again, I was reminded of the verse, "I being in the way, the Lord led me!" (Genesis 24:27 KJV).

ARE YOU A GROANER OR A PRAISER?

My evangelist friend, Ken Poure, who has been greatly used of God in family conferences throughout the nation, suggests that our reaction at times like this exhibits our spiritual maturity. He proposes that the time lapse between one's knowledge of a disappointing experience and praising the Lord by faith will reveal the strength of one's spiritual life. If you can rejoice in a matter of moments, you are spiritually mature. If it takes you fifteen minutes to an hour, you are still growing. If an hour or several days pass, "you are in real trouble," Ken warns. Then he asks a very perceptive question: "Are you a praiser or a groaner?" Most people are one or the other. The sooner you learn to praise God in the face of adverse circumstances or frustrated expectations, the happier you will be and the more likely you will live a depression-free life.

Chapter 18

How to Help Your Children Avoid Depression

To our dismay as parents, the tendency toward depression sometimes begins at a very early age. The depressed child will usually withdraw and become abnormally quiet and seclusive. He will sulk or hide from group activities at play, hoping someone will notice his pain. Because parents are often the last to recognize depression in their children, their frustration and anger at the child's withdrawal may compound the difficulty before they become fully aware of it.

If the depressed child does not withdraw, he tends to nurse his resentments until they erupt in such erratic behavior that he earns the reputation of being "a problem child." He may break things to get attention, fight with other children, and in general become the family troublemaker. Such behavior may indeed be interpreted by his parents as a cry for help. He craves love, affection, and reassurance from them, but their exasperation at his behavior only amplifies his feeling of rejection. This lowers his self-esteem, increases his anger, and produces further obnoxious behavior. If his brothers or sisters are more lovable by nature, he may conclude his parents love them more than him, which compounds the problem.

Statistics indicate that suicide may well accompany such a condition. Because children often live in a fantasy world and through television feed upon violence, they may have no true comprehension of the finality of death. Therefore, they may determine to get even with their parents by some act of self-destruction, while at the same time hoping to return to life (as some individuals do on television). The increasing number of depressed children who resort to suicide is an alarming tragedy of our times. And even if the depressed child escapes self-destruction, he or she is almost certain to develop the harmful habit of self-rejection. A negative thinking pattern or failure complex can well leave him or her emotionally and mentally scarred for life.

The adopted son of a couple caused such concern because of his erratic behavior that his parents came for counseling. Although the boy had developed a reputation in school for being "stupid," "inept," and "bungling," in reality he had an IQ in excess of 145 and knew as much about science and electronics as many engineers. By drawing deeply upon spiritual resources and administering great love, acceptance, and approval, the parents brought that boy out of his tendency to depression. In the process, we developed the following checklist of children's needs, which when met, will help them lessen or avoid depression.

GIVE LOVE AND AFFECTION

The primary cause of depression in children—lack of love and affection from their parents—sets up thought patterns of resentment, self-rejection, and self-pity. God has so constructed the mental mechanism of children that they automatically look to their parents for affection. Our children's emotional need for love matches their physical need for food.

In my opinion, one reason so many adults encounter recurring depression today is that they were not breastfed as babies. Humanistic man in his determination to effect a way of life independent of God has made many mistakes through the years; one of them was in suggesting to young mothers that modern science had produced a substitute for mother's milk. Unfortunately, they failed to take into account that a bottle in a crib is no substitute for a mother's love.

A group of Jewish doctors set up a special clinic in New York for Jewish orphans. They spared no hygienic means to protect the babies from germs, even to using special germ-killing lights, filtering the air, and requiring that attendants put on new sterile uniforms and rubber gloves when feeding the little ones. Much to their horror, they discovered that the mortality rate in their hospital was three times higher than in a similar hospital in Mexico. An investigator was dispatched to find what the Mexican hospital contained which theirs did not. When the report came back, they could hardly believe it! The understaffed Mexican hospital, lacking in registered nurses, unsanitary by New York standards, and totally inadequate according to the rules of modern medicine, adhered faithfully to a rather "odd rule." Every baby was held in the arms of an attendant at feeding time.

As important as the mother's milk is to the child physically, so is the tenderness and reassurance of a mother's love to the child's emotions. I am deeply convinced that the Creator had this vital relationship in mind when he designed both the mother's body and the child's emotions. All children crave affection, even the most choleric child. If he receives it at this stage, he tends to develop into normality and finds it easy to express affection. The love-starved child often becomes either cold emotionally or develops an obsessive compulsion for affection. When our first child was a preschooler, we boarded children. I will never forget the olive-skinned four-year-old named Carol who lived in our home for one year. She had been abandoned by her mother, no one knew the identity of her father, and she had lived in eight different homes by the time she came to us. I never saw a child who craved so much kissing. Whenever I showered kisses on our Linda, Carol would demand many more—and always insisted that I kiss her squarely on the mouth. Sometimes it took the supernatural love of God to bestow sufficient love upon that child, but I can testify that he supplies that need.

SHOWER ACCEPTANCE

The need for acceptance by those closest to us in life is well known. In fact, many children are afraid they really do not belong to their parents or seem apprehensive lest a mistake was made in bringing them home from the hospital. Not only their relationship with parents in the home, but also their appearance, capabilities, and habits are in need of acceptance. The child who is conscious that he is approved by his parents and was desired by them before his birth is a fortunate child indeed. By contrast, many counselees begin the sad narration of their life story, "I was a mistake; my parents never wanted me in the first place." Such a mental hurdle is very difficult to overcome.

It is a sign of maturity in a parent when he does *not* react negatively to his child's weaknesses that parallel his own. Most parent-child personality conflicts are caused by the parents' reaction to their own weakness manifested in their child. They hate the thing in themselves; consequently, they despise it in their child and they overreact. The child should not be expected to understand that the parents' rejection is not against the child personally, but against those traits that remind the parents of themselves. As a child, he or she will interpret the parents' actions as total rejection.

Mature parents will recognize themselves in their child—emotionally, physically, and mentally. If a mother and father have learned to accept themselves, they can easily accept their child. Once having communicated that acceptance, they can lovingly help him toward overcoming his weaknesses.

AVOID ANGER IN THE HOME

Destructive anger erupts in many forms, all of which prove harmful to children, who are so self-centered by nature that parental irritation automatically makes them regard themselves as the cause of the upset and the object of the anger. Such anger produces an insecure and resentful child, which, as we have seen, compounds his negative behavior and increases his parents' expression of anger. Young parents in particular are often very impatient. When confronted with the immature and often exasperating activities of a child, this impatience bursts into harsh language or angry discipline, which only aggravates the child's self-rejection and insecurity and prepares him for self-pity and depression.

OPENLY DISPLAY PARENTAL LOVE IN THE HOME

Another good thing parents can do to promote a sense of security and love in a child is to demonstrate love regularly in the home. As a result of the rising divorce rate, children are forced to choose sides between the two people on earth they love most—mother and father—whose angry outbursts toward each other confuse the child emotionally and cause him to build up defenses against giving himself in love to someone else. If the home disintegrates, and he is forced to leave one parent, he may resent the one he accompanies and fantasize about the one he leaves. Remember, the child who watches his mother and father demonstrate affection for each other will develop a predisposition toward security, affection, and a good mental attitude.

Looking back on my childhood, I recall being raised during the depression. My father died before my tenth birthday, leaving my twenty-eight-year-old mother a widow with three small children, including my five-year-old sister and my seven-week-old brother. I have never had to deal with a sense of insecurity, largely because I have never known what it is like to feel unloved. My father had a great capacity to love, and although he was taken from us at an early age, as a child I could understand his absence through death (a sharp contrast to the problem of divorce).

My mother's love for me and her great faith in God always sustained the optimistic idea that no matter what problems arose, a reasonable solution could be found. Every child has a right to such love and acceptance. As I conjure up fond memories of my parents, I especially remember my father coming into the kitchen, putting his arms around my mother, and lifting her three inches off the floor in a warm, affectionate embrace. That scene always gave me a sense of security. Even the memory of that scene made me feel good. Many of the emotional neuroses children reflect today could probably have been avoided had they experienced such obvious demonstrations of their parents' love.

SET RULES FOR GUIDELINES

Just as a swinging bridge with guardrails is easier to walk across than the same bridge without protection, so every child needs fences or limits set by his parents to direct behavior. These rules should be simple and well-defined, administered with love. They will constantly change with the age of the child, but whenever you set a rule, prepare for the child to test it, and don't expect him to thank you for it. I have watched children chafe at rules, badger their parents about them, and then, when they have forced their parents to revoke the rule, indicate a loss of respect for the parent.

DISCIPLINE WISELY

Too much parental leniency begets undisciplined children. The Bible makes it very clear that if you spare the rod, you will undoubtedly spoil the child. "Folly is bound up in the heart of a child, but the rod of discipline will drive it far from him" (Proverbs 22:15). Educators tell us that knowledge accompanied with emotion provides the surest form of learning. A vigorous spanking or other appropriate form of discipline when delivered in love makes a profound impression on the mind of the child. Yes, he may feel rejected at the time, but every child needs to discover that some things in life are off-limits. If he is not exposed to discipline, he will fail to learn many valuable lessons that he desperately needs to know. In addition, discipline is cathartic.

A child can feel true guilt when he has done wrong. Consequently, even though his punishment hurts, it provides a welcome mental relief. That is why children are frequently in a good mood shortly after being disciplined. Those parents who refuse to discipline their children cheat them out of that much needed alleviation of conscience.

Roger came to live in our home against my better judgment. Still in our twenties, my wife and I were not prepared to cope with a teenager. But the welfare worker assured us that if we didn't take him, he would be sent to a boy's detention home. Caught in the crossfire of parental hostility, he was assigned to his mother but desperately wanted to live with his father.

We got along fine as long as we let Roger do pretty much as he pleased. Gradually we had to assign him some chores as we did our own children. Day after day he got worse. Wantonly destructive, he refused to comply with our minimal standards, becoming verbally abusive and nasty. Then it happened! When my wife asked him to do the dishes one Sunday afternoon, he refused, sassed her back, and became downright insulting.

One of the things I had learned from my father the hard way was that no man worthy of the title would suffer his wife to be verbally or physically abused by anyone—including his own children. Stepping into the kitchen, I demanded that Roger apologize, but he steadfastly refused. When I gave him a choice between a spanking and an apology, he said, "You wouldn't dare!" That challenge couldn't be passed up—so I took him into the bedroom and administered the board of education to the seat of learning.

Within fifteen minutes Roger was out in the kitchen talking affectionately and happily. He even pitched in and helped me dry the dishes. Somehow that spanking taught him that we loved him along with our own children and also cleared his conscience of the heavy load of guilt for his misconduct. Life once again became livable for the whole family.

Contrary to popular opinion, discipline does not crush or stifle a child's spirit when properly administered. Instead, it often creates quite the opposite effect. The child who is disciplined when he is wrong gains the assurance of his parents' love. It is not at all uncommon for the obstreperous child, whose guilt-laden activities make him irrepressible, to become more considerate, obedient, and loving after proper discipline. By contrast the undisciplined child will have difficulty in achieving a sense of acceptance.

One factor about parental discipline should be stressed. Parents absolutely must be united on rules and standards of behavior. The child will naturally work one parent against the other, much to the disruption of the family and the breakdown of effective discipline. Disagreement on principles should never be aired in front of the child, but thoroughly discussed until a united position and joint policy statement can be shared with the child, whether both parents are present or absent. I have seen perfectly normal children, particularly in their teen years, turn into maladjusted monsters because the mother let it be understood that as soon as father went off to work, his rules were no longer enforced. Equally as harmful is the immature father who finds he can win the affection of his children by lowering the mother's standards. That is a short-term love that sows the bitter seeds of confusion and rebellion.

BE CONSISTENT

The most important part of discipline is consistency. This relates not only to individual problems in the life of one child, but also to equal consideration of all the children in the family. Maintain few rules whose violation results in spanking, but once established, make sure you exact the penalty without hesitation!

BE FAIR—NO CHILD IS PERFECT

Most young people want their day in court. For that reason, the parents should project the image that they are willing to discuss the rules. Children always feel better when they have been able to air their feelings in the family court of justice, even when regulations are not altered. Besides, the parents should train their children to reason matters out, not merely respond emotionally.

COMMUNICATE GOD'S LOVE EARLY

The child raised by Christian parents is most fortunate, for next to parental love, every human being needs to be assured of God's love. Such a message is best communicated by the parents early in life. The little Sunday school song, "Jesus loves me, this I know, for the Bible tells me so," sung fervently by young children every week, acts as a source of reassurance to them. In some of their lives, only such reassurance can compensate for the lack of parental love and help to generate a normal attitude toward life.

LEAD YOUR CHILD TO CHRIST
WHEN HE OR SHE IS YOUNG

Every human being needs to accept Christ as personal Lord and Savior. The sooner he or she does, the better are his or her chances of avoiding unnecessary pitfalls that induce emotional trauma. The new

Christian then can develop a mature, confident emotional pattern that helps to prepare him or her for the uncertain circumstances of life.

GUARD AGAINST NEGATIVE THINKING

One's thinking pattern is learned early in life. Watch your child carefully for signs of negativism or defeatism. Foster in the child the assurance that he or she *can* do all things through Christ who strengthens us. Let the child understand that today's impossibility may well become tomorrow's achievement. A child must develop the mental attitude espoused by the old adage, "You can learn to do *anything* if you want to badly enough." But a positive approach to life does not just happen; it results from consistent, patient reassurance on the part of the parent.

A child will never benefit from constant criticism or condemnation. In an airport lounge I overheard a parent instructing a second grader how to purchase a paper from a coin-operated newsstand. With a leap of joy the child returned with the paper, obviously expecting his father's approval. His smile instantly turned to dismay and fear as his father berated him publicly for being "stupid." It was yesterday's paper! The father had not learned that family unity and personal responsibility are not promoted by public humiliation.

AVOID THE MALADY OF GRIPING

We have already discovered that griping is very harmful, for verbalized criticism has a way of entrenching negative thoughts not only in the mind of the speaker, but also in the mind of all hearers. Children who go about griping are establishing a predisposition for consistent periods of depression. Refuse to allow your children the luxury of cluttering up your house with criticism.

At fifteen, one of our children was a professional griper. No matter what the occasion, he could find something critical or negative to say. Nothing ever pleased him. Finally we decided to take some long overdue parental action. On the basis of 1 Thessalonians 5:18 we showed him that his griping was contrary to the will of God. The first thing he said was, "But . . ." I stopped him and said,

"No buts about it! From now on you are not permitted to gripe in this house. We have a happy household here, and we want your help in keeping it that way." Within three weeks we could see definite signs of improvement. Today, my son has a different and better personality than he would have if we had permitted him to let that habit become more deeply ingrained in his nature.

CORRECT THE INFIRMITY OF SELF-PITY

Self-pity is a natural mental escape pattern for the child who cannot keep up with or compete in an adult world, or for the melancholy perfectionist who is rarely pleased with himself or others. Even the third child, contending with older brother and sister, tends to struggle with self-pity more than most children.

Gentle and consistent instruction in avoiding this tendency will guard the child from a thought pattern that will have to be broken forcibly later in life to avoid depression.

BE THANKFUL

Every Christian should learn that the spirit of thanksgiving brightens drooping spirits and eliminates depression. Children who are taught to be thankful to God first and then to their parents are well on their way to depression-free living. Teach them early to give thanks for food, love, shelter, health, teachers, and friendship. Children have an amazing ability to learn spiritual truths, and it is often easier for them than for adults to understand that God has a plan even in adverse circumstances. Train your child to give thanks in everything (1 Thessalonians 5:18), in the expectation that, "when he is old he will not turn from it" (Proverbs 22:6).

SEE YOUR CHILD AS HE OR SHE IS BECOMING

Most parents tend to view their children as they *are* rather than as they will *become*. I can remember looking at my sons and wondering whether they would ever amount to anything. Today I am very proud of two young men. As children they fought so fiercely I was afraid they would become mortal enemies. Today they are best of friends. When children are little, picture them on your imagination screen as they are becoming, for then you will empathize to them that you sense their latent potential. Otherwise the reality of the present may only illuminate a selfish, intemperate, grimy little urchin. Be careful to maintain an attitude of affection and patience, for a child cannot easily distinguish between whether his parent is displeased with him or his deed. Happy is the child whose parents recognize that by God's grace, their child will grow up to be a well-adjusted, successful adult someday.

SET A GOOD EXAMPLE

The best learning tool for any child is the example of his parents. If they see you indulging in negativism, self-deprecation, or self-pity, they will follow suit. But if you manifest practices conducive to winning over depression, your children will imitate those good habits.

Almost every authority on depression, both modern and ancient, observes that depression seems to run in families. We know two reasons for this: inherited temperament and home training. You cannot control the temperament of your child, but you can govern his training. I am inclined to believe that although some is genetic, as we saw in chapter 13, depression runs in families primarily because children tend to copy the bad habits of their parents. I have long observed that depressed children of depression-prone parents display similar vocabularies and thinking patterns.

Have you ever heard the expression, "When you talk to him, it's just as if you're talking to his father"? Every parent should ask, "If my child grows up to think and talk like me, will he manifest a happy spirit and emotional stability or exhibit those symptoms that anticipate depression?"

Chapter 19

How to Help a
Depressed Friend

When Vince Foster, special legal counsel to the president of the United States, committed suicide in an obscure park in Washington, D.C., on July 20, 1993, everyone was surprised. Bill Clinton, a boyhood friend, couldn't believe it! He had talked to him just two days before. Webb Hubble, the number-three man at the White House, also a longtime personal friend from Little Rock and an occasional golfing partner, also could not believe it. None of his intimate friends at the highest positions of power could believe a man at the prime of his life would point a .38 caliber gun into his mouth and pull the trigger. Most of his friends didn't know he was even depressed—certainly not depressed enough to commit suicide.

However, if we can believe the many conflicting bits of information coming out of the many investigations of this tragedy, he left ample signs of depression. The problem was that no one seemed to pay any attention to them. If someone had, Vince Foster might still be alive.

Obviously, the man was under enormous pressure. It was his job to supervise the Clintons' finances in ongoing investigations with the IRS and securities officers. He had been deeply troubled by the "Travel Gate" scandals that led to the firing of five thirty-year nonpolitical employees, and according to his suicide note, he was deeply troubled by the criticism of the Washington press—which admittedly, can be pretty brutal when it wants to be.

Had his colleagues known anything about temperament they could have anticipated his depression and perhaps have done something that would have saved his life. First of all, he had a high degree of melancholy temperament, the one temperament most susceptible to depression. He was reported to have a high IQ and was very conscientious, consequently he took any slights to his integrity or competence very personally. It seemed he dreaded the investigations, reports, and charges that he knew would be aimed at his friends in the White House. The pressure, long hours, and overwork with no end in sight that Mr. Foster faced is a formula that contributes to many of the 30,000 suicides each year.

Unfortunately, like Mr. Foster, the friends of the depressed often do not seem to notice the symptoms, or in some cases don't care enough to do anything about them until after it is too late. Oftentimes, a "friend in time of need" who does notice can spend time with the individual and help him or her over that "hump" in life or over that period of depression, turning the individual from the idea of taking his or her own life. Obviously, that is "a friend indeed"!

Depressed people need help! Their erratic behavior notwithstanding, they require the support of those around them, even though their actions make it difficult. Some will display an angry or irritable face that rebuffs their friends when they need them most. Many withdraw into silent isolationism, lending the impression that they want to be alone. Don't believe it! Your assistance will be more valuable at that point than at any other time.

Frequently the family of a depressed person, unaware of his depression, becomes exasperated by his behavior. Consequently, when he needs understanding and empathetic love, he may be subjected to unkind words and disapproval, which only compound his depression. Even when he withdraws, he is really afraid to be alone. Don't expect such a person to reach out for support, but confer it anyway. The Bible teaches that love is kind. If you really love a person, you will befriend him and be considerate of him, not only when he is strong, but when he needs you most in the chasm of weakness. The following suggestions for extending aid to the depressed will furnish a basic list to which the Holy Spirit will add in light of your own special circumstances.

Be there!

The most important thing you can do for a depressed person, humanly speaking, is to be present when he needs you. No matter how much he reacts adversely to your presence, he needs you to save him from his self-destructive emotions, mental attitudes, and, in some cases, physical violence. You need not talk or probe or offer advice to be of help. Your presence during a time of intense despondency affords mute evidence of your love and will tend to counteract the rejection that has contributed to his depression.

I remember one instance when I almost didn't go to the aid of a depressed friend because I really didn't know what to say to him. I knew that if I had been rejected by my family the way he was, I would have been depressed too. Consequently I couldn't think of anything to say. But I went anyway. For years afterward I felt like a jerk; all I did was sit with him for a couple hours, read Scripture and pray with him. Years later he thanked me and said how much it had meant to him adding, "If you hadn't come, I don't know what I might have done to myself." Needless to say, I'm glad I went!

Don't sympathize with him.

He has slipped into the slough of despond because he has been indulging in self-pity. Don't help him justify his self-pity, but at the same time don't condemn him. He requires understanding and empathy, not condemnation.

Program hope on the screen of her imagination.

The depressed person universally projects hopelessness and despair; her goals have been destroyed, her outlook is negative, and the light at the end of her tunnel has gone out. For some time, her thought patterns have continually concentrated on failure and hopelessness, thus causing her circumstances to appear bleaker than they are. Therefore, any kind and gentle whisper of hope in the face of her present circumstances will be beneficial.

Many times in the counseling room during the first interview, I succeed only in projecting on the depressed person's imagination screen the certainty of hope, based on the fact that with God all things are possible. If a man or woman leaves my office with a ray of hope that someone honestly can foresee an imminent solution to their dilemma, their mental state often improves between interviews.

One woman was so convinced of her hopeless condition that she left my office equally as dejected as when she arrived. To my surprise, she returned for her second appointment much improved. Even though she retained no inner confidence, she had been somewhat buoyed up by my confidence that Christ really was her answer and hope was in sight. First she drew strength from my assurance in Christ; then gradually we programmed on the screen of her imagination what he could supply for her. Finally, she began to appropriate the principles of hope for herself through the Word of God.

Be encouraging, but do not argue.

In the midst of programming the hope that is available in Christ, ignore your friend's defense mechanisms of defeatism and negativism and refrain from being excessively positive. Your friend may resent your faith at that moment, so be gentle and understanding.

Get him to think about something besides himself.

Self-occupation is a hallmark of the depressed. Whenever possible, guide his thinking toward others. One depressed counselee announced that she had found help from the taxi driver on the way to my office. Evidently he was an outspoken, self-pitying character who freely expressed his misery. She admitted, "I feel better after having listened to him. He's got more problems than I have."

Take threats of suicide seriously!

All threats of suicide should be taken seriously until proven false. As a friend untrained in suicide prevention, get the person to the pastor, a biblical counselor, or a medical doctor for professional help. If that is impossible, and you are the only person between that individual and eternity, you might ask some of the questions the therapist asked my friend, Don Baker, mentioned earlier. It seems he engaged him in a discussion, asking him to answer questions similar to those that follow, and may have saved his life.

- "How would you commit suicide?" The options are usually a gun, a knife, or hanging. The point is not to be morbid, but most of those who talk about suicide haven't really thought of some of the repugnant details of the act—and certainly not its consequences.
- "Where would you do it?" Most have not thought of that, either. Some may say "in the kitchen." Usually, if they have thought about it they will say "in the bedroom."
- "What would that do to the room?" Few potential suicides have thought about their blood all over the wall or the bed or even the carpet. They only think of ending their pain.
- "Who do you think would find your body first?" When the therapist asked this question of my friend Don, Don was stripped of any more thoughts of suicide. For only then did he realize it would probably be the daughter he loved so dearly. Even in his darkest hours that possibility could no longer be a consideration.

Such questioning is not something you would use lightly, but usually the questions will make your friend think seriously about the consequences of suicide on those he loves. In the process, you will help your friend get his eyes off himself.

Try to engage her in activity.

There is something therapeutic about body motion, for it stimulates the flow of blood, gets the heart pumping strongly, and tends to activate the glands. I have found that jogging after a heavy preaching schedule is equally as beneficial as sleeping, and in some cases better. Emotional exhaustion leaves us spent, whereas activity tends to clean out the system. You may wish to become involved in your friend's favorite sport or activity as a suggestion to get her started.

Help him to gradually assume his normal responsibilities.

Everyone faces responsibilities in life, and sooner or later he must resume these responsibilities. Be careful that you do not dump the full load on him at first, because the heavy weight of responsibility may be the original cause for depression.

Don't be too cheerful!

The wise man in Proverbs 25:20 states, "Like one who takes away a garment on a cold day, like vinegar poured on soda, is one who sings songs to a heavy heart." A depressed person finds a loud, cheerful person a great source of irritation.

I found this graphically illustrated in my study the day after our church was defeated by the San Diego City Council in our request to build a new church. A dear friend had heard the bad news and came to cheer me up. He wanted to be helpful, but he proceeded injudiciously. With a big smile on his face, he slapped me on the shoulder and laughingly cried, "PRAISE THE LORD!" Strange as it may seem, my reaction was one of intense anger. I not only resented his lack of sensitivity and understanding but even his cheerful grin. The fact that he was right and I was 100-percent wrong did not help a bit. I did not require sympathy, but was in need of understanding. He gave me neither. One must attempt to cheer up a depressed person graciously, gently, tenderly, and slowly.

Get him into the Word of God.

Nothing relieves a depressed person more than rehearsing the promises of God. Unfortunately, his depression makes him resentful of God, and thus he avoids the only solution to his emotional problem. If he will permit you to read portions from the Word, do so. Suggest key portions *he* could read. Perhaps he would be helped by some of the great psalms of David, who experienced depression and knew how to cure it. Suggest also that he read a good book that you can personally recommend. It is my hope that this book will become a therapeutic tool which many can present to their depressed friends.

Pray with her in a thankful spirit.

Even the depressed will rarely refuse prayer, which they usually recognize as their last hope. But make sure that you pray to God *about* them and their problem, not *at* them. Remember, you are extremely vulnerable at this moment, for your prayer will reveal your understanding of your friend's problem. Be very careful not to condemn her for her resentment and self-pity. Let the Holy Spirit do the work of conviction. Pray with thanksgiving for what God has done and is able to do in her life. Just hearing your prayer of thanksgiving and understanding can be therapeutic. It also reminds her of the resources of God that are readily available to her.

Spend time with him.

The Bible teaches that the first characteristic of love is patience, meaning endurance. If you really love a person, confirm that love when he is depressed by spending time with him, affording reassurance that someone really loves him.

HELPING THOSE IN THE DESPAIR OF GRIEF

The death of a loved one naturally induces grief. This is even true of the most warmhearted Christian. Many times I have heard Christians admit after the loss of a loved one, "You can never really prepare yourself for death." Although that is certainly true, Christians do not "grieve like the rest of men, who have no hope" (1 Thessalonians 4:13).

First Thessalonians 4:13–18 was written to a young church to dispel their sadness at the loss of loved ones. The comfort of that passage is founded on the promise that we shall see our believing loved ones again. That is one of the most treasured truths in the Bible. Because Jesus Christ is coming again, all those who trust him will be reunited someday. A person who realistically programs that fact on the screen of his or her imagination will sharply reduce the tragedy of grief. The pain of bereavement cannot be removed immediately but it will gradually diminish.

Consoling a non-Christian at the time of grief is most difficult, for he is "without hope and without God in the world" (Ephesians 2:12). Sometimes such individuals will cry out to God in their desperation and be saved. Whatever their plight, they need companionship, for being alone becomes the worst feature of their experience at this time. Fortunately an intuitive consciousness of this fact exists in almost every human being, which explains why relatives and loved ones rush to the side of a person who has just lost a partner, parent, or child. We all recognize a common need at such a time.

Assistance to a grieving individual includes rehearsing for him the promises of God. Under severe grief it is not uncommon for the mind to go blank. Thus, a friend who spends time with one grieving, providing reassurance of God's promises and faithfulness, will be a tremendous inspiration. It takes love, love, and more love to be that kind of friend.

Chapter 20

The Miserable Majority

Why are you downcast, O my soul?
Why so disturbed within me? Hope in God.
Psalm 42:5

Sooner or later everyone becomes depressed! One's mental condition may not be severe enough to require hospitalization due to catatonia, and one may not be so despairing of life as to attempt suicide, but inevitably everyone encounters depression.

For most people, particularly Christians, depression is a transient experience that overtakes them when the circumstances of life hit a low ebb at the same time their spiritual battery is down and their mental thinking pattern is negative. Usually the depression passes within a limited time provided the person straightens out his spiritual life, as previously explained, and changes his thinking pattern toward himself, the problem, or the person causing the problem. To eliminate the depression, it is not necessary to change the problem, but it is essential to adjust one's mental attitude. The situation is compounded if the person made some major decision during the depression, such as running away from home, getting a divorce, quitting school, leaving a job, or attempting suicide. Usually it is dangerous to make a major life decision when you are depressed. It is preferable to eliminate the depression first, then proceed to the decision.

For many people, depression is a way of life. They learned the habits of resentment and self-pity early and develop a carefully honed and well-entrenched thought process that needs changing. Such individuals should be encouraged by the fact that although depression creates a good deal of misery, it need not be fatal.

EXAMPLES FROM THE BIBLE

A close examination of the Bible reveals that some of the greatest servants of God had no small problem with depression. If the old adage is true that "misery loves company," depressed people will enjoy this chapter.

Job the Patient

One of the greatest men in the ancient world was the patriarch Job. Some feel he was a contemporary of Abraham, and therefore he lived about 400 years before Moses. Some historians believe he may have been the mastermind behind the construction of the pyramids of Egypt. (Read the book of Job in the Old Testament for more information.)

In the early years of Job's life, he was exceedingly blessed of God. Among his assets were seven sons and three daughters, 7000 sheep, 3000 camels, 1000 oxen, 500 donkeys, and "a very great household." No wonder the Scriptures report that this man "was the greatest man among all the people of the east" (Job 1:3).

Naturally Job had no problem with depression in those days— not with everything going well for him. But suddenly, all that changed. His animals were stolen or slain, and a tornado destroyed the home of his oldest son during a party, killing all his children. To make matters worse, his body was covered with boils "from the soles of his feet to the top of his head" (Job 2:7).

Although Job did not realize he was being tested by God to prove his genuine faithfulness, throughout all this tragedy he did not sin, even when his wife encouraged him to "curse God and die!" (Job 2:9). His positive reaction to all this tragedy, which would have plunged the average person into the pit of despair, has earned him the reputation of being the world's most patient man.

Everyone has his breaking point however, even Job. The final straw occurred when his three best friends came over to encourage him to confess the sin in his life that brought on this series of tragedies. After sitting on the ground in silence for several days, Job spoke. His words clearly reveal depression, for he had finally indulged in the sins of resentment and self-pity. A careful reading of Job 3 and 7 bears this out. Some of his thoughts indicating his self-pity are as follows:

3:1   "Job opened his mouth, and cursed the day of his birth."

3:3   "May the day of my birth perish."

3:4   "That day—may it turn to darkness; may God above not care about it; may no light shine upon it."

3:6   "That night—may thick darkness seize it; may it not be included among the days of the year, nor be entered in any of the months."

3:10 ". . . for it did not shut the doors of the womb on me to hide trouble from my eyes."

3:11 "Why did I not perish at birth?"

Only a heart of solid granite would find it difficult to understand Job's sinful response, but that does not excuse or mitigate it. This great man was depressed by the same sinful mental attitude that causes today's depression—self-pity. When he confessed his sin (7:20–21), indicating that he had maintained his faith in God in spite of his awful tragedy, Job was forgiven and his spirits lifted. He then entered into a debate with his friends attesting to the faithfulness of God. Job's increasing spirit and faith are apparent in chapters 9 through 40, *before* his circumstances improved. As a result, God blessed Job with "twice as much as he had before" (42:10). Not only were his riches restored, but he and his wife were granted seven more sons and three beautiful daughters. In addition, long life and health were bestowed upon Job, who lived 140 more years and saw four generations of his sons.

The primary lesson to learn from Job is not only that we must rejoice in spite of unbelievably tragic circumstances, but that even when we don't at first, it is still possible to gain forgiveness by looking to God in faith. He is always faithful to his children, for he knows how much we can bear, even if we don't. God does not carry a grudge just because we react improperly at first, but is ever ready to forgive and restore. Job was used mightily of God *after* his time of depression.

The World's Greatest Leader

When judged by his personal achievement and the impact he made on humanity, Moses stands as the greatest leader in all of history. He not only led three million griping Jews out of Egypt and continued with them for forty years in the wilderness, but he also served as the instrument of God, giving to the world the highest law code and standard of ethics ever produced.

In a previous chapter, I gave Moses' self-pitying prayer recorded in Numbers 11:10–15 as a classic illustration of harmful prayer. In verse 15 he became so depressed that he asked God, "Put me to death right now." Fortunately for Moses and the children of Israel, God ignored that request, but that Moses would ask is evidence that his sin of self-pity must have been habitual. A careful review of his life likewise indicates a serious problem with anger or resentment. Put these two sins together and you have the perfect formula for depression.

That Moses' self-pity and consequent depression were forgiven and that God continued to use him for thirty-eight more years again illustrates that depression need not be fatal, either physically or spiritually. A depression-prone person can be used of God if he will repent of his evil thinking pattern and trust God for the future. This is particularly true if the biblical principles for living are firmly established in his mind so that in a fit of depression he does not make a serious blunder that will so ensnare his life that after the depression is past he becomes a "castaway" and is no longer usable for God's perfect will in his life.

Another great leader who came on the world scene about twelve centuries after Moses offers a good example by contrast. Having triumphed over the Western world by the time he was thirty-three years old, Alexander the Great became depressed because there were no more worlds for him to conquer. During his depression he turned to drink, and it is said that he literally drank himself to death. Moral values and biblical principles for living, when programmed into the filing cabinet of the mind, will keep such tragedies from occurring.

The Father of the Prophets

Next to Moses, Elijah was probably the greatest man in the Old Testament, possessing miraculous power to heal the sick, raise the dead, prevent rain for three years, and even call down fire from heaven. On one occasion he single-handedly killed 450 evil prophets of Baal who had committed the worst sin known to man—deceiving men about God. He established the school of the prophets, which was used mightily of God to keep Israel and Judah from going into paganism and idolatry sooner than they did.

Even though he was a great man of God, Elijah also knew the defeat of depression. On one occasion he became so despondent that he asked God to let him die (1 Kings 19:4).

Rather fanciful suggestions have been offered by some Bible teachers in an attempt to justify his depression: "He suffered a psychological letdown after the public confrontation with the prophets of Baal on Mount Carmel"; "He was discouraged with the children of Israel because so many of them had gone to worshipping Baal"; or "Queen Jezebel was after him, and she had a vicious reputation." Like all excuses, however, they are nothing more than intellectual meringue—all froth and no substance. Elijah was depressed merely because he was indulging in self-pity! First Kings 19:10 shows his thinking pattern clearly: "I have been very zealous for the LORD God Almighty. The Israelites have rejected your covenant, broken down your altars, and put your prophets to death with the sword. I am the only one left, and now they are trying to kill me too."

As a matter of record, 7000 other prophets were true to God, but in Elijah's mind he was the only faithful one left. Self-pity always blinds one's eyes to resources and maximizes difficulties.

Who has escaped such thoughts? "I am the only one who has to do this chore"; "I am the only person who can't sing"; "Mom and Dad always pick on me, never the others." Such disobedient thinking ultimately produces depression, which will continue until the thinking pattern changes. Fortunately for Israel and for Elijah, he repented of his sin, the Lord protected him, and he outlived both Jezebel and her wicked husband, King Ahab.

The Disgruntled Prophet

If the number of souls converted to Christ through a man's preaching were the measure of greatness, the prophet Jonah has to be recognized as the greatest preacher of all time. It is estimated that over one million Ninevites repented as a result of his preaching. Instead of being elated at the way God used him to bring salvation to so many people, this prophet became strangely depressed. He actually prayed, "Now, O LORD, take away my life, for it is better for me to die than to live" (Jonah 4:3).

A secular counselor would understandably probe for some deep-seated emotional problem in Jonah's life to account for this depressed state. Some might even attribute it to the emotional letdown that followed his frenetic preaching schedule. But the simple fact remains that Jonah was "greatly displeased" and "angry"! He was angry at God because God had forgiven the sins of the Ninevites and spared their lives. Jonah hated the Ninevites! His hatred was not without human justification, of course, for they had cruelly persecuted the children of Israel for years. He probably was overjoyed that God was finally going to destroy them, which no doubt is why he originally refused to go there and preach to them. So when God forgave them, his fury was unrestrained. His anger led to self-pity and ultimately to such a state of depression that he asked God to let him die. What an example of turning an undeniably joyous occasion into a depressing experience! Jonah should have trusted God for the outcome that he did not understand. Instead, his self-pity short-circuited his potential for rejoicing, so he withdrew into the anguish of seclusion, muttering to himself and complaining to God.

We may be tempted to excuse Jonah, for the New Testament command, "Give thanks in all circumstances" (1 Thessalonians 5:18), had not yet been written. But you can be sure that if he had thanked God for the great spiritual revival in Nineveh, he would never have been depressed.

The Weeping Prophet

Some men rose out of the pages of history at a time when the most appropriate service to perform for their nation was to weep. Jeremiah lived at such a time! And he wept. And his tears were justified. Israel, the great nation once blessed of God, had so apostatized that she had been led away into captivity 135 years before. For their own safety, all the faithful Israelites had fled to the southern kingdom of Judah. Only a spiritual revival under King Hezekiah and the prophet Isaiah had saved Judah. In spite of the mighty hand of God in delivering this little nation, the Jews eventually forgot the God of their ancestors. To such a nation God called Jeremiah, the weeping prophet.

With deep concern and open weeping, he warned the people that if they did not repent of their sins and return to God, the Babylonians would destroy their city and lead them away as captives. Instead of appreciating his honest warnings and exhortations to repent to avoid the impending judgments of God, the people turned unmercifully on Jeremiah. He was imprisoned several times and on one occasion was placed in stocks. Although he responded in the Spirit most of his life, at one time he was obviously depressed—as demonstrated in his prayer life. In the fifteenth chapter of the book that bears his name, we find a prayer that establishes the depth of his self-pity. "Alas, my mother, that you gave me birth, a man with whom the whole land strives and contends! I have neither lent nor borrowed, yet everyone curses me" (v. 10).

Finally he turned on the Lord and erupted with this tragic outburst, "I never sat in the company of revelers, never made merry with them; I sat alone because your hand was on me and you had filled me with indignation. Why is my pain unending and my wound grievous and incurable? Will you be to me like a deceptive brook, like a spring that fails?" (vv. 17–18). The Lord responded to Jeremiah, "They will fight against you, but will not overcome you: for I am with you to rescue and save you.... I will save you from the hands of the wicked and redeem you from the grasp of the cruel" (vv. 20–21).

God seems to understand when his children lapse into self-pity, particularly when the pressures of life become too heavy. But that does not exempt them from the depression which naturally follows. Jeremiah accepted God's assurances when God said, "I am with you to save you" and went on to serve God many years. In fact, his external condition grew worse, but he looked to God and avoided a recurrence of his depression.

We can all profit by the lesson Jeremiah learned through this difficulty reflected in one of his short prayers: "When your words came, I ate them; they were my joy and my heart's delight" (15:16). The best source of joy for the depressed child of God comes through looking to the Lord in his Word.

Chapter 21

An Eighty-Five-Year-Old Optimist

Give thanks in all circumstances, for
this is God's will for you in Christ Jesus.
1 Thessalonians 5:18

It isn't often that one meets a genuine optimist in life, particularly one who is eighty-five years old. A contemporary of Moses and Joshua, this man's infectious faith makes him a classic illustration of the principles of this book. To my knowledge, not one negative thing is recorded about this great man. Although he had ample reason to indulge in self-pity, it seems evident that he never did, even as an octogenarian. In addition to a vital faith in God, he possessed an exceedingly positive mental attitude and vision that everyone should imitate. If they would, I am confident the seventies would be known as a decade of optimism rather than as "the decade of depression."

MY FAVORITE CHARACTER

The exploits of hundreds of great men are recorded in the Bible. The one who stands head and shoulders above them all is the little-known man of God named Caleb. Although not listed in the New Testament "Who's Who" of Hebrews 11, this man and his optimistic spirit should inspire everyone interested in studying people.

The first time he appears in the pages of Holy Writ, the nation Israel was facing a crucial test. The Lord had led them out of Egypt, spoken to them at Sinai, and brought them to the southern border of the land he had promised to give them. To encourage his people, God instructed Moses to select a leader from each of the twelve tribes to "search the land of Canaan" (Numbers 13:2).

THE GODLY SPY

Caleb was forty years old and a leader of his tribe when selected to go in and spy out the land. Commissioned to discover the strength of their adversaries, the location of their cities and strongholds, and the condition of the land, he did his work well. Not content to bring back merely a verbal report, he and his friend Joshua, Moses' chief lieutenant, returned with some of the fruit of the land, including grapes so large that a giant bunch was carried on a pole between two men.

On their return to Kadesh-barnea, where the people waited for the report, a great crowd gathered around them. To Caleb's amazement, ten of the spies presented a very negative report. In spite of the fruitfulness of the land flowing "with milk and honey," they were more impressed with the strength and size of the opposition. (Unbelief has a strange way of magnifying difficulties and minimizing resources. In addition, it is contagious!) The ten faithless spies summed up their report about the giants in the land by saying, "We can't attack those people; they are stronger than we are. . . . We seemed like grasshoppers in our own eyes, and we looked the same to them" (Numbers 13:31, 33).

This "evil report" of the ten faithless spies reveals a common malady of unbelief. The spies underestimated their own abilities, exaggerated the prowess of the enemy, and totally ignored God's power and continued direction in the affairs of Israel.

Consequently, they came to a negative conclusion that was entirely unrelated to the facts. This tendency seriously limited God's use of their lives and jeopardized the lives of their families.

Caleb leaped up and "silenced the people before Moses and said, 'We should go up and take possession of the land, for we can certainly do it. . . . If the LORD is pleased with us, he will lead us into that land and give it to us, a land flowing with milk and honey" (Numbers 13:30; 14:8).

Unfortunately for Israel, the people believed the negative report of the majority instead of the faithful testimony of Caleb and Joshua. Consequently, instead of possessing their inheritance, they were banished to a forty-year sojourn in the wilderness. Of all the adults living at that time, only Caleb and Joshua were permitted to enter the land thirty-nine years later. The rest perished in the wilderness because of their unbelief!

FORTY-FIVE YEARS LATER

When the time finally came for the children of Israel to possess the land of Canaan, even the great leader Moses was dead. Joshua, his successor, led the new generation of Israelites into the land God had promised them. Contrary to popular misconception, taking the land away from the giants was no easy matter. In fact, it took six years of fierce fighting before the twelve tribes found it safe to establish their dwellings in the land. Under Joshua's direction, Caleb had been an active leader during those awful years of war.

One day, near the close of the fighting, the two survivors of the wilderness wanderings were walking together. Caleb reminded his old friend Joshua of the promise Moses had given him forty-five years before:

> So on that day Moses swore to me, "The land on which your feet have walked will be your inheritance and that of your children forever, because you have followed the LORD my God whole-heartedly." Now then, just as the LORD promised, he has kept me alive for forty-five years since the time he said this to Moses, while Israel moved about in the desert. So here I am today, eighty-five years old! I am still as strong today as the day Moses sent me out; I'm just as vigorous to go out to battle now as I was then. Now give me this hill country that the LORD promised me that day. You yourself heard then that the Anakites were there and their cities were large and fortified, but, the LORD helping me, I will drive them out just as he said. (Joshua 14:9–12)

Caleb knew when he made his request that all the remaining giants in the country had fled to this mountain, but that did not daunt his eighty-five-year-old spirit one bit. Though his enemies were well-entrenched and had made the mountain a stronghold of giants, he said, "Give me this hill country." He knew his God was well able to deliver it to him—and he did!

The Bible does not tell us how old Caleb was when he died, but the inference is that he lived many years on his mountain. In fact, he probably cleared off a beautiful view where he could look out over the land below.

THE SECRET OF CALEB'S MENTAL ATTITUDE

If self-pity can ever be justified, humanly speaking, Caleb was certainly entitled to indulge in that sin. Banished to chewing dust out in the wilderness for thirty-nine years because of someone else's sins, he could have turned out to be a notorious griper. He could have spent his time thinking, "If those unbelieving people had listened to Joshua and me, we could have been settled in the land when I was in my prime." Every time a dust storm blew up, he could easily have blamed his plight on the unbelievers.

Interestingly enough, not one self-pitying or griping word is written of him. Instead, he fathered several children, and together with his wife, raised them to serve the Lord. And throughout those years he had his goal set on one day building his home on that beautiful mountain he had seen as a spy. He didn't know how he would do it, but he had absolute confidence that eventually God would fulfill his promise. Even though he had to wait forty-five years, he not only found God faithful, but he finally experienced the "exceedingly abundant blessing" for which our God is famous.

The real secret to Caleb's greatness appears in God's description of him: "my servant Caleb" who "had *a different spirit* and follows me wholeheartedly" (Numbers 14:24, italics added). That other spirit that characterized Caleb means the Holy Spirit, the hallmark of any Spirit-filled, obedient, trusting Christian. You can have that same Spirit. It is certainly *God's will for your life.*

Be sure of this, the spirit of Caleb that so valiantly shielded him from depression is available to you if, like Caleb, you learn the primary spiritual lesson that all Christians must learn in order to face all the emotional pressures of life: "Give thanks in all circumstances." Whether or not you understand the circumstances of life, you can look forward to God's ultimate deliverance from your problem, and his assurance to supply all your needs as you go through those problems. The result? You will never again be defeated by depression. It is entirely up to you!

Notes

Introduction

1. "Coping With Depression," *Newsweek,* 8 January 1973, 51.

Chapter 1: The Problem of Depression

1. Aaron T. Beck, *Depression: Causes and Treatment* (Philadelphia: University of Pennsylvania Press, 1967), 4.
2. Ibid., 5.
3. Ibid.

Chapter 4: The Cycles of Depression

1. "Coping with Depression," *Newsweek,* 8 January 1973, 51.
2. Kenneth Hildebrand, *Achieving Real Happiness* (New York: Harper, 1955), 139.
3. Ibid., 141.
4. Mortimer Ostow, *The Psychology of Melancholy* (New York: Harper and Row, 1970), 87–88.

Chapter 5: The Causes of Depression

1. Mortimer Ostow, *The Psychology of Melancholy* (New York: Harper and Row, 1970), 82.
2. Ibid., 72–73.

Chapter 7: Is There a Cure for Depression?

1. Leonard Cammer, *Up From Depression* (New York: Pocket Books, 1971), 133.
2. Mortimer Ostow, *The Psychology of Melancholy* (New York: Harper and Row, 1970), 114–15.
3. Cammer, 137.

4. Ibid., 139.

5. John Rush, *Beating Depression* (Toronto: John Wiley and Sons, Canada Ltd., 1983), 111.

6. J. Raymond DePaulo and Keith Russell Ablow, *How to Cope with Depression* (New York: Fawcett Crest, 1989)

7. Clark Barshinger, et al., "The Gospel According to Prozac," *Christianity Today,* 14 August 1995, 34.

8. Ostow, 117.

9. Cammer, 152.

10. Ibid., 154.

Chapter 8: The Place of Anger in Depression

1. Mortimer Ostow, *The Psychology of Melancholy* (New York: Harper and Row, 1970), 72

2. Ibid., 18.

3. Ibid., p. 75–76, 78–79.

Chapter 9: Self-Pity and Depression

1. "Your Emotional Stresses Can Make You Sick," *Chicago Tribune,* 18 July 1972, sec. 1, p.1.

Chapter 12: Depression and Your Self-Image

1. Maxwell Maltz, *Psycho-Cybernetics and Self-Fulfillment* (New York: Bantam, 1970), 96.

Chapter 13: Depression and Your Temperament

1. J. Raymond DePaulo and Keith Russell Ablow, *How to Cope with Depression* (New York: Fawcett Crest, 1989), 98–99.

2. David Myers, *The Pursuit of Happiness: Discovering the Pathway to Fulfillment, Well-Being, and Enduring Personal Joy* (New York: Avon, 1993), 57.

Chapter 14: Grief Is Not the Same as Depression

1. David Gelman and Daniel Pedersen, "Count Your Blessings," *Newsweek,* 24 May 1993, 57.

Chapter 15: Depression and the Occult

1. "The Campus Life Forum: Does This Girl Look Like a Witch?" *Campus Life,* January 1973, 16.

2. Ibid., 14.

3. Ibid., 13.

4. Hal Lindsey, *Satan Is Alive and Well on Planet Earth* (Grand Rapids: Zondervan, 1972), 157.

5. "The Campus Life Forum," 18.

Bibliography

Adams, Jay E. *Competent to Counsel.* Nutley, N.J.: Presbyterian and Reformed, 1971.

Adolph, Paul E. *Release from Tension.* Chicago: Moody Press, 1965.

Arieti, Silvano, ed. *American Handbook of Psychiatry.* 2 vols. New York: Basic Books, 1959.

Baker, Don, and Emery Nester. *Depression—Finding Hope and Meaning in Life's Darkest Shadow.* Portland, Ore.: Multnomah Press, 1983.

Beck, Aaron T. *Depression: Causes and Treatment.* Philadelphia: University of Pennsylvania Press, 1967.

Berne, Eric. *Games People Play.* New York: Bantam, 1972.

_____. *What Do You Say After You Say Hello?* New York: Bantam, 1972.

Brandt, Henry R., and Homer E. Dowdy. *Christians Have Troubles, Too.* Old Tappan, N.J.: Revell, 1968.

Cammer, Leonard. *Up from Depression.* New York: Pocket Books, 1971.

Christenson, Larry. *The Christian Family.* Minneapolis: Bethany Fellowship, 1970.

Collier, Robert. *The Secret of the Ages,* rev. ed. Tarrytown, N.Y.: Robert Collier Publication, 1951.

DePaulo, Jr., J. Raymond, and Keith Russell Ablow. *How To Cope with Depression.* New York: Fawcett Crest, 1989.

Dobson, James. *Dare to Discipline.* Wheaton: Tyndale, 1991.

Haggai, John Edmund. *How to Win Over Worry.* Grand Rapids: Zondervan, 1959.

Hallesby, O. *Temperament and the Christian Faith.* Minneapolis: Augsburg, 1962.

Harris, Thomas A. *I'm OK—You're OK.* New York: Harper and Row, 1967.

Hart, Hornell. *Chart for Happiness.* New York: Harper and Row, 1967.

Hildebrand, Kenneth. *Achieving Real Happiness.* New York: Harper, 1955.

Hyder, O. Quentin. *The Christian's Handbook of Psychiatry.* Old Tappan, N.J.: Revell, 1971.

Jabay, Earl. *The God-Players.* Grand Rapids: Zondervan, 1969.

Ketterman, Grace H. *You Can Win Over Worry.* Old Tappan, N.J.: Revell, 1984.

Koch, Kurt E. *Christian Counseling and Occultism.* Grand Rapids: Kregel, 1965.

Kreeft, Peter. *Making Sense Out of Suffering.* Ann Arbor, Mich.: Servant, 1986.

LaHaye, Tim. *I Love You, But Why Are We So Different?* Eugene, Ore.: Harvest House, 1992.

_____. *Spirit-Controlled Temperament.* Wheaton: Tyndale, revised, 1994.

_____. *Transformed Temperaments.* Wheaton: Tyndale, 1971.

_____. *Understanding the Male Temperament.* Old Tappan, N.J.: Revell, 1977.

_____. *Why You Act the Way You Do*. Wheaton: Tyndale, 1984.

Lindsay, Hal. *Satan Is Alive and Well on Planet Earth*. Grand Rapids: Zondervan, 1972.

Lloyd-Jones, D. Martyn. *Spiritual Depression: Its Causes and Cure*. London: Pickering and Inglis, 1965.

McMillien, S. I. *None of These Diseases*. Old Tappan, N.J.: Revell, 1963.

Maltz, Maxwell. *Psycho-Cybernetics and Self-Fulfillment*. New York: Bantam, 1970.

Murphy, Joseph. *The Power of Your Subconscious Mind*. Englewood Cliffs, N.J.: Prentice-Hall, 1963.

Nelson, Marion H. *Why Christians Crack Up*. Chicago: Moody Press, 1960.

Osborne, Cecil. *The Art of Understanding Yourself*. Grand Rapids: Zondervan, 1967.

Ostow, Mortimer. *The Psychology of Melancholy*. New York: Harper and Row, 1970.

Rush, John. *Beating Depression*. Toronto: John Wiley and Sons Canada Limited, 1983.

Saparina, Y. *Cybernetics Within Us*. Hollywood: Wilshire, 1967.

Schuller, Robert H. *Self-Love: the Dynamic Force of Success*. New York: Hawthorn, 1969.

Schwartz, David J. *The Magic of Thinking Big*. New York: Cornerstone Library, 1959.

Solomon, Charles R. *Handbook of Happiness*. Denver: Grace Fellowship Press, 1971.

Steveson, George S., and Harry Milt. *Master Your Tensions and Enjoy Living Again*. Englewood Cliffs, N.J.: Prentice-Hall, 1959.

Szasz, Thomas S. *The Myth of Mental Illness*. New York: Dell, 1961.

Tournier, Paul. *The Healing of Persons*. New York: Harper and Row, 1965.

Wilson, Margery. *Kinetic Psycho-Dynamics*. Englewood Cliffs, N.J.: Prentice-Hall, 1963.

Wiersbe, Warren W. *Why Us? When Bad Things Happen to God's People*. Old Tappan, N.J.: Revell, 1984.

Other books by Tim LaHaye

Anger Is a Choice
The Act of Marriage
How to Be Happy Though Married
I Love You, But Why Are We So Different?
Spirit-Controlled Family
Spirit-Controlled Temperament
Why You Act the Way You Do
Understanding the Male Temperament

LaHaye Temperament Analysis

- *a test to identify your primary and secondary temperaments*
- *a description of your predominant characteristics*
- *information regarding your vocational aptitudes and possible vocations suited to you*
- *recommendations on improving your work habits*
- *a list of your spiritual gifts, in the order of their priority*
- *suggestions for where you can best serve in your church*
- *steps for overcoming your ten greatest weaknesses*
- *counsel on marital adjustment and parental leadership*
- *special advice to singles, divorcees, pastors, and the widowed*

Your personal 13- to 16-page evaluation letter from Dr. Tim LaHaye will be bound in a handsome portfolio.

*...your opportunity
to know yourself better!*

$10.00 Discount Certificate

Off regular price of $29.95

Name _____

Address _____

City _____

State/Zip _____

*Send this Discount Certificate
and your check for $19.95 to:*

Family Life Seminars
370 L'Enfant Promenade #801
Washington, D.C. 20034